TORONTO
ALIGHT

Patrick Lemieux

Published by
Across The Board Books™
Toronto, Ontario, Canada

Toronto Alight, Copyright © 2020 by Patrick Lemieux. All Rights Reserved. This book may not be used or reproduced, in whole or in part, without written permission from the copyright holder except in the case of limited Fair Dealing or Fair Use (or similar with respect to territorial legislation) excerpts for critical articles and reviews. For information address Across The Board Books at: info@acrosstheboardbooks.ca

The right of Patrick Lemieux to be identified as Author of this Work has been asserted by him in accordance with the Copyright Act of Canada, 1997.

ISBN: 978-1-926462-19-6

First Print Edition: November, 2020

Also by Patrick Lemieux

Fiction, Art & Illustration:
- *Play of Light: The Art of Patrick Lemieux*
- *Revenge of the Dark Witch of Oz: The Illustrated Screenplay*
- *Horizon Line – Volume 1* (Comic Book Collection)

Fiction:
- *The Prisoner of Orchard Bend*
- *The Murder Ballad of Orchard Bend*
- *The Lost Sheriff of Orchard Bend*

Non-Fiction:
- *The Queen Chronology: The Recording & Release History of the Band* (co-written by Adam Unger)
- *The Mike Oldfield Chronology: The Recording & Release History*
- *The Barenaked Ladies Chronology: The Recording & Release History of the Band*
- *The Rush Chronology: The Recording & Release History of the Band*
- *The David Bowie Chronology, Volume 1: 1947-1974: The Recording & Release History*

To Emily, Natalie, Sandra & Kirsten,
Hercinia Arts Collective
&
to Molly,
The Silver Starlets & The Farmer's Daughter Show

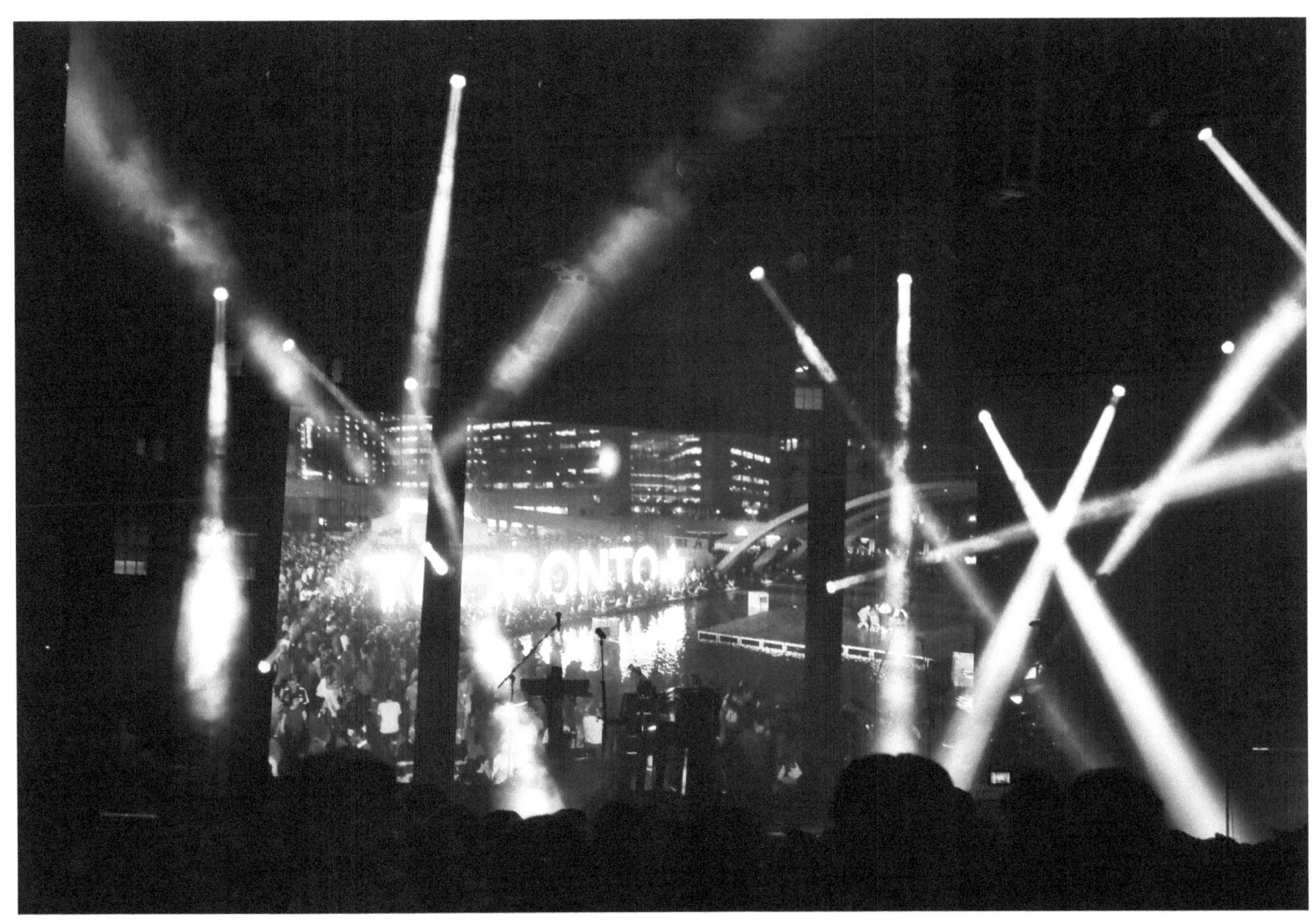

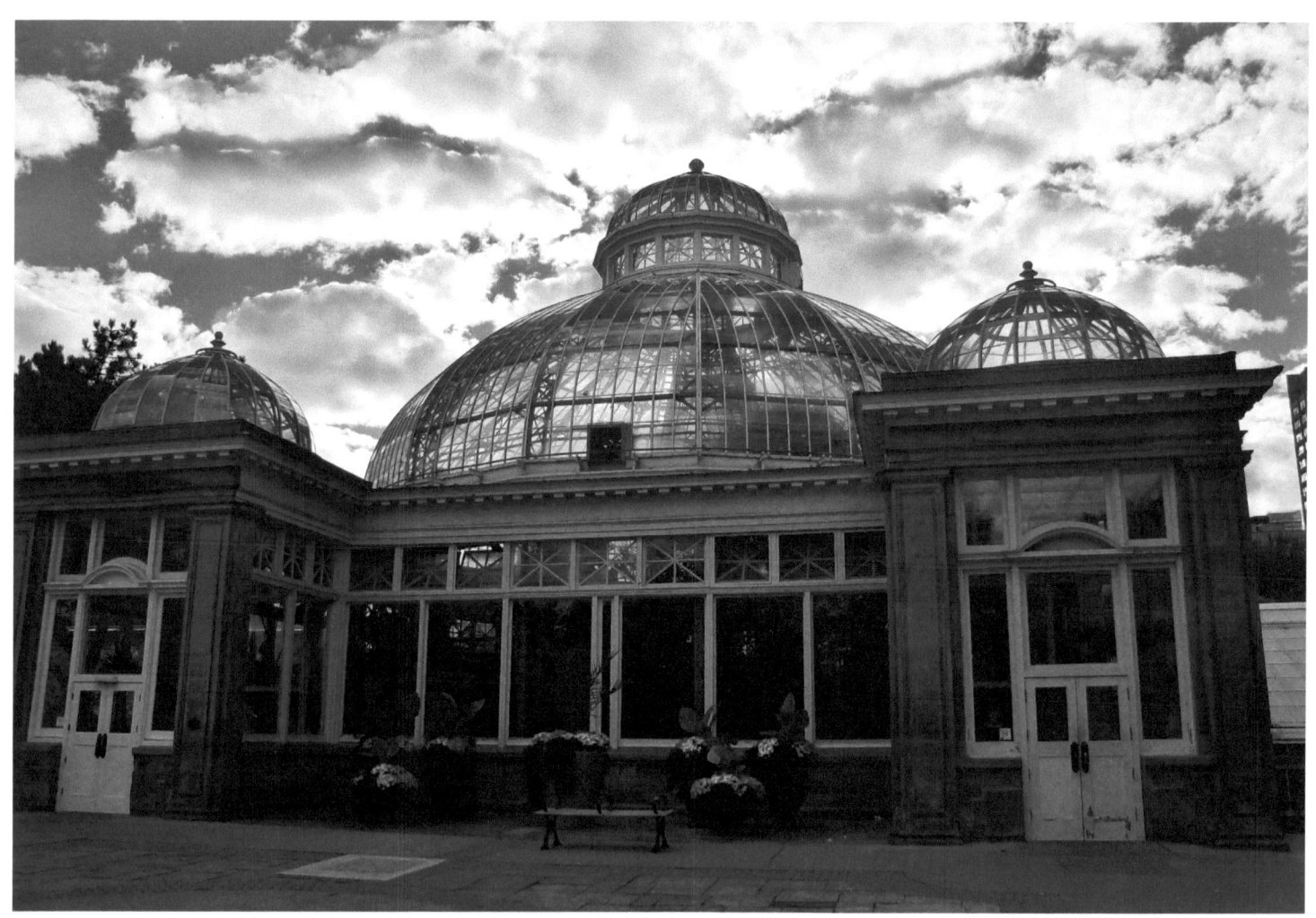

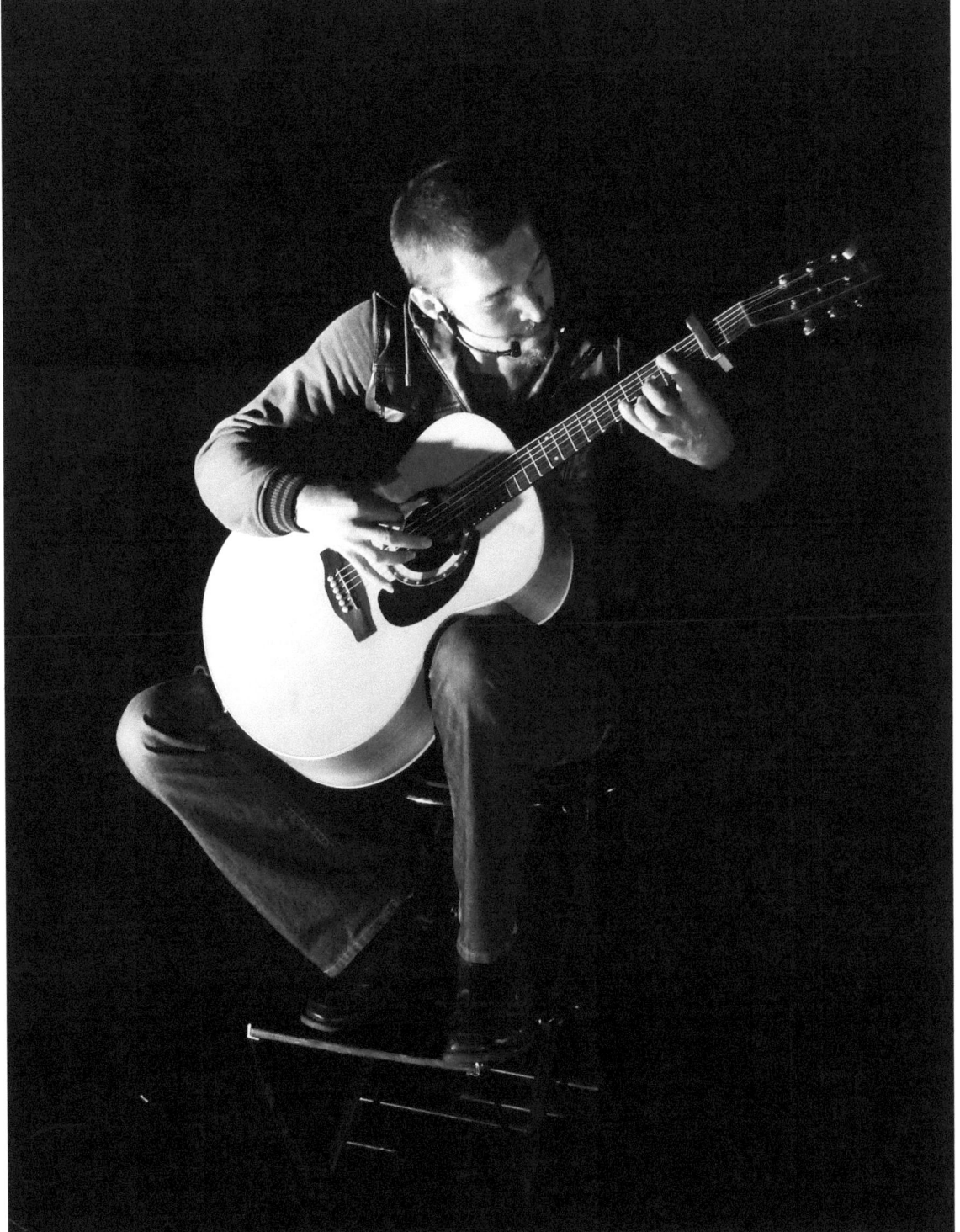

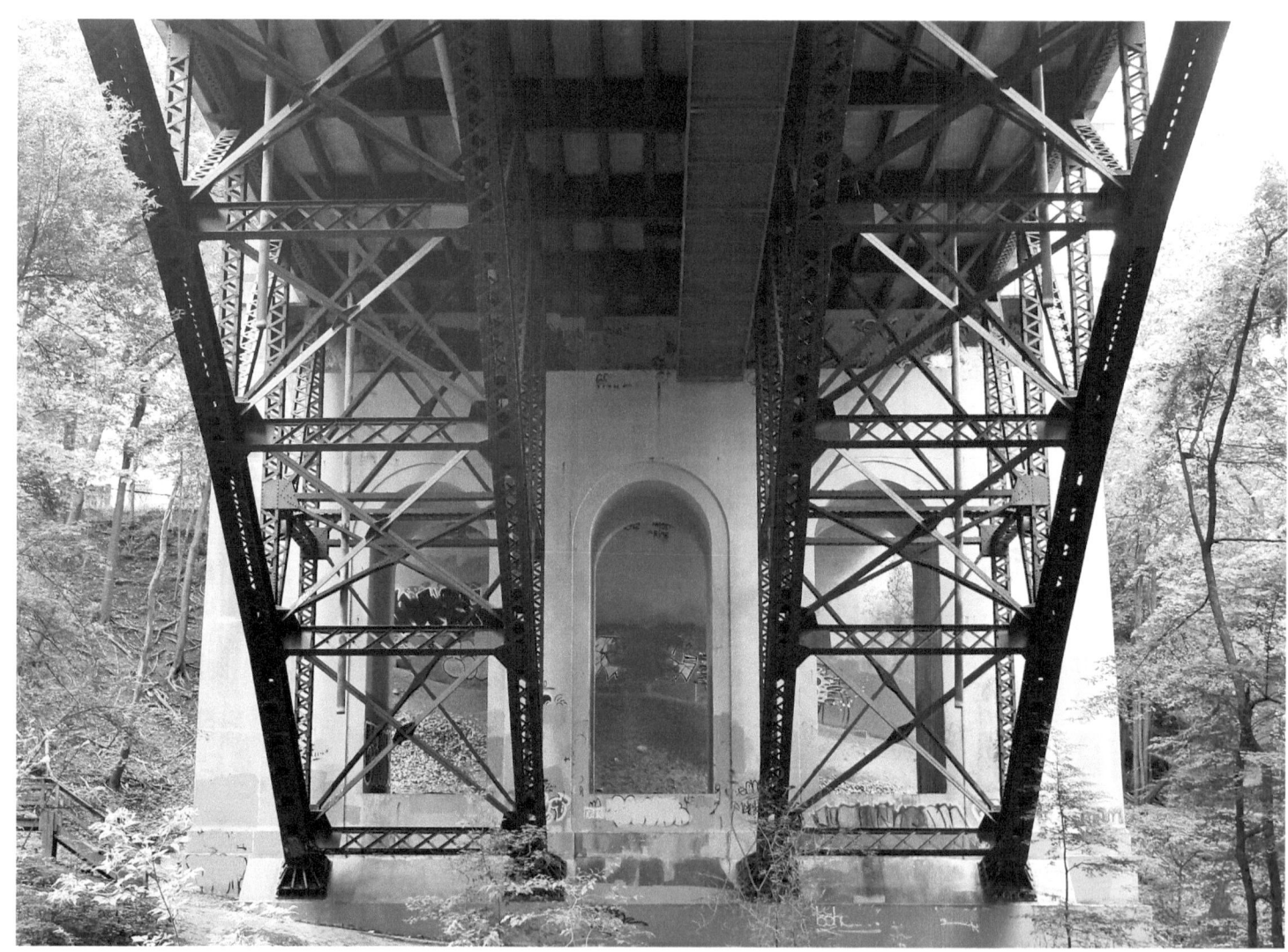

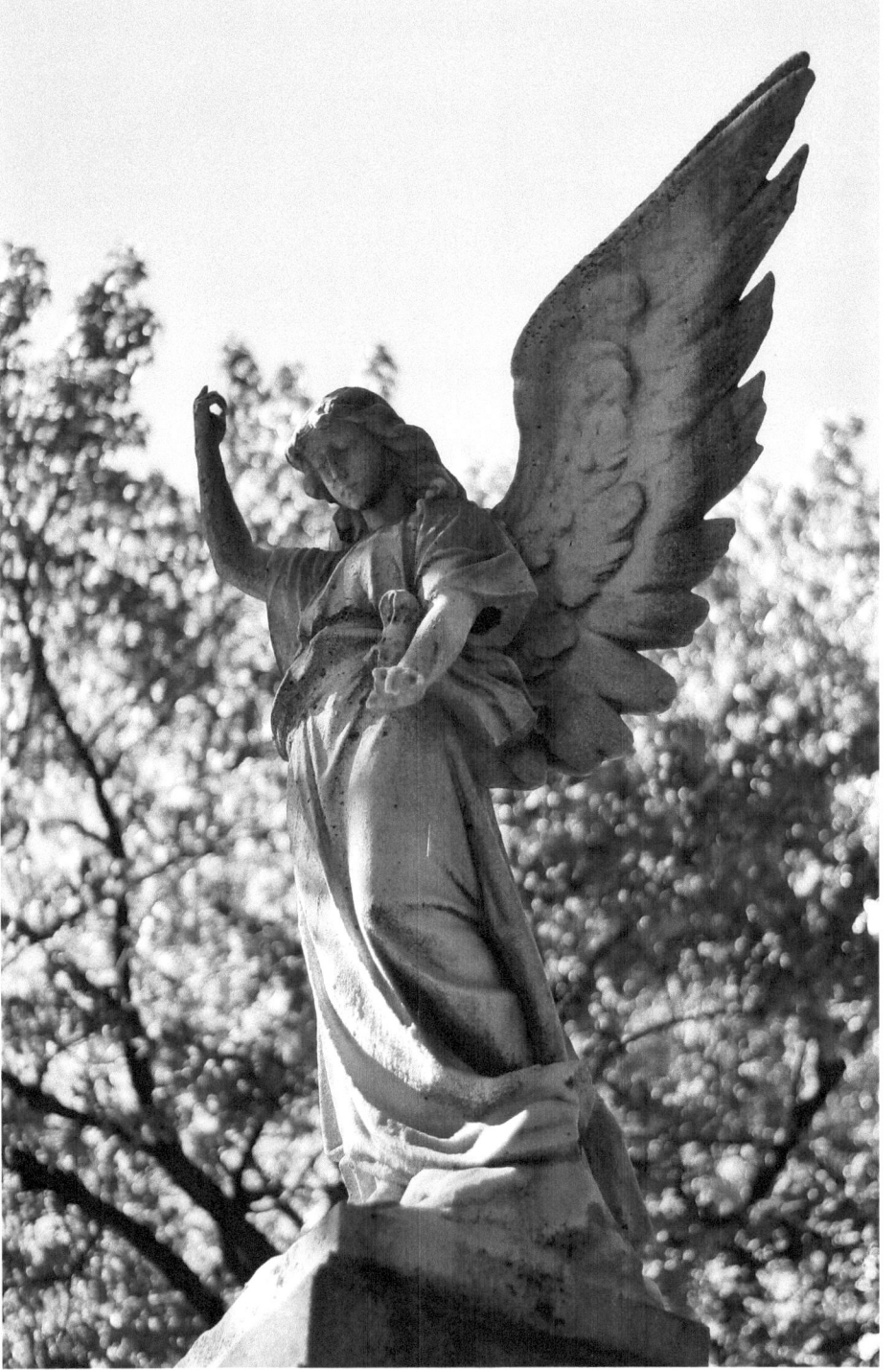

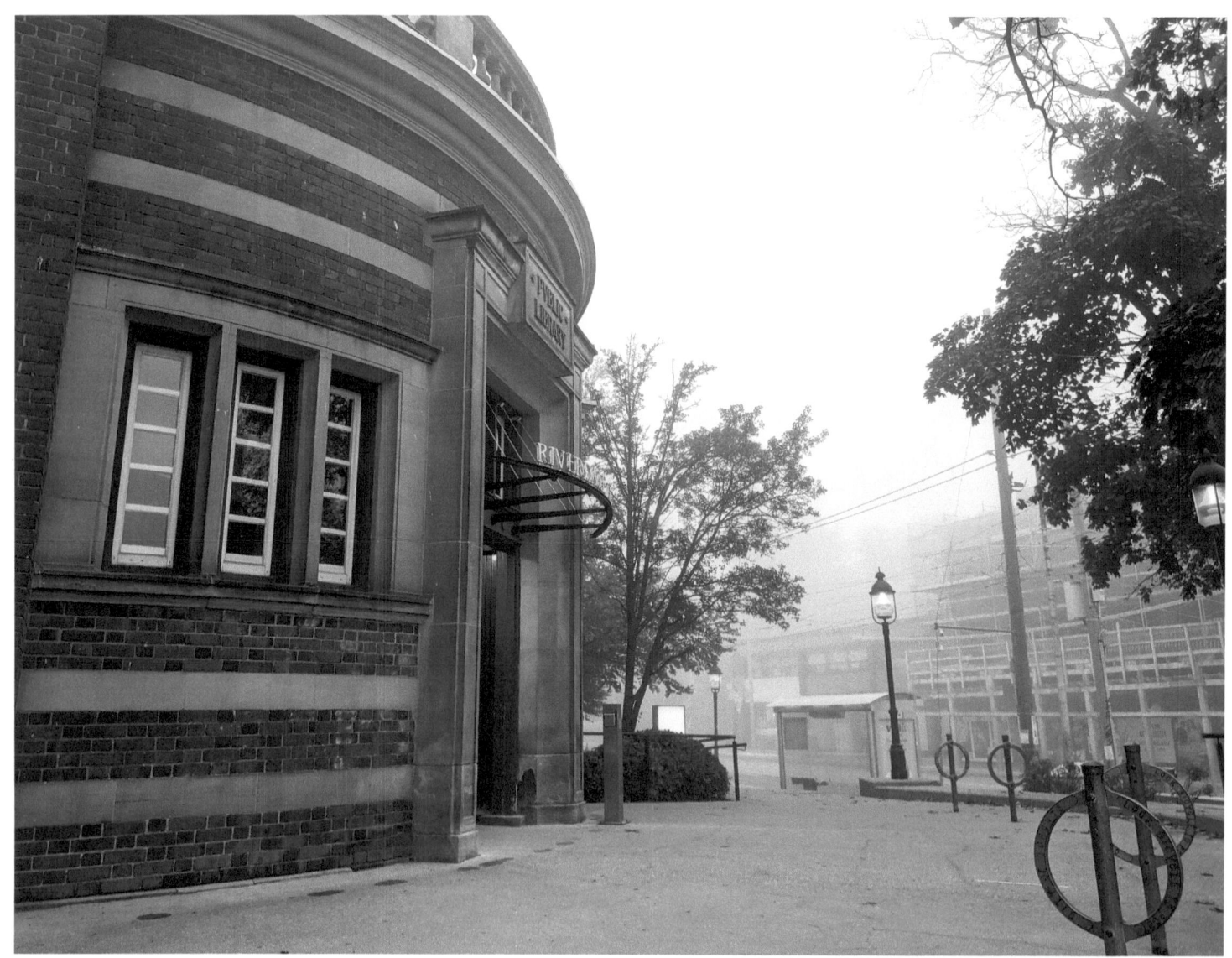

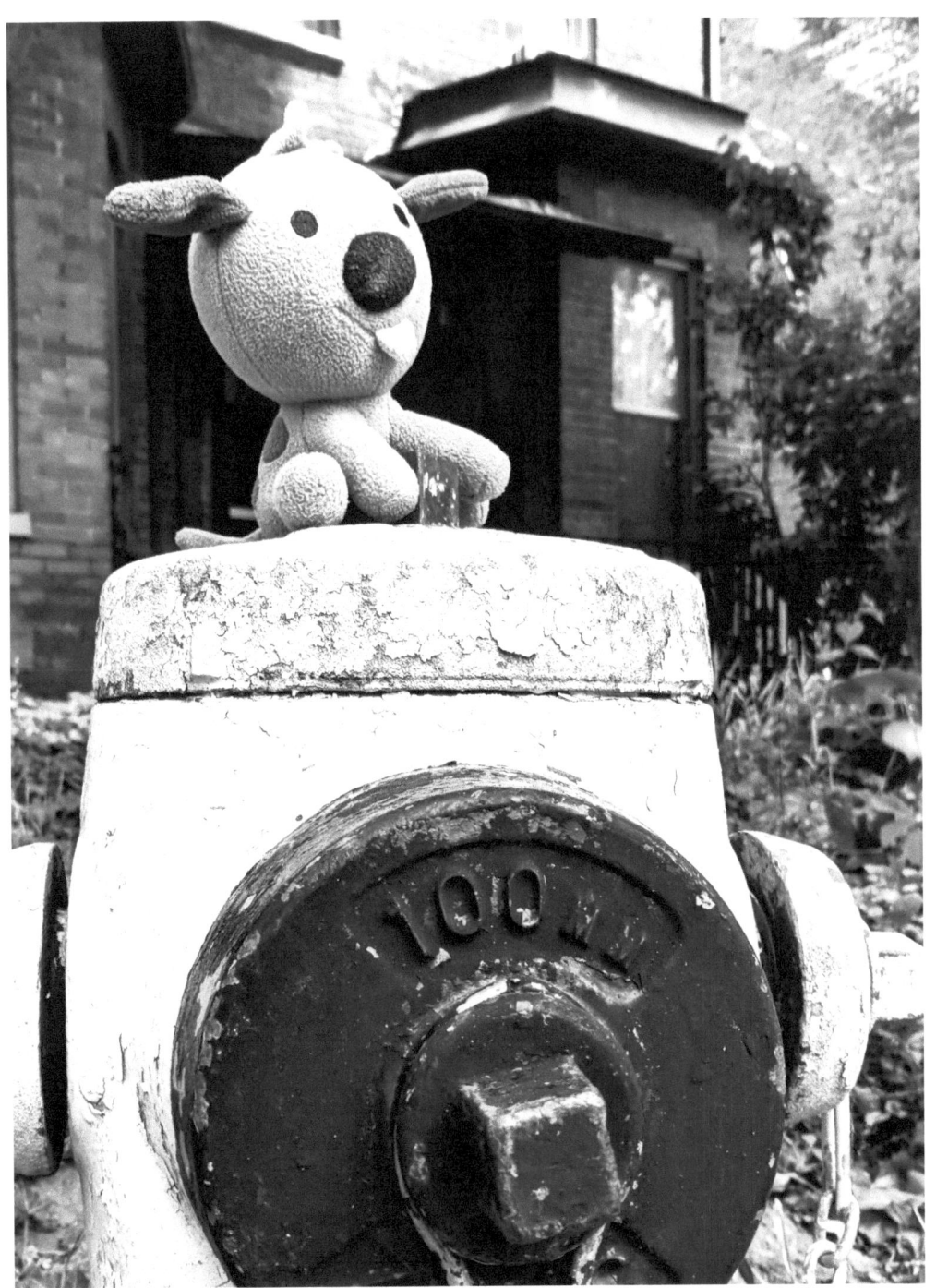

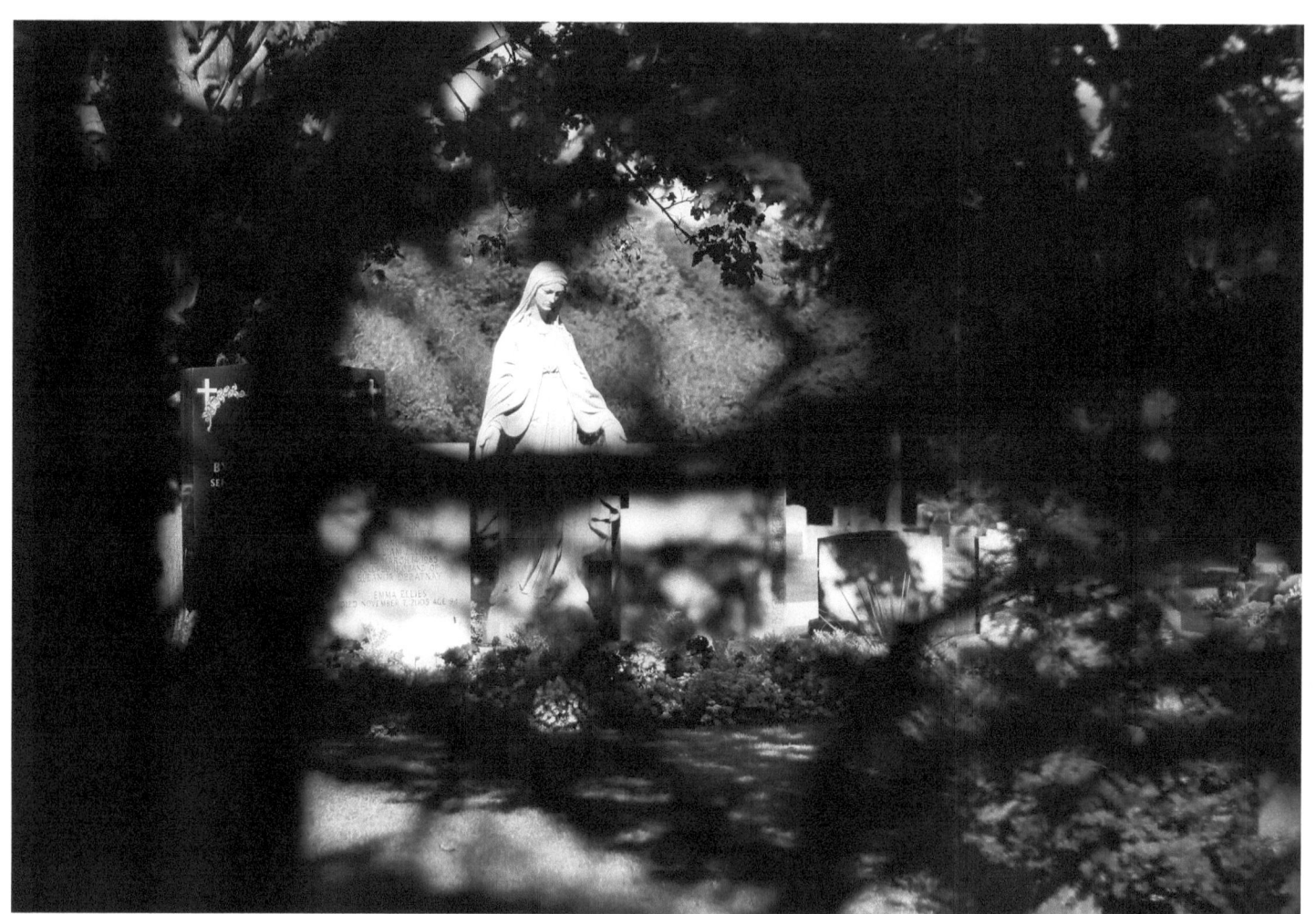

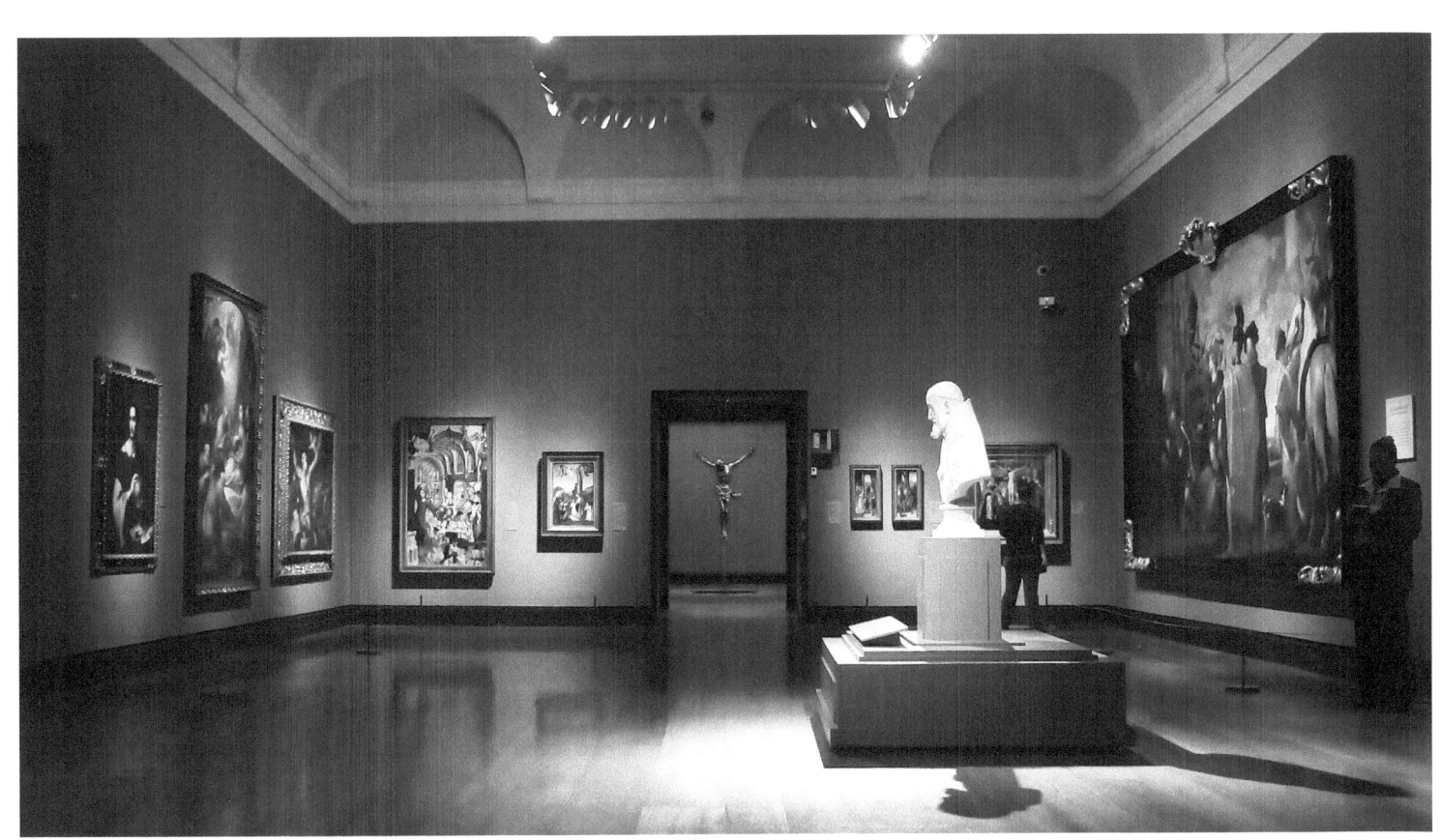

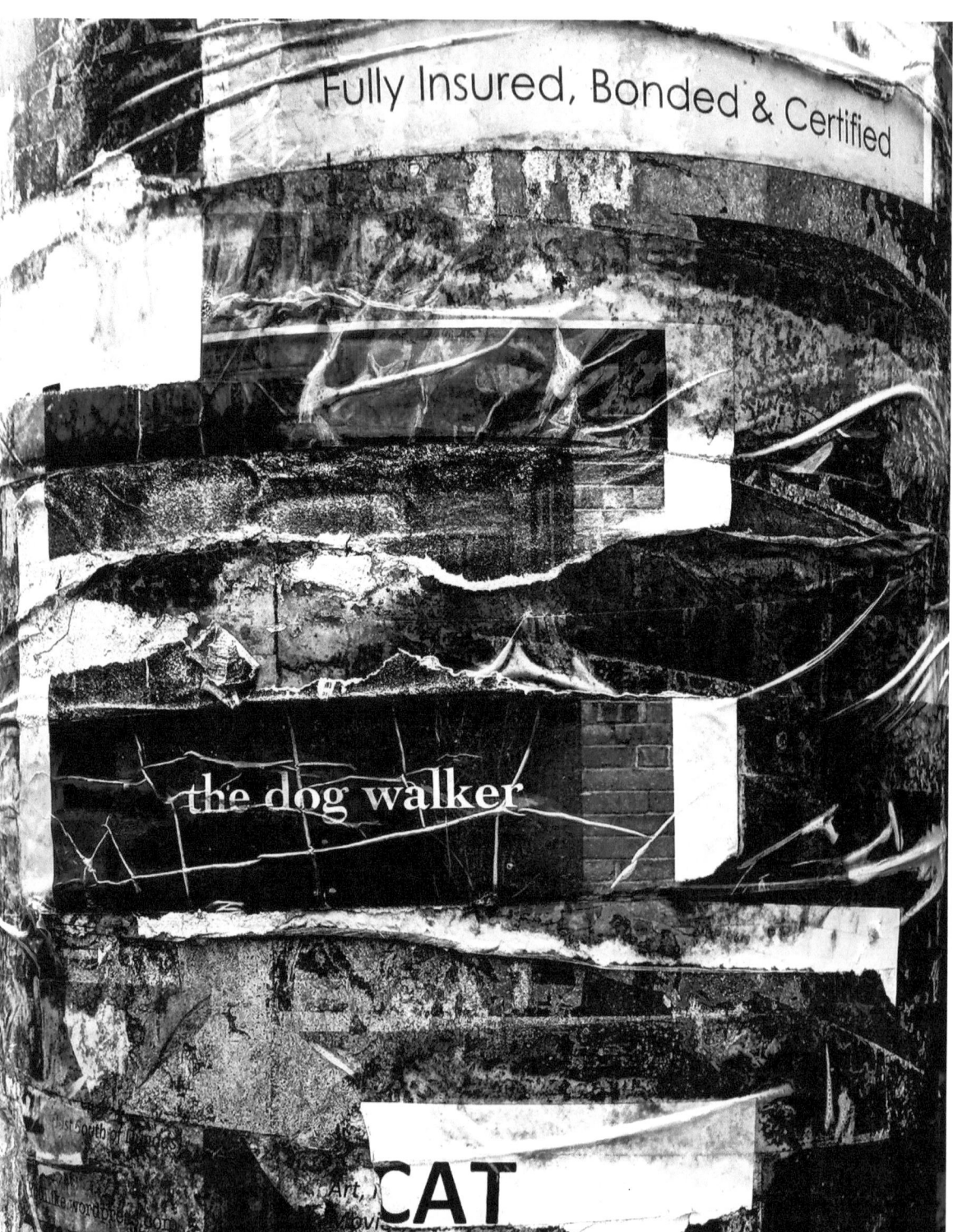

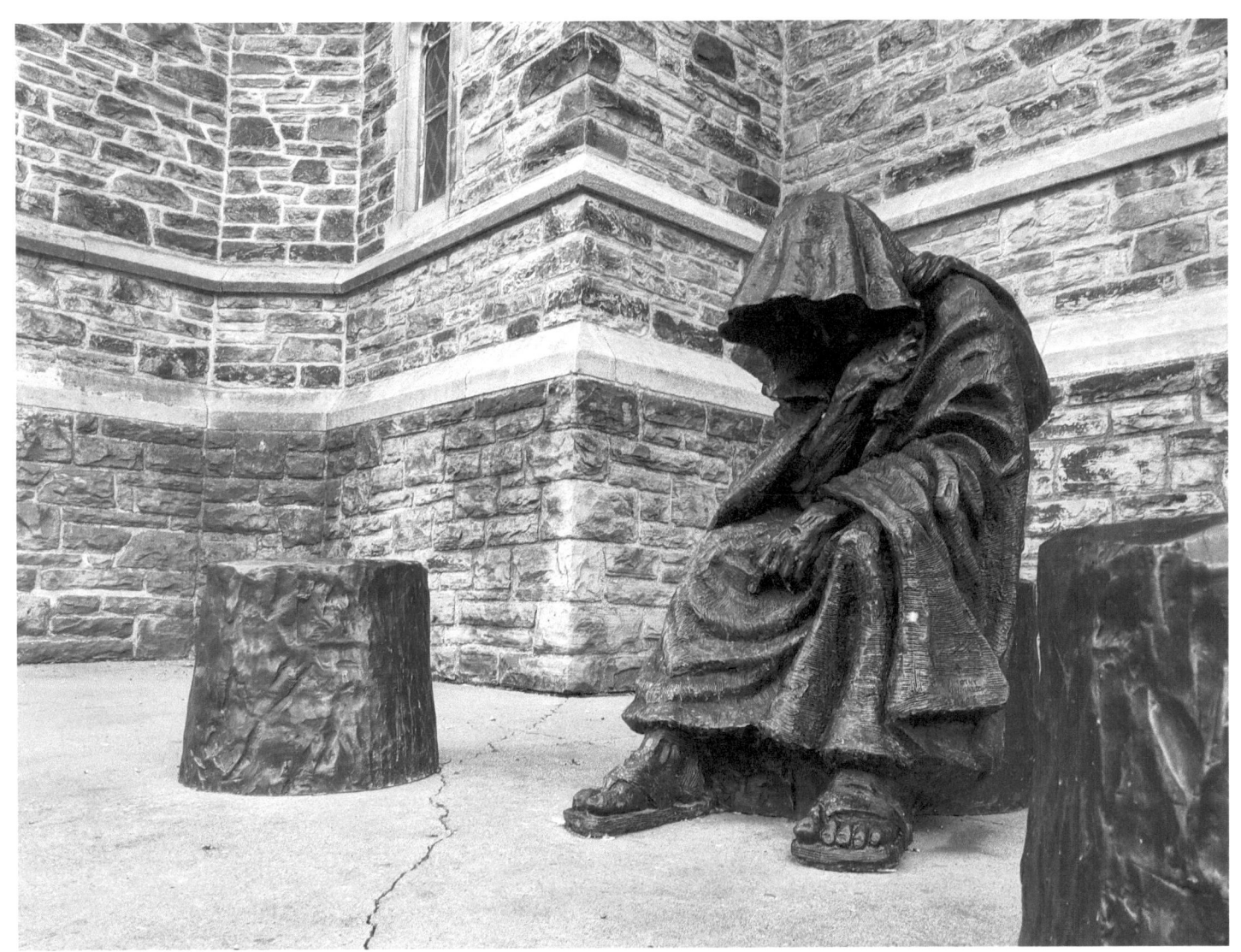

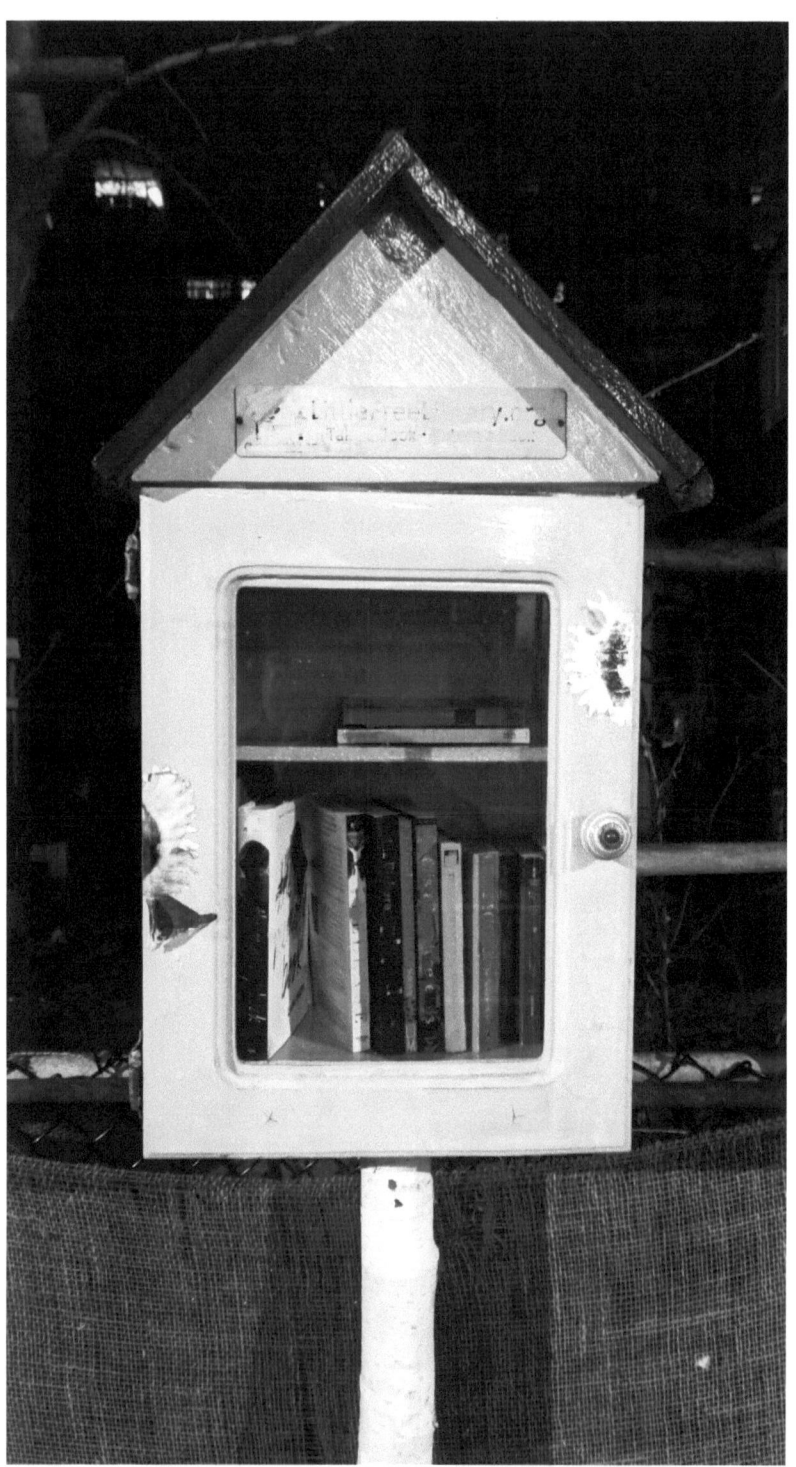

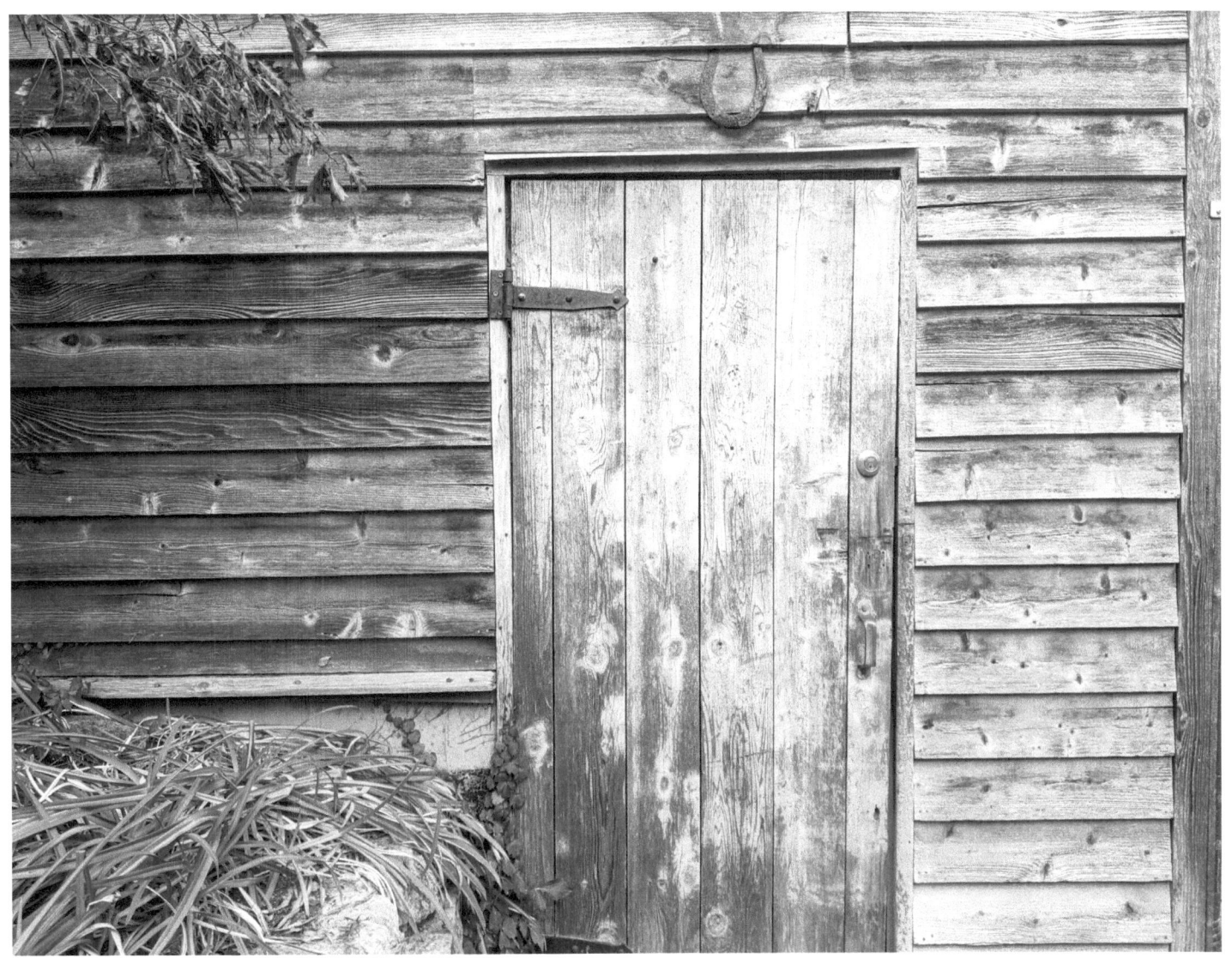

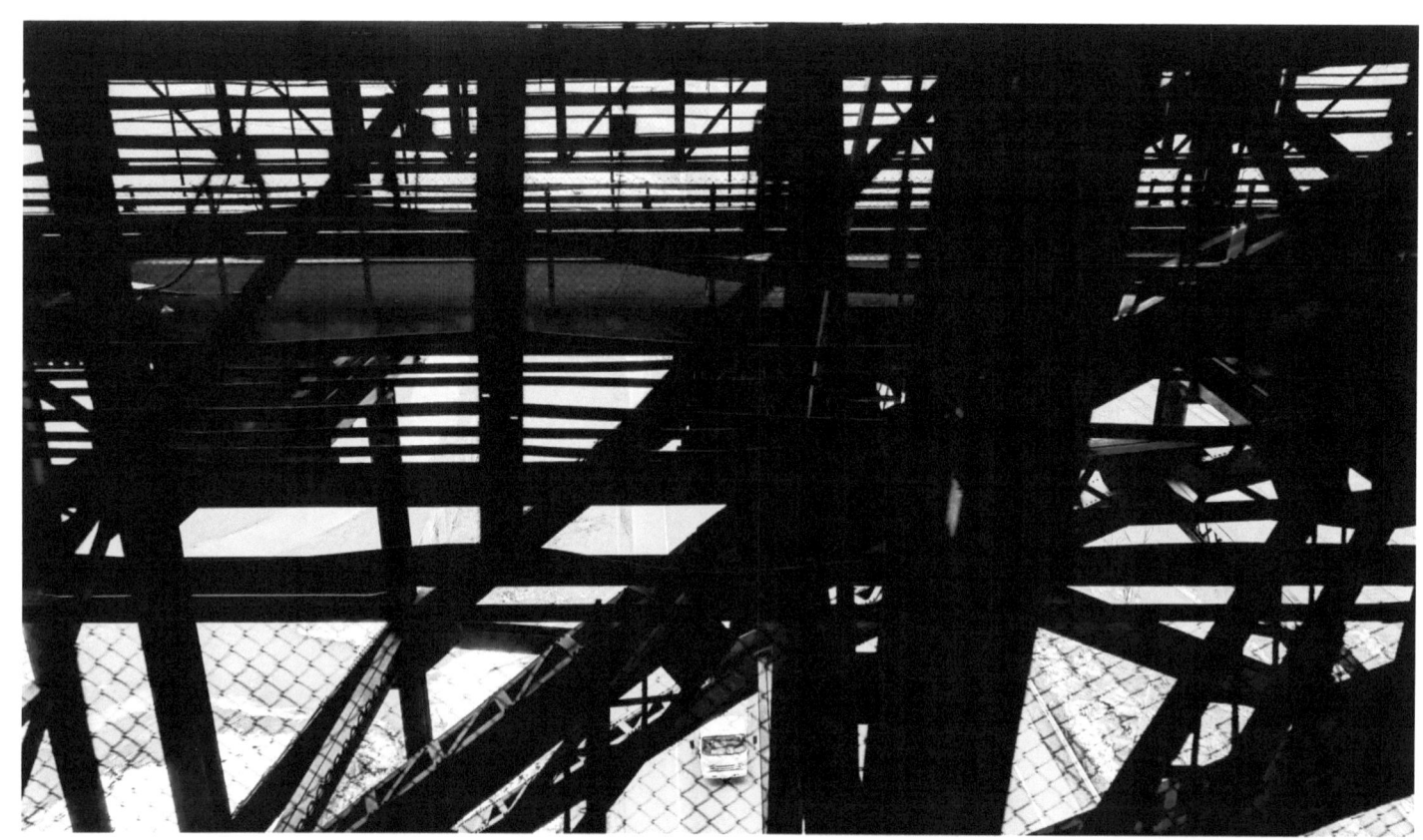

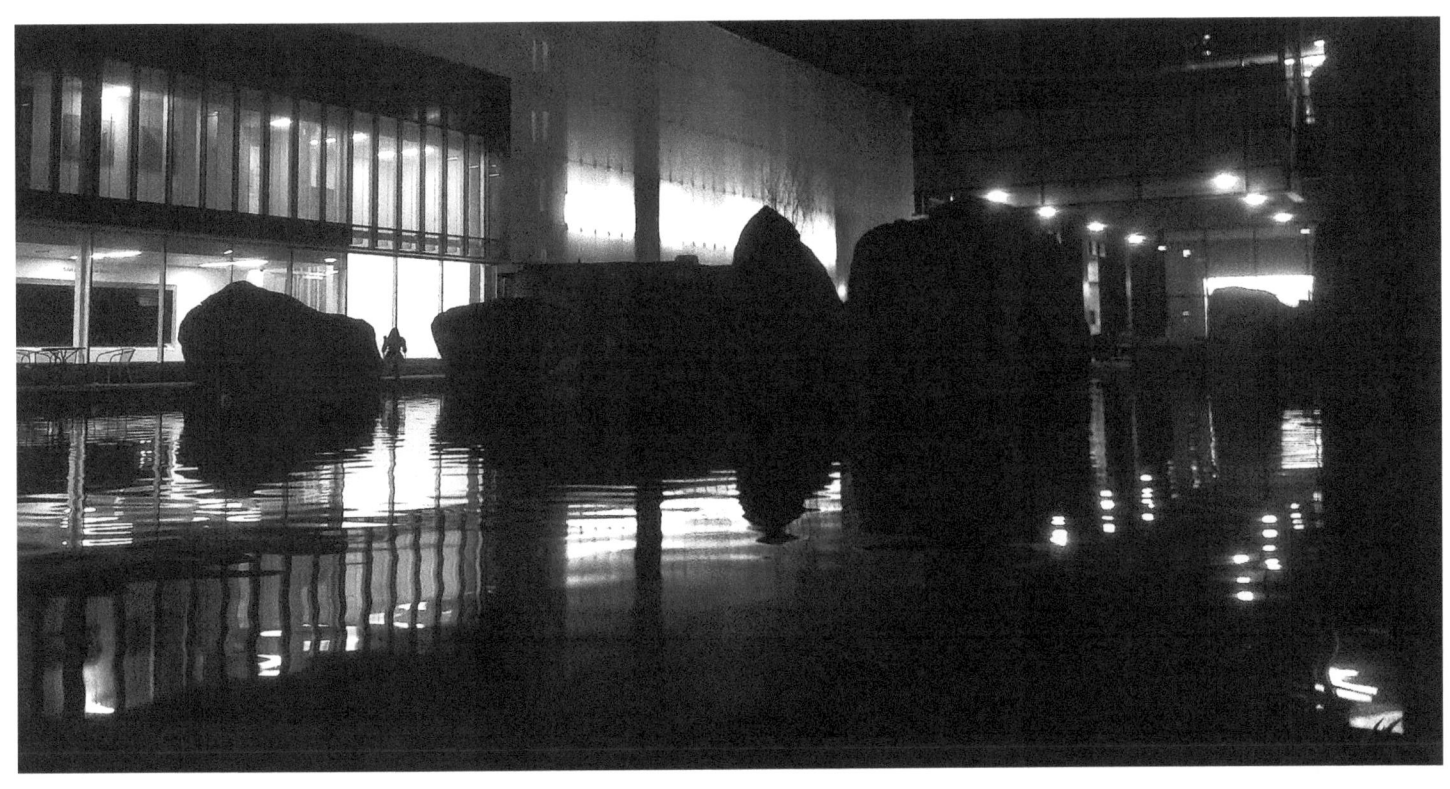

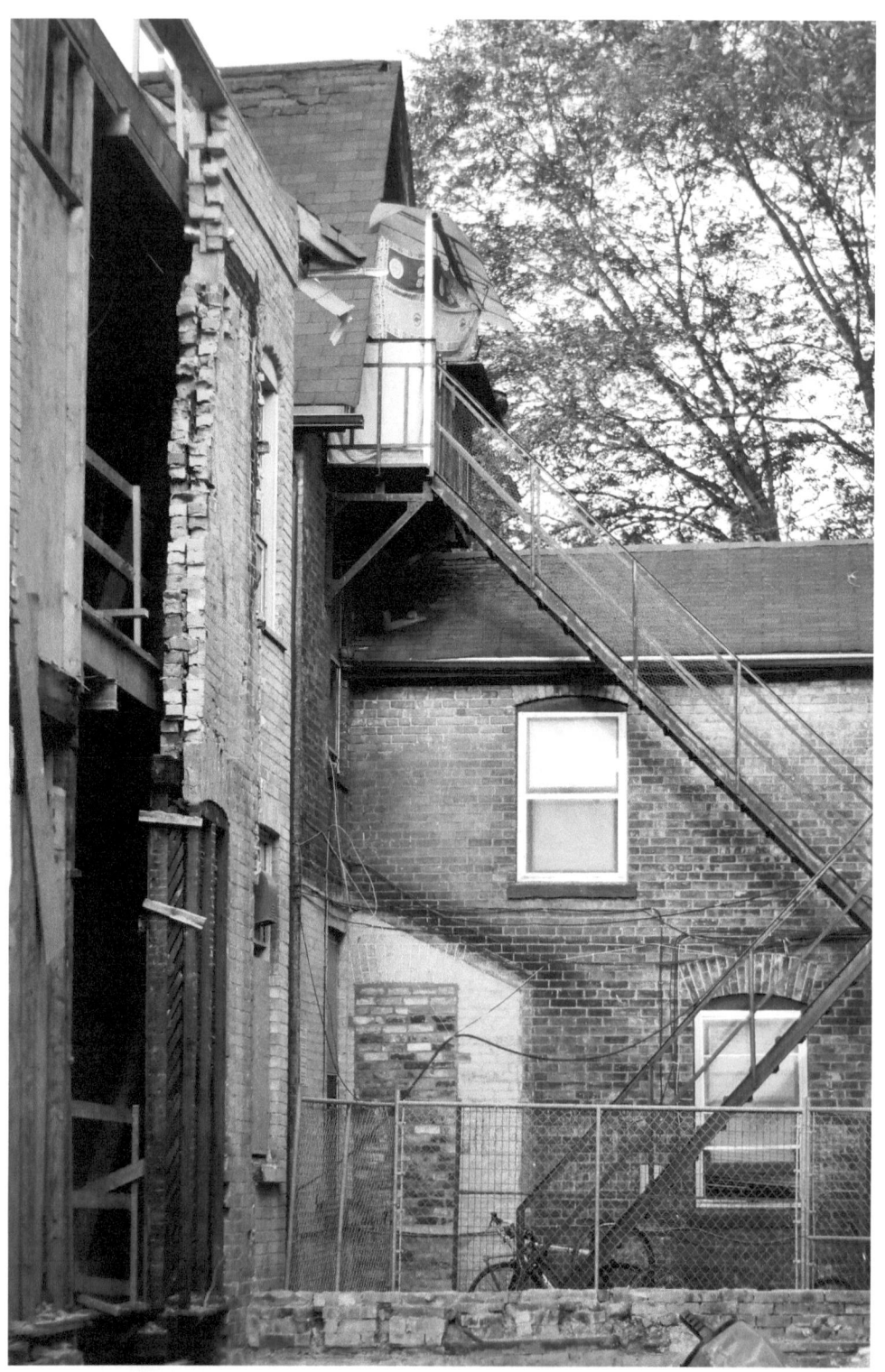

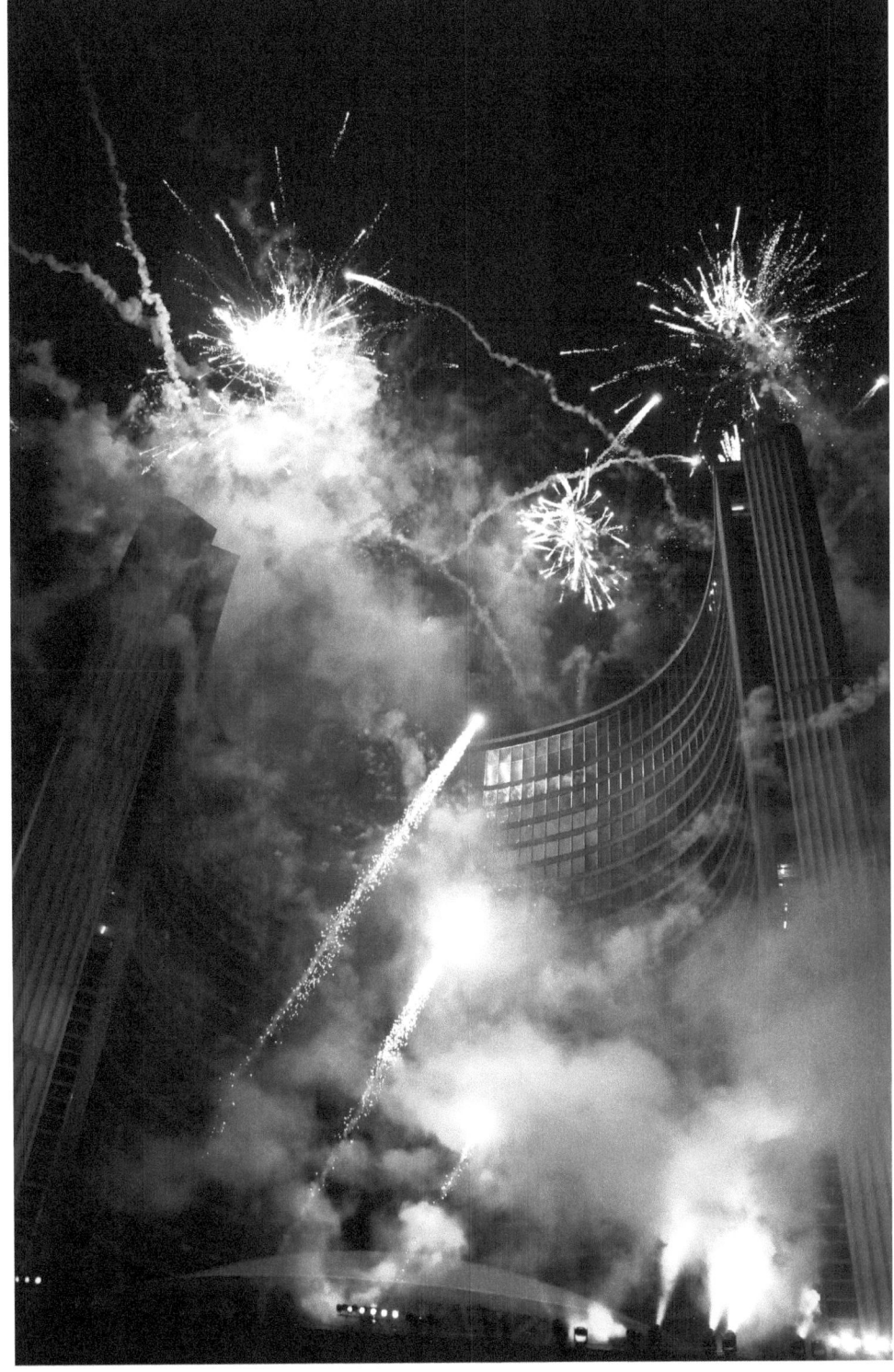

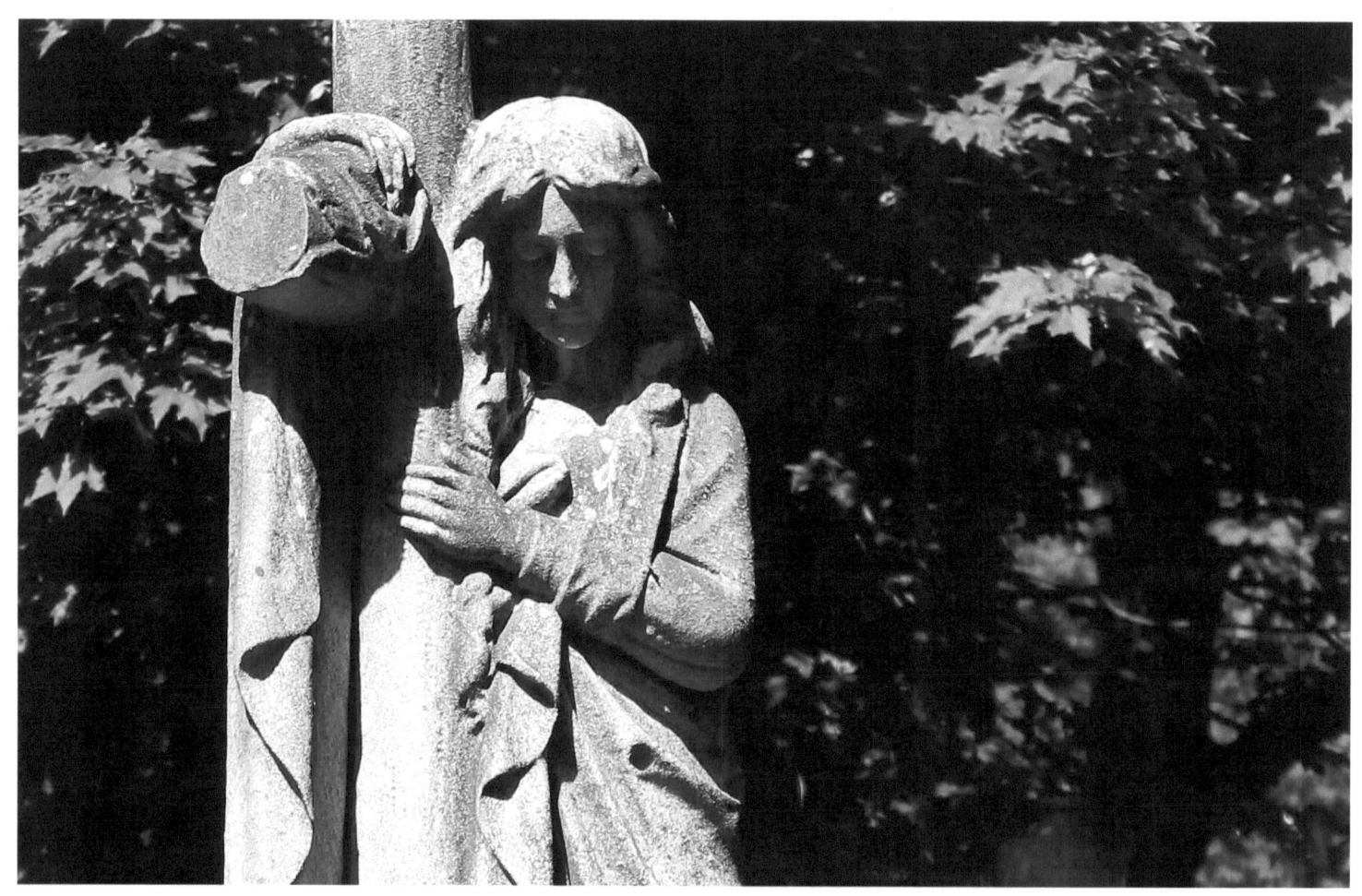

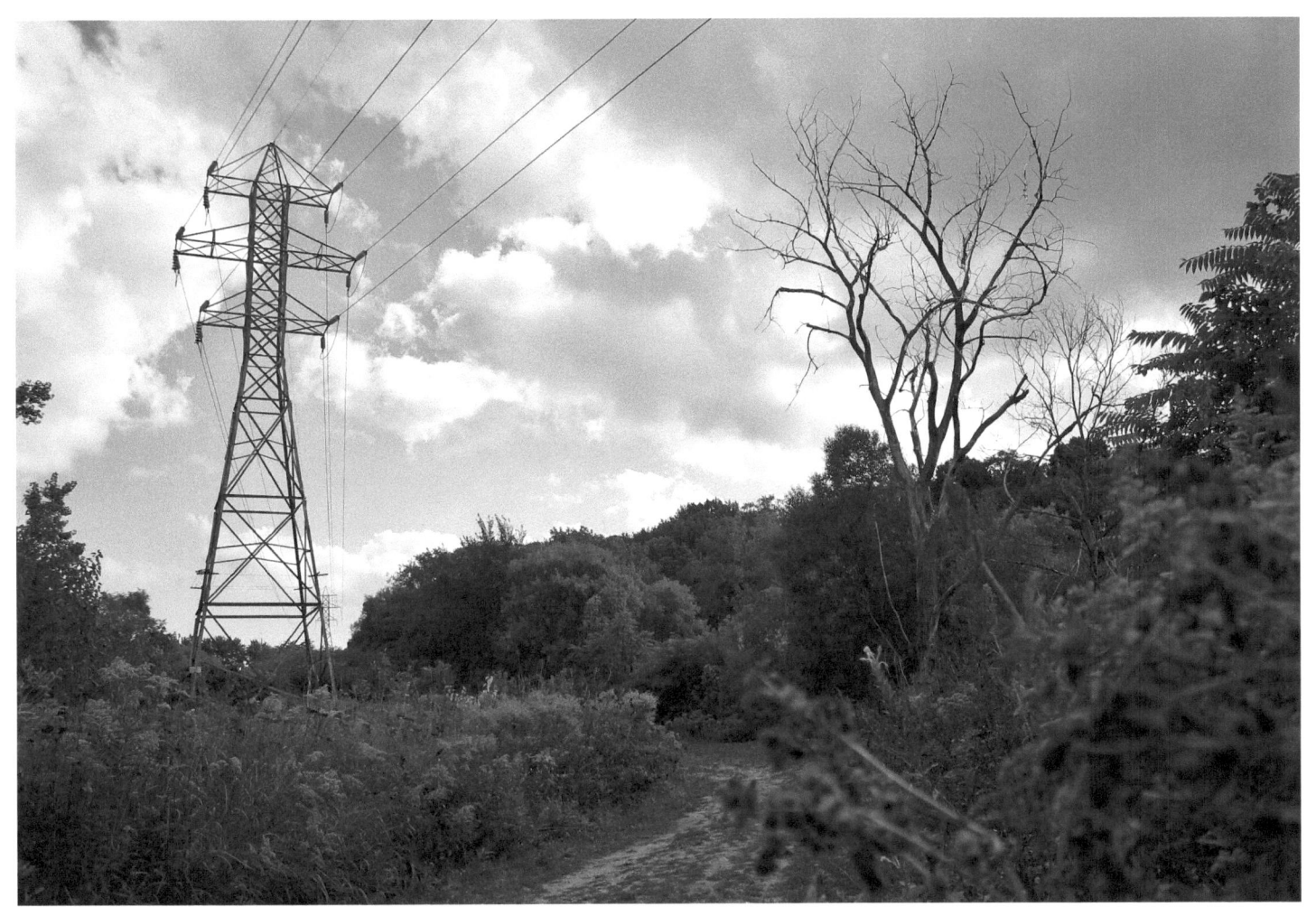

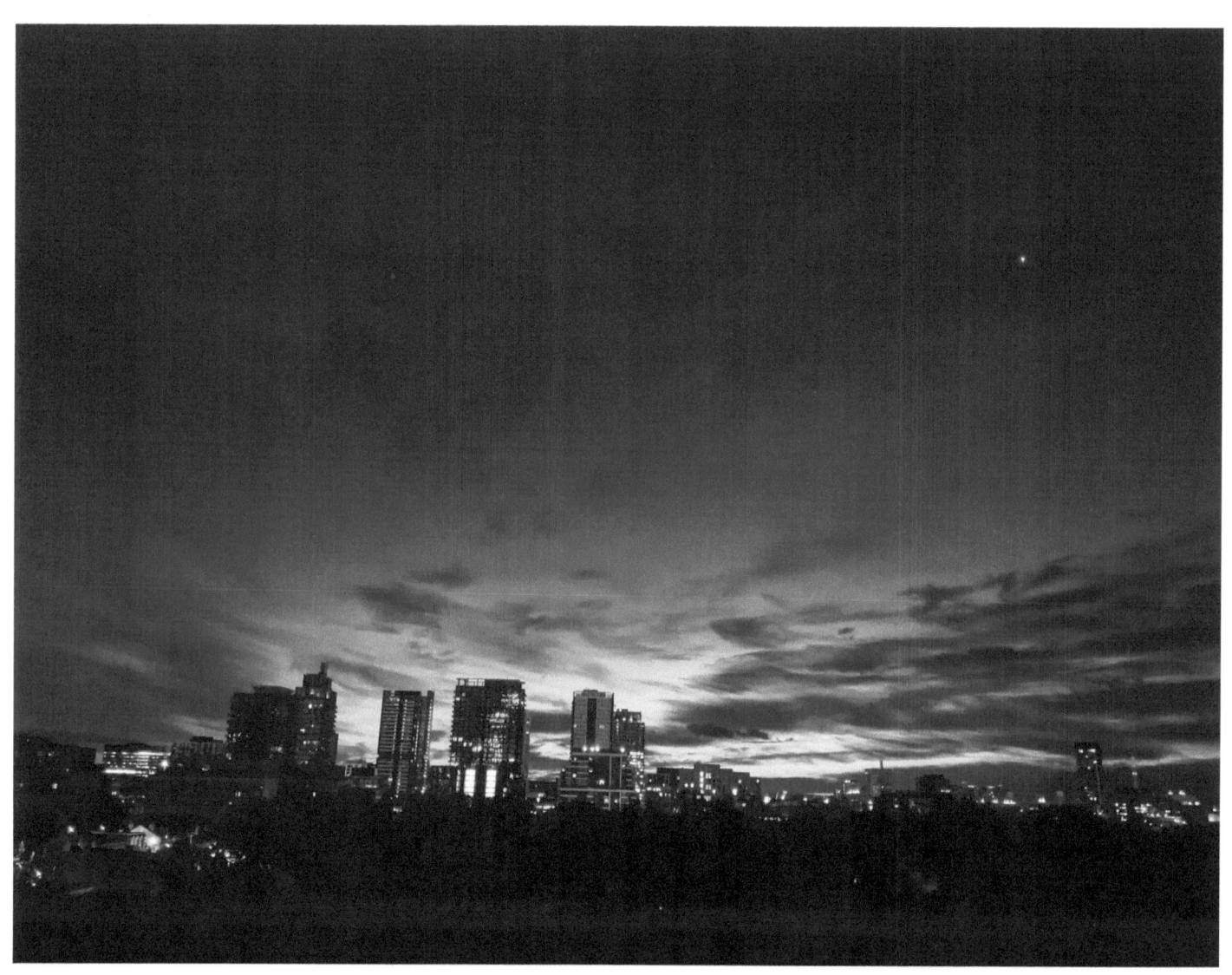

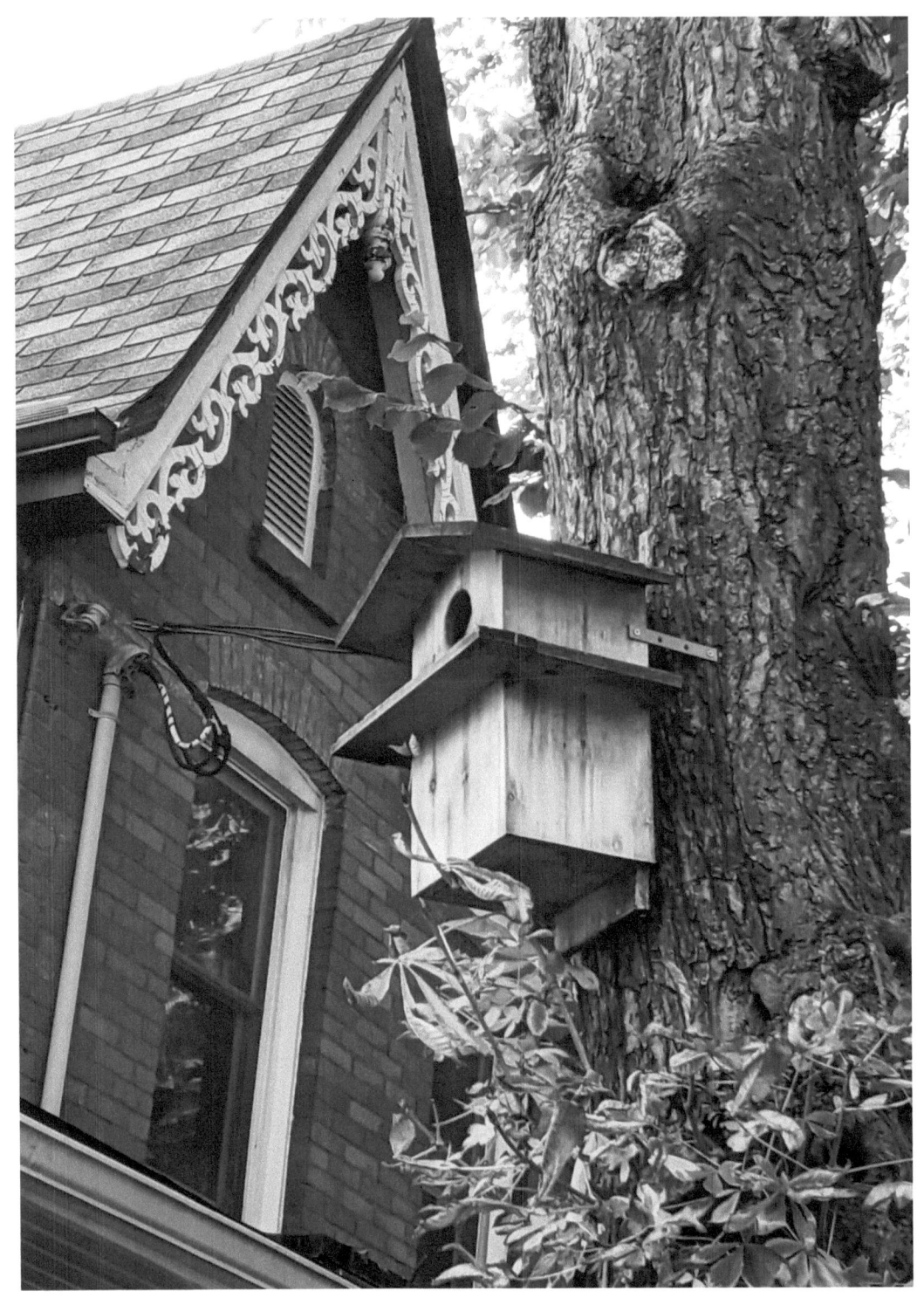

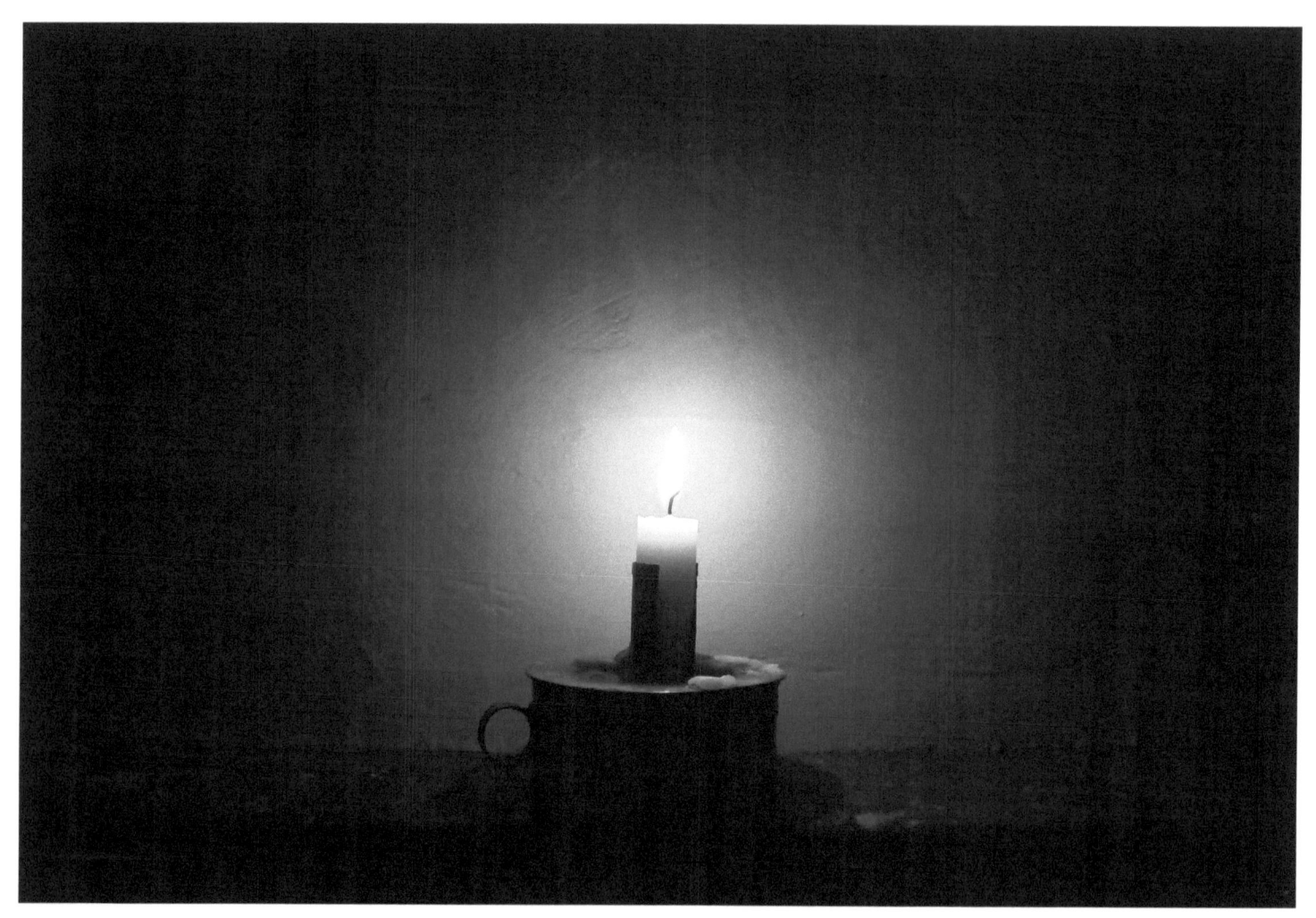

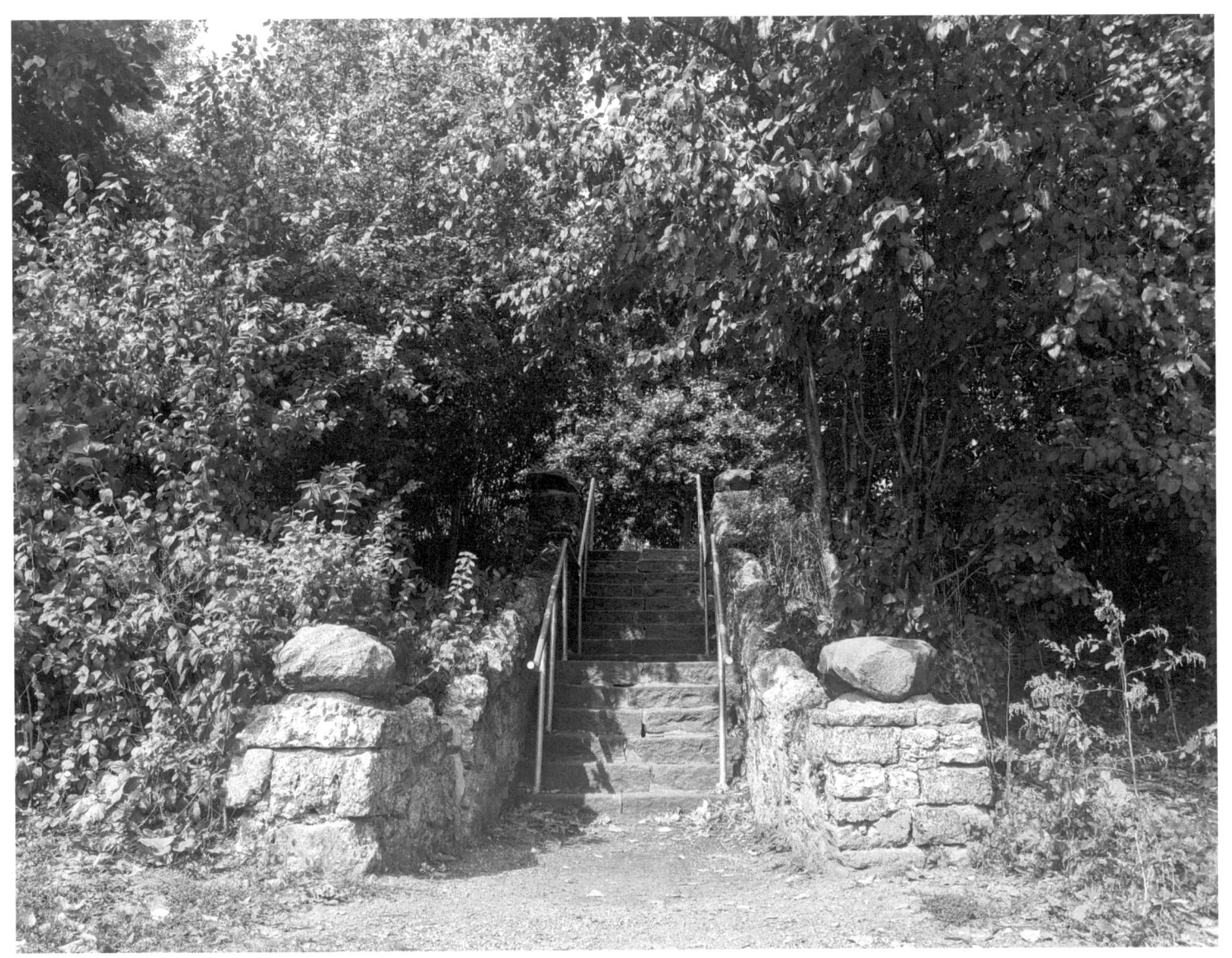

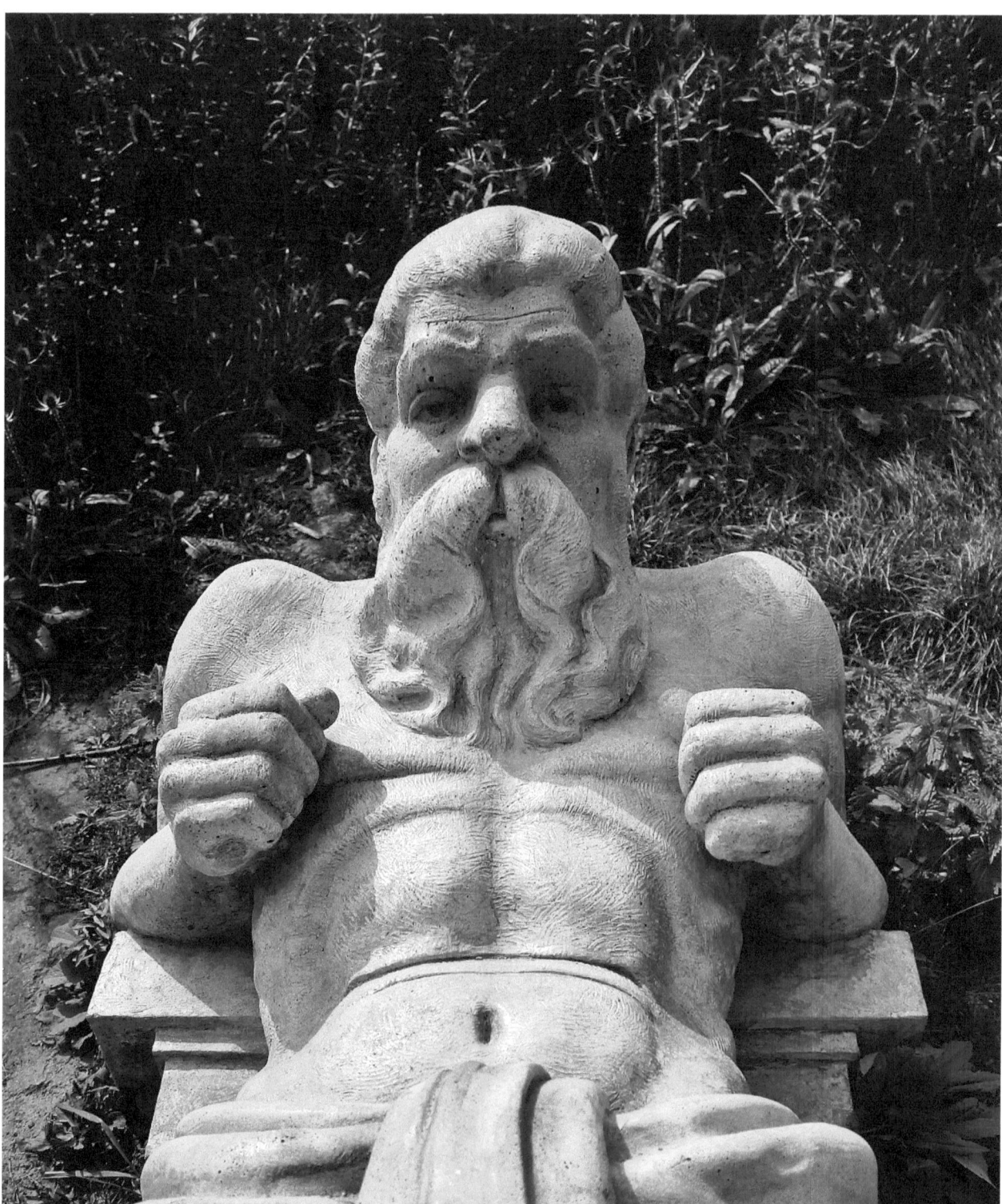

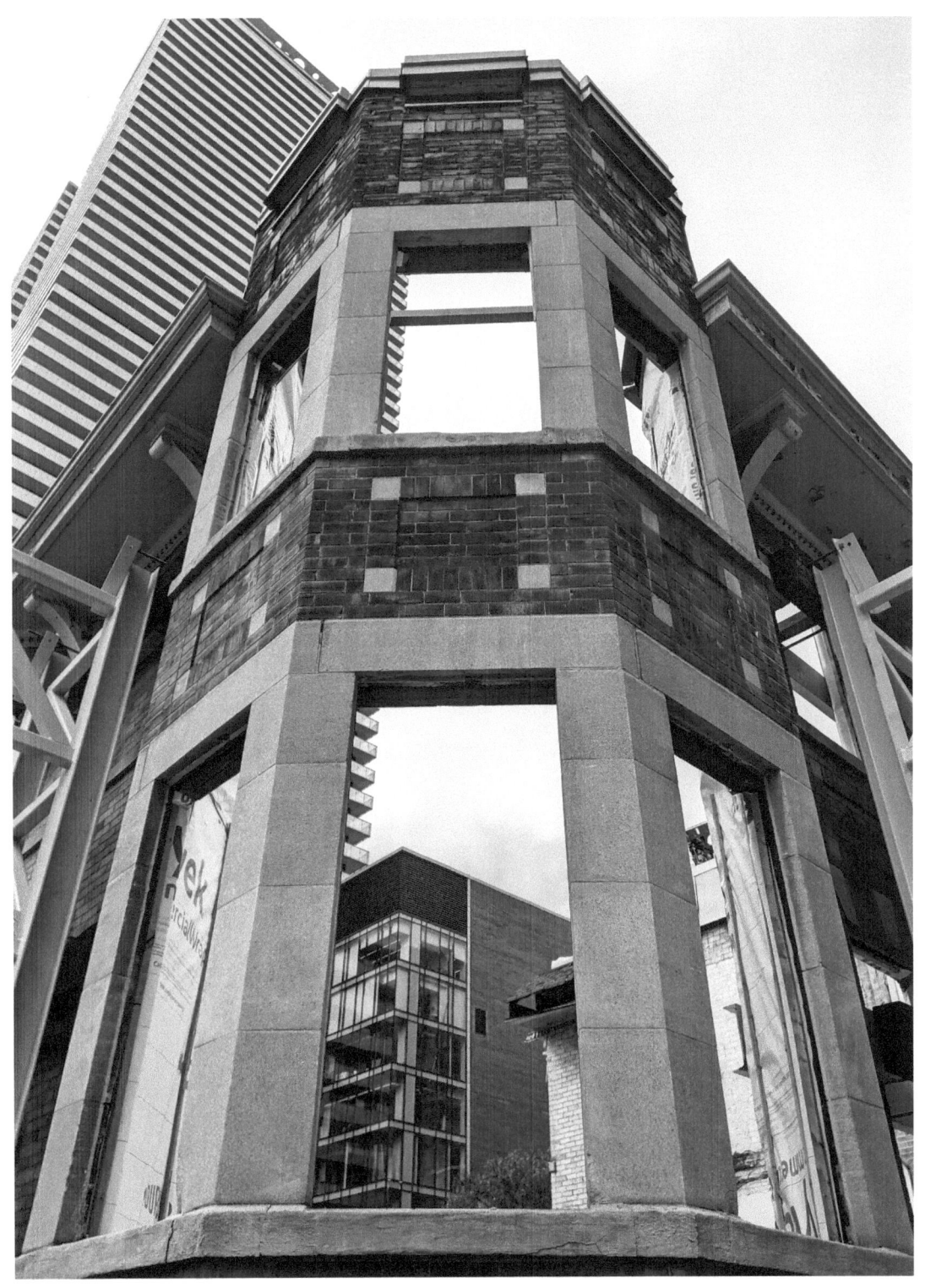

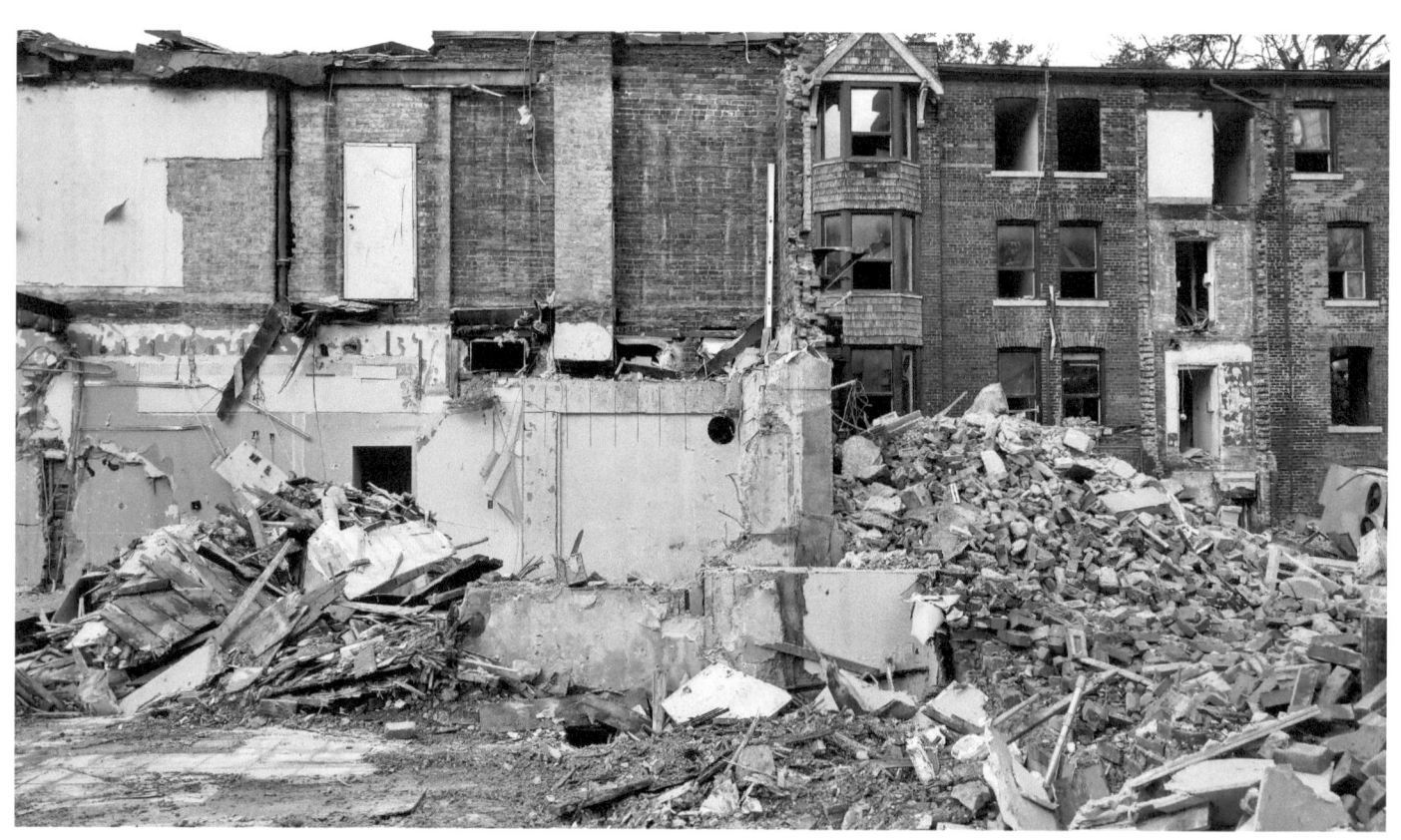

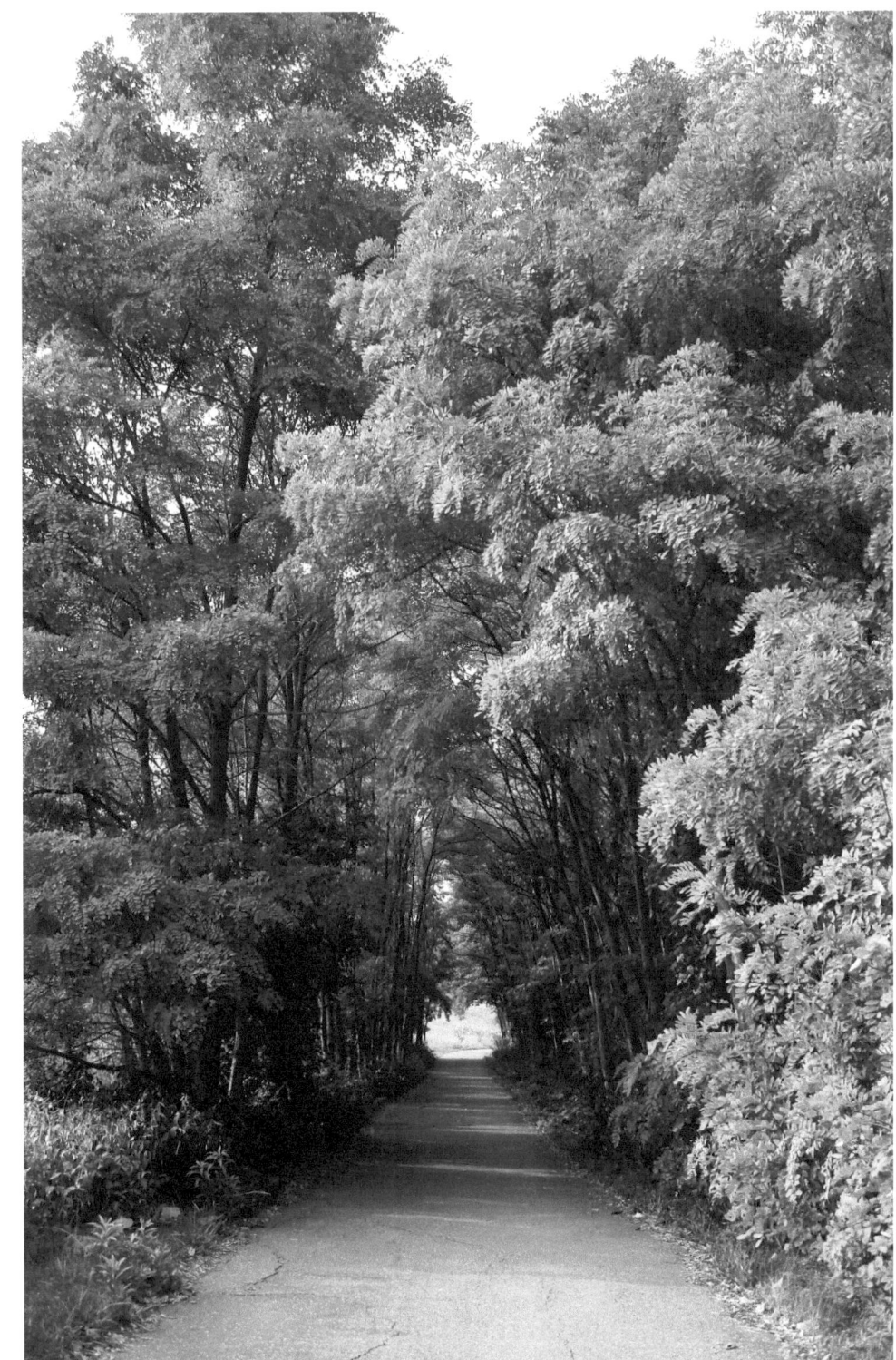

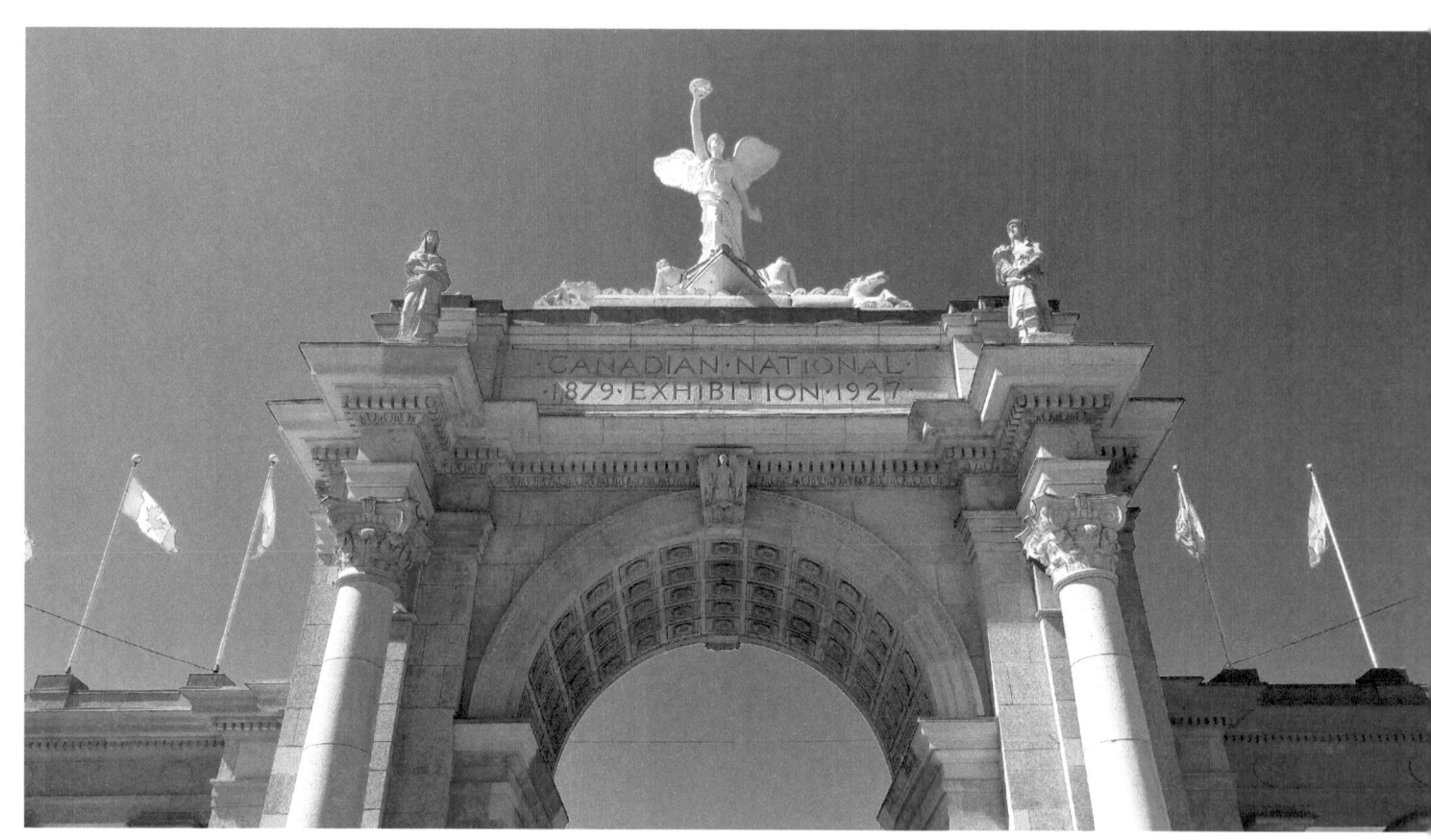

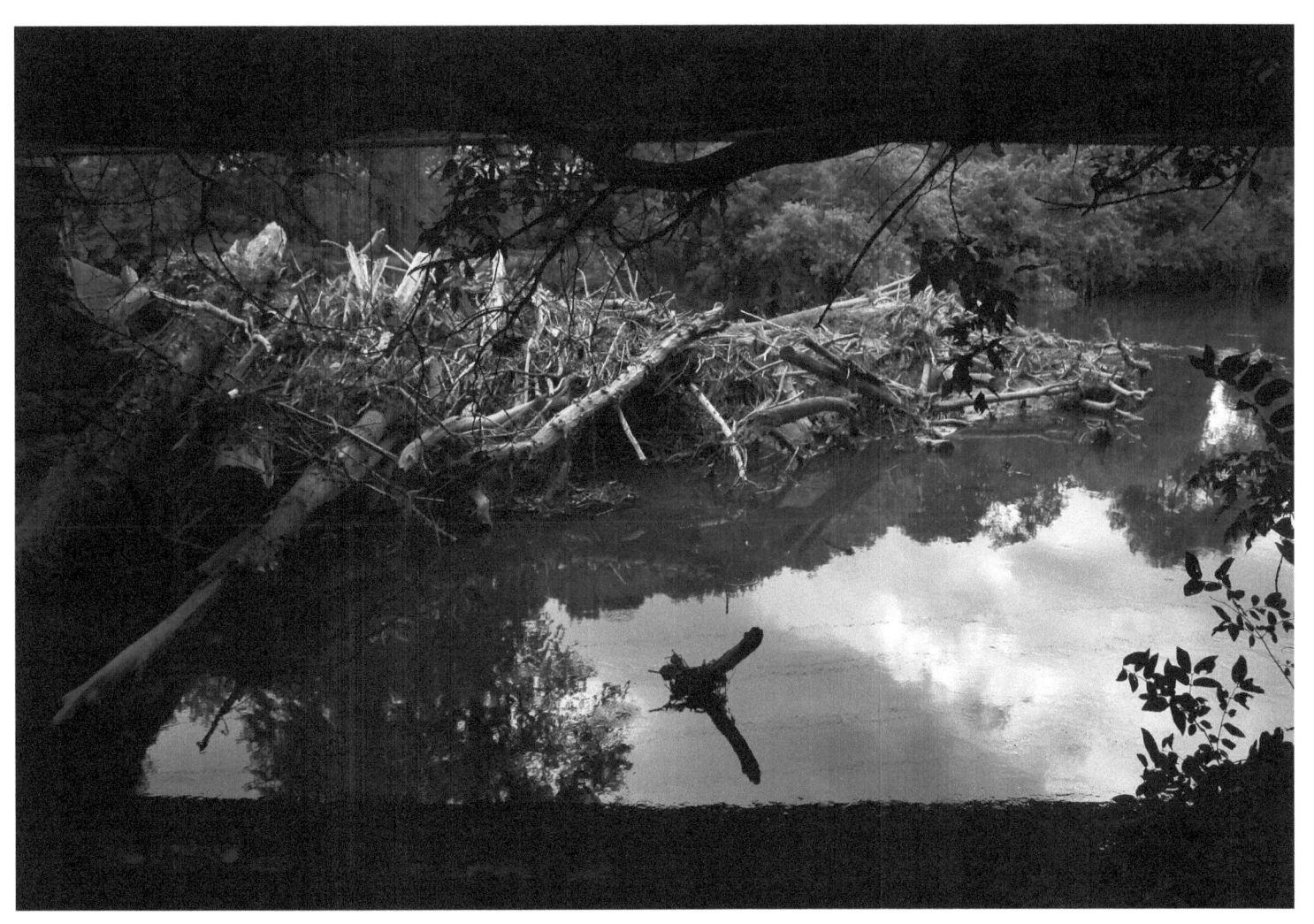

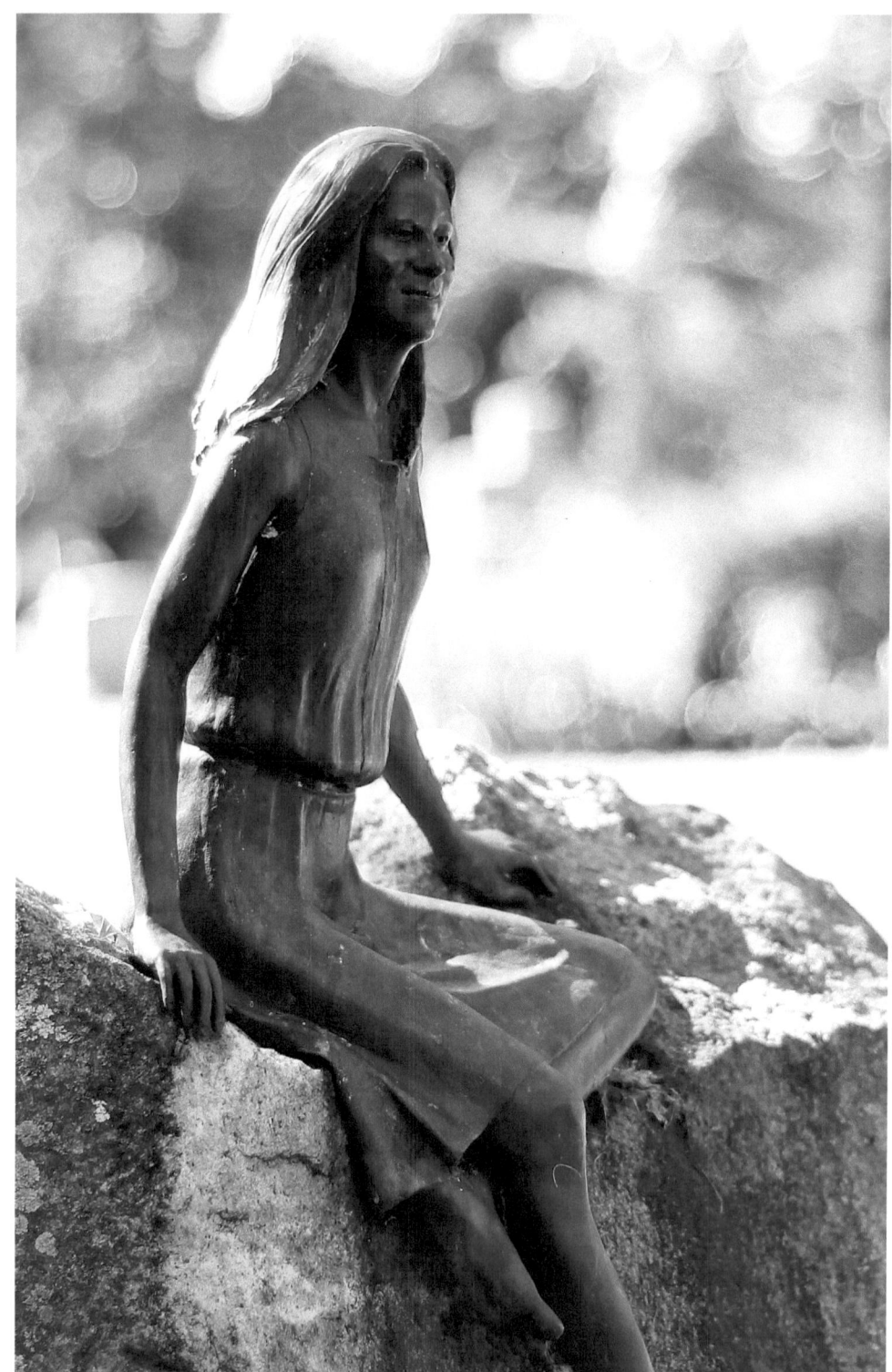

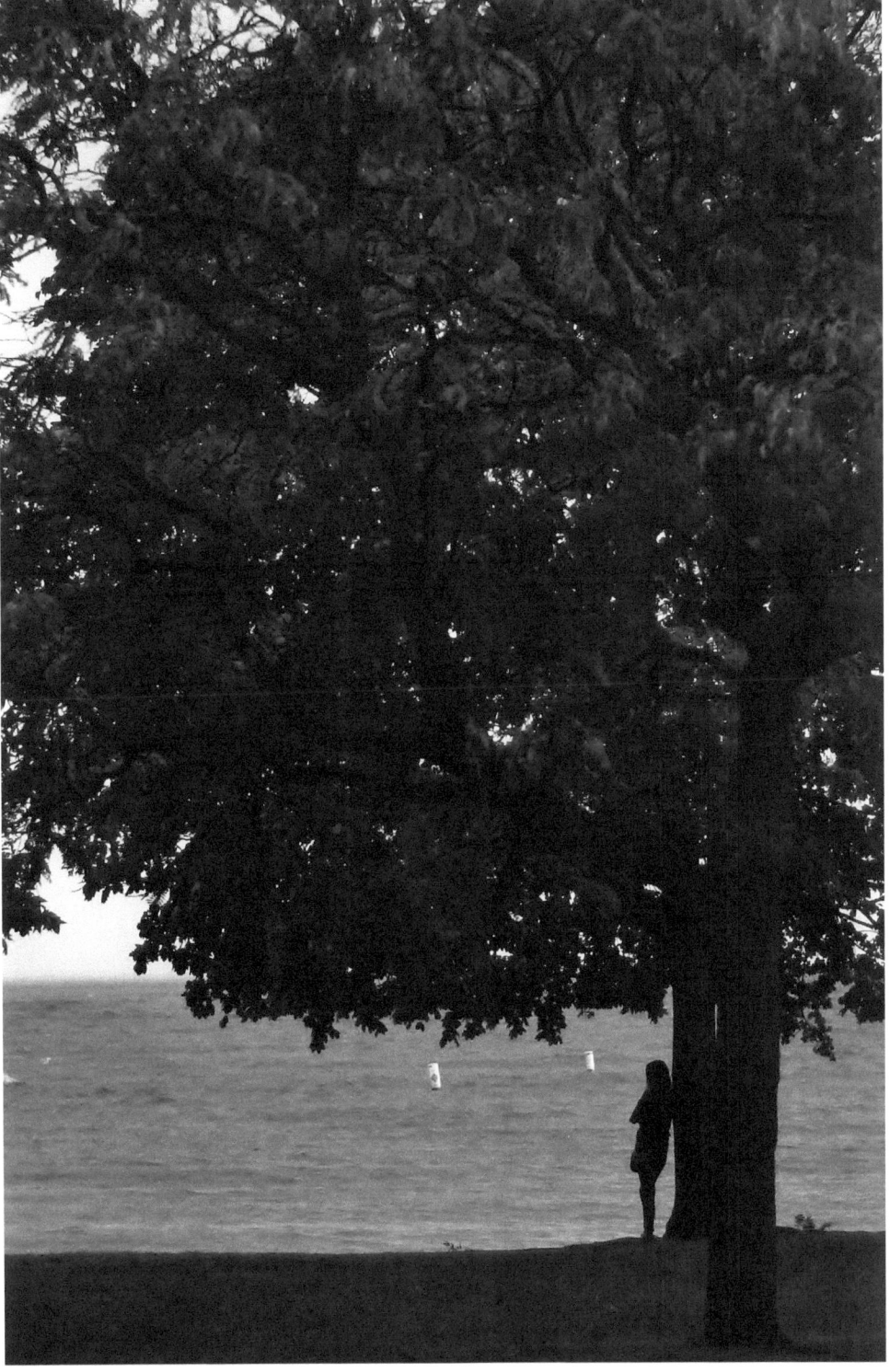

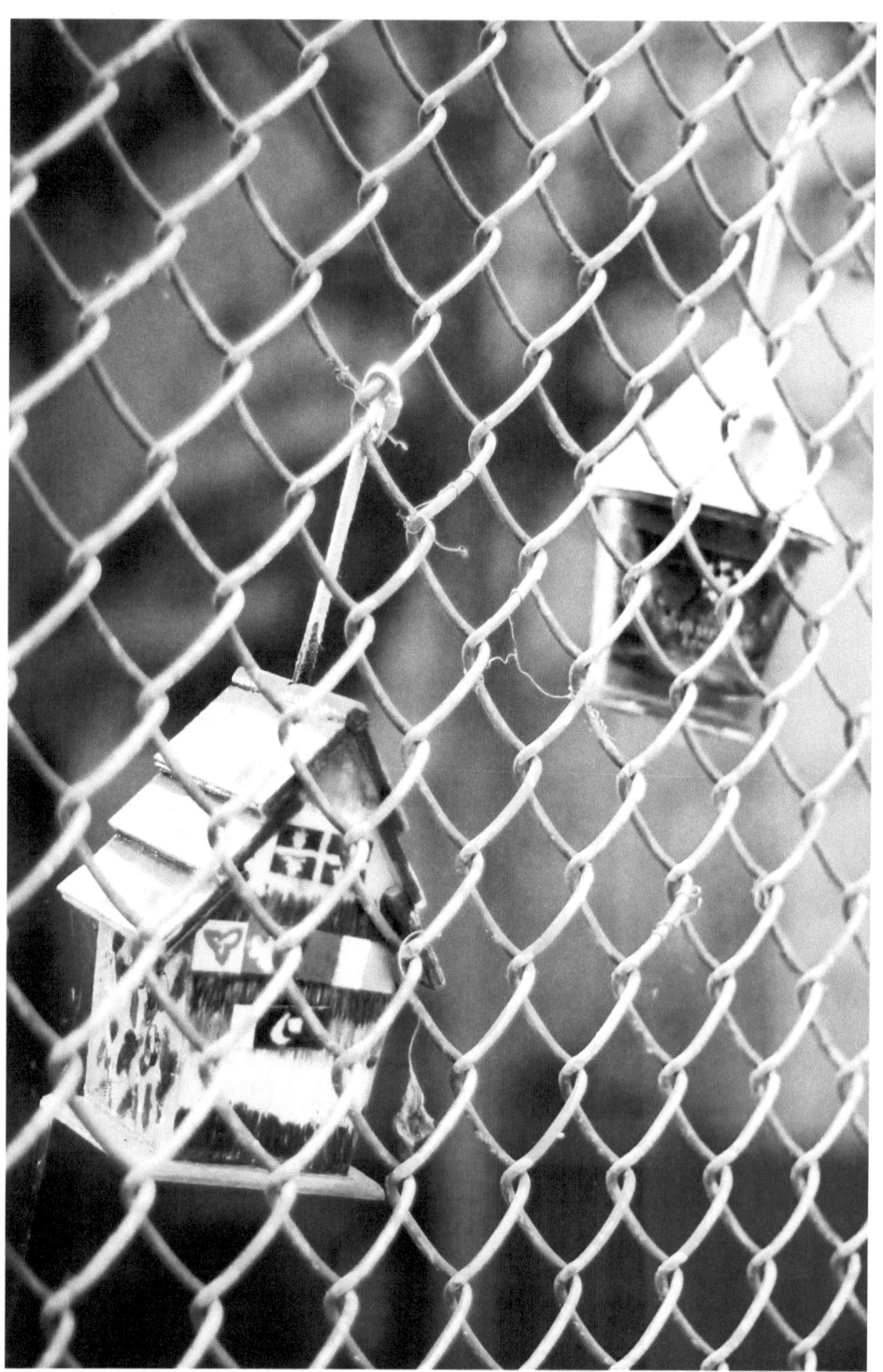

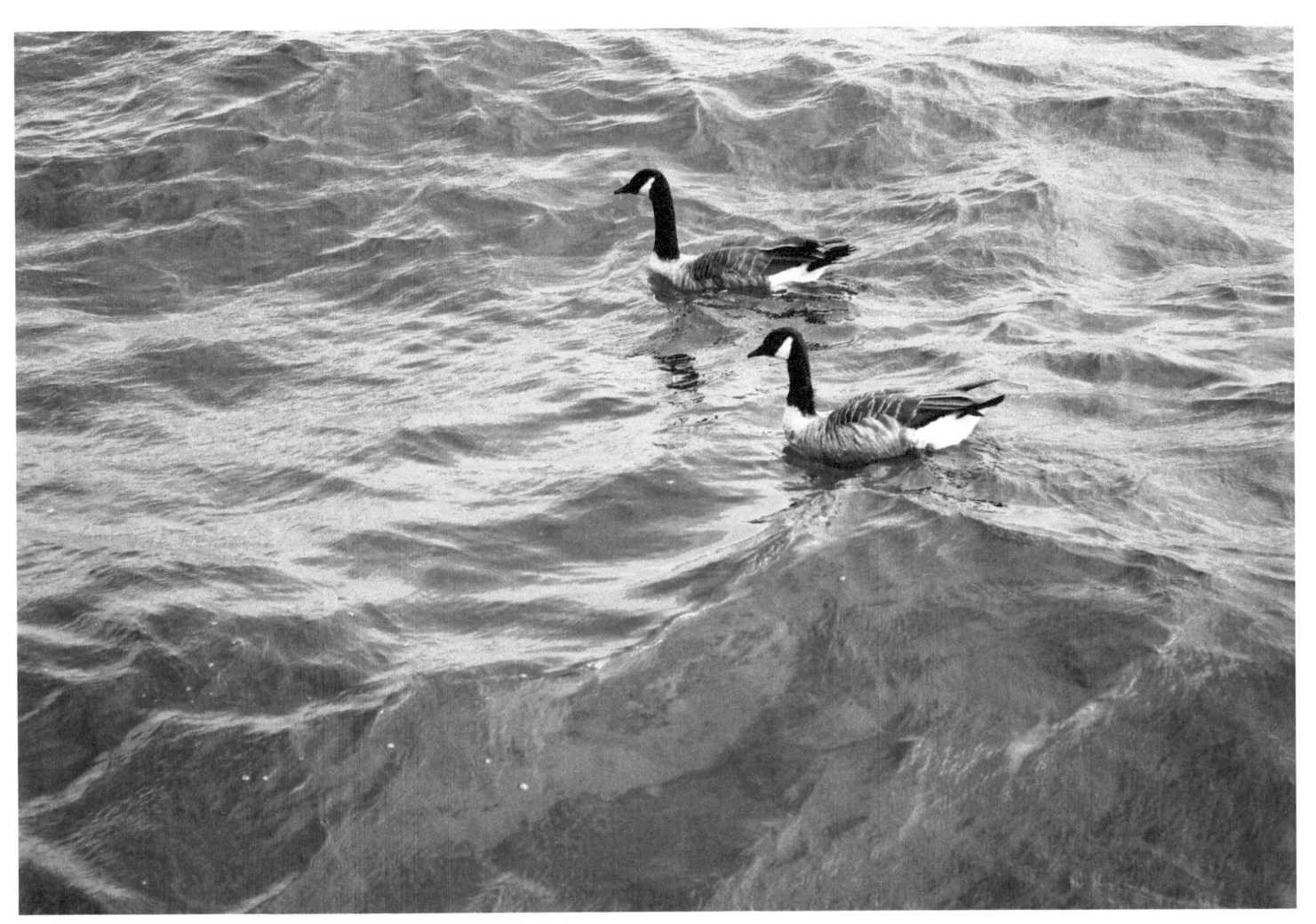

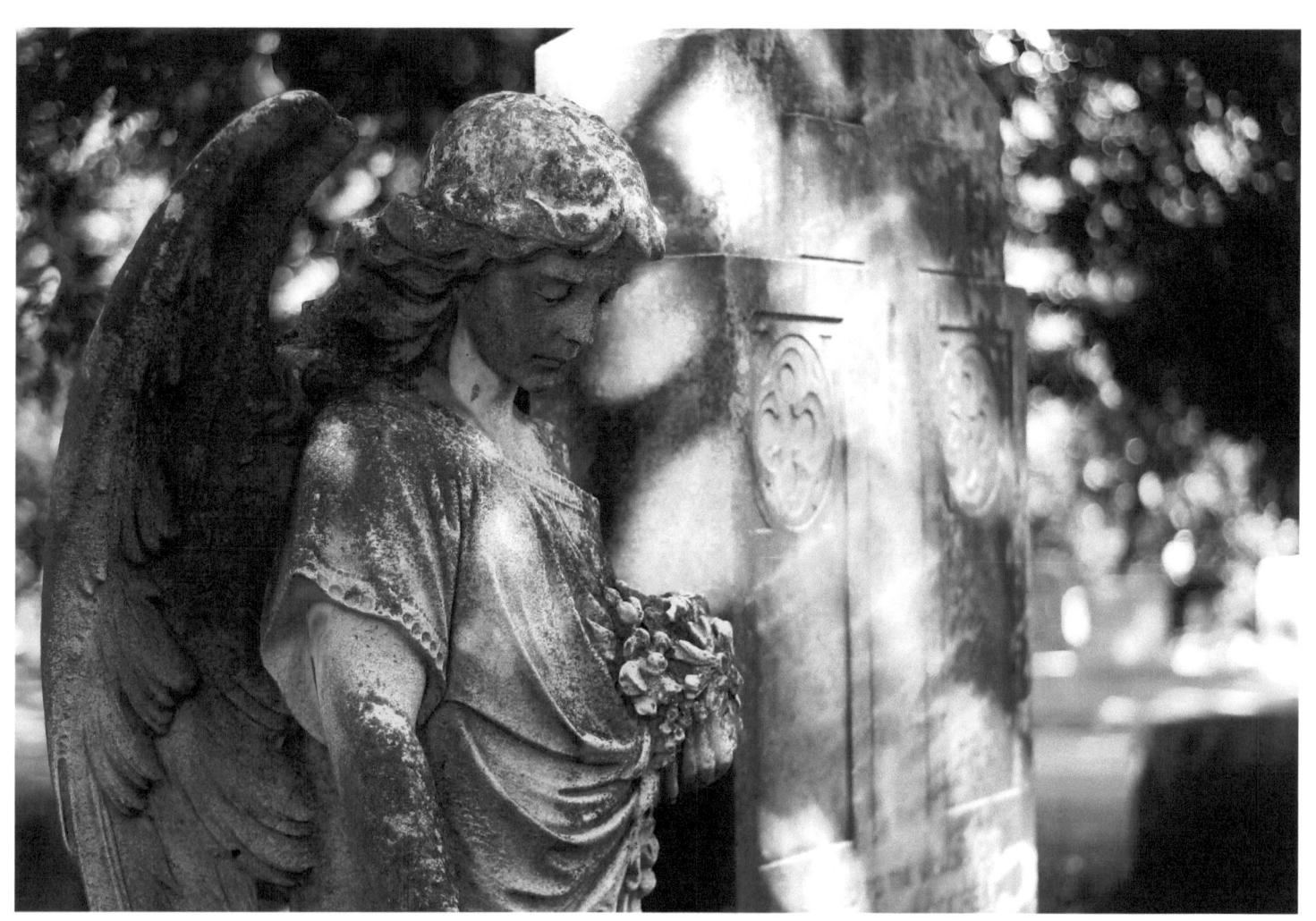

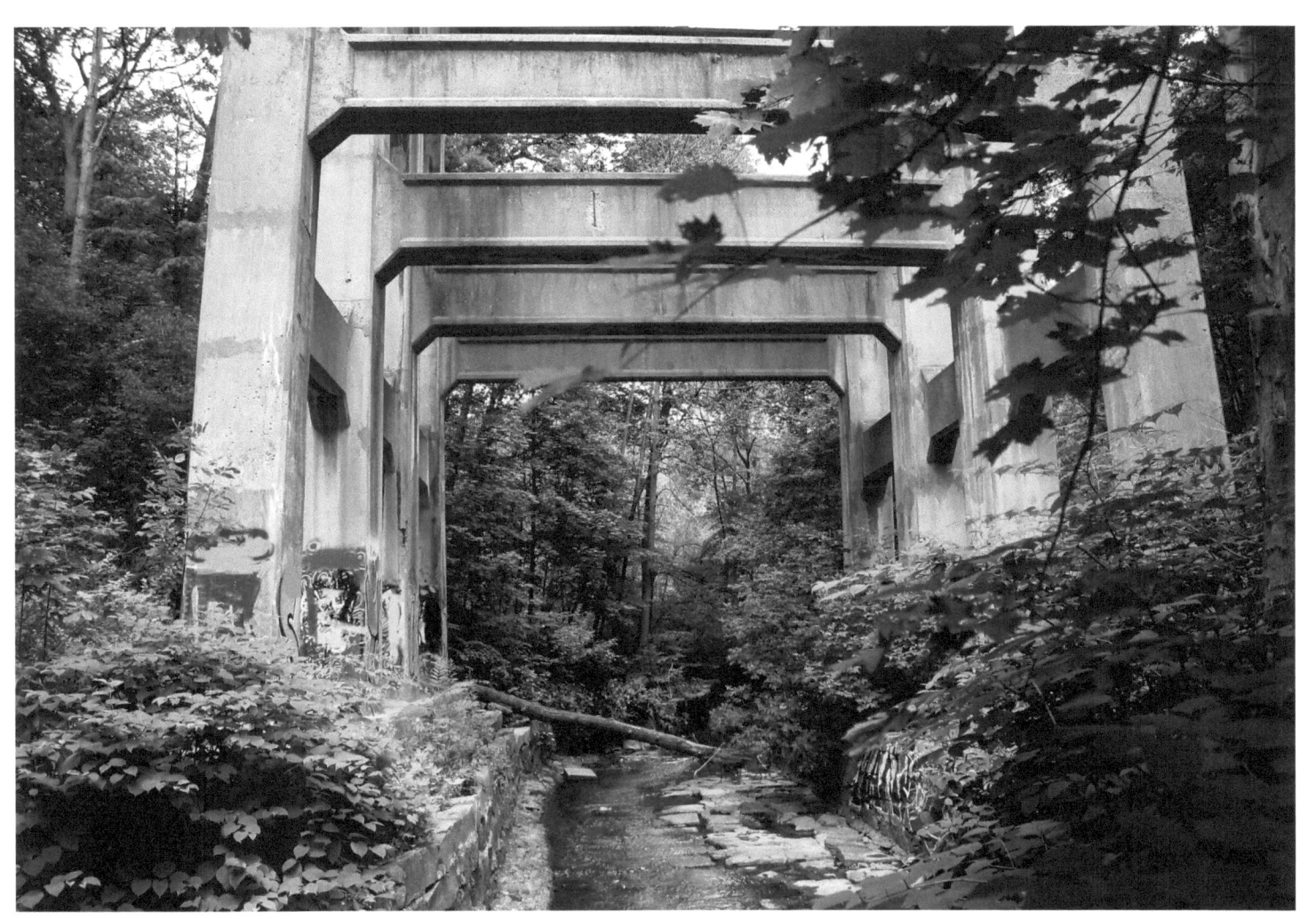

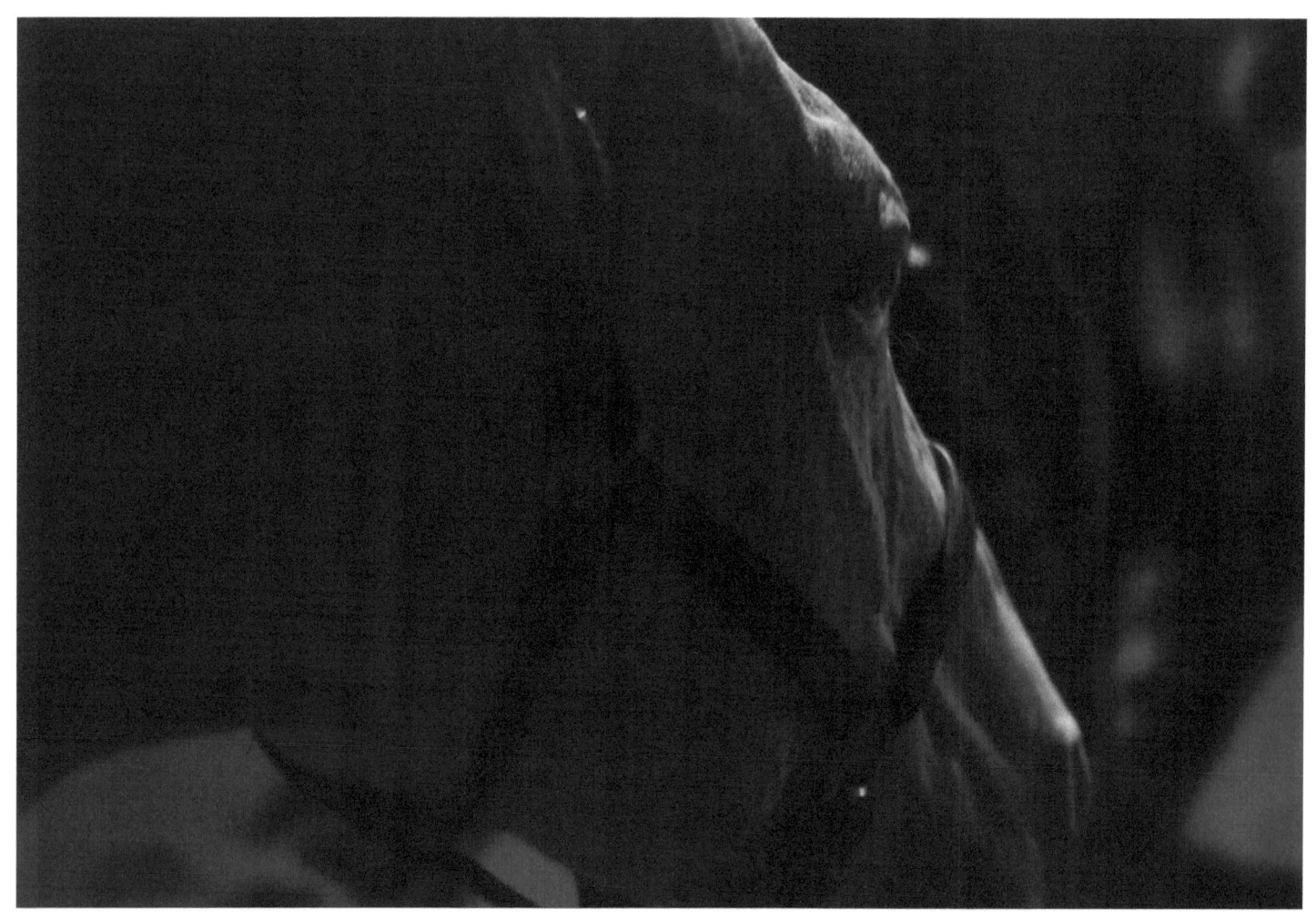

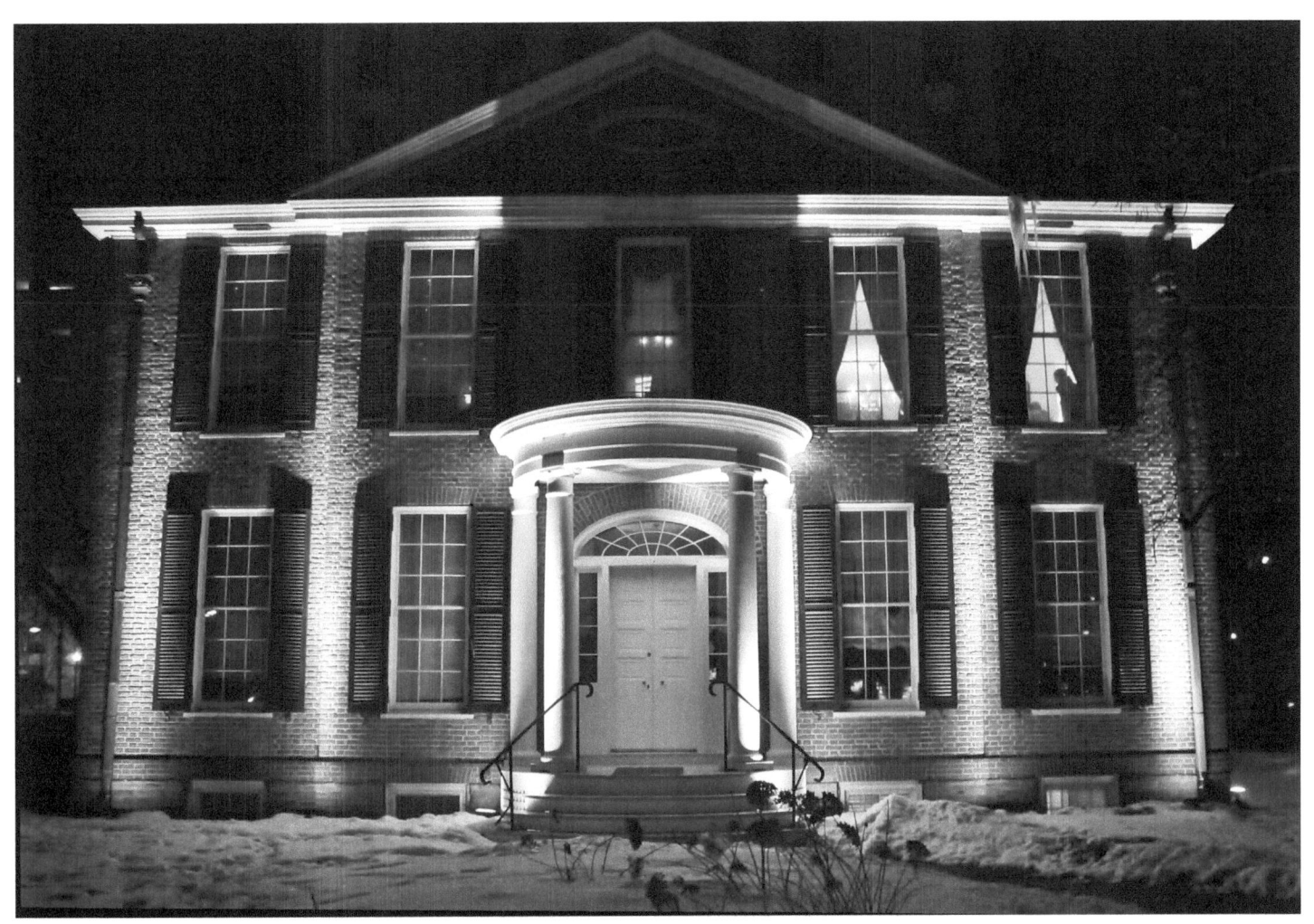

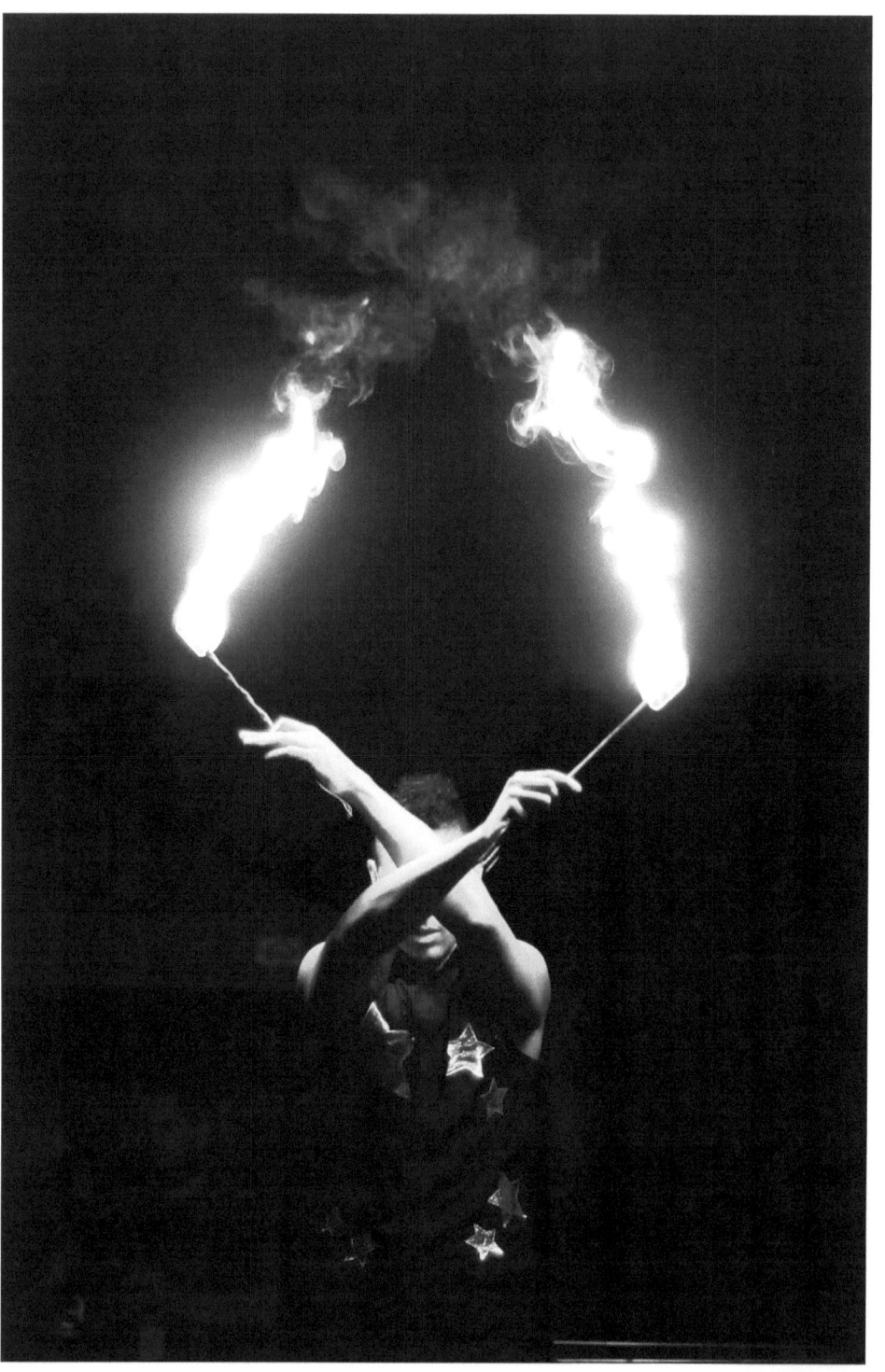

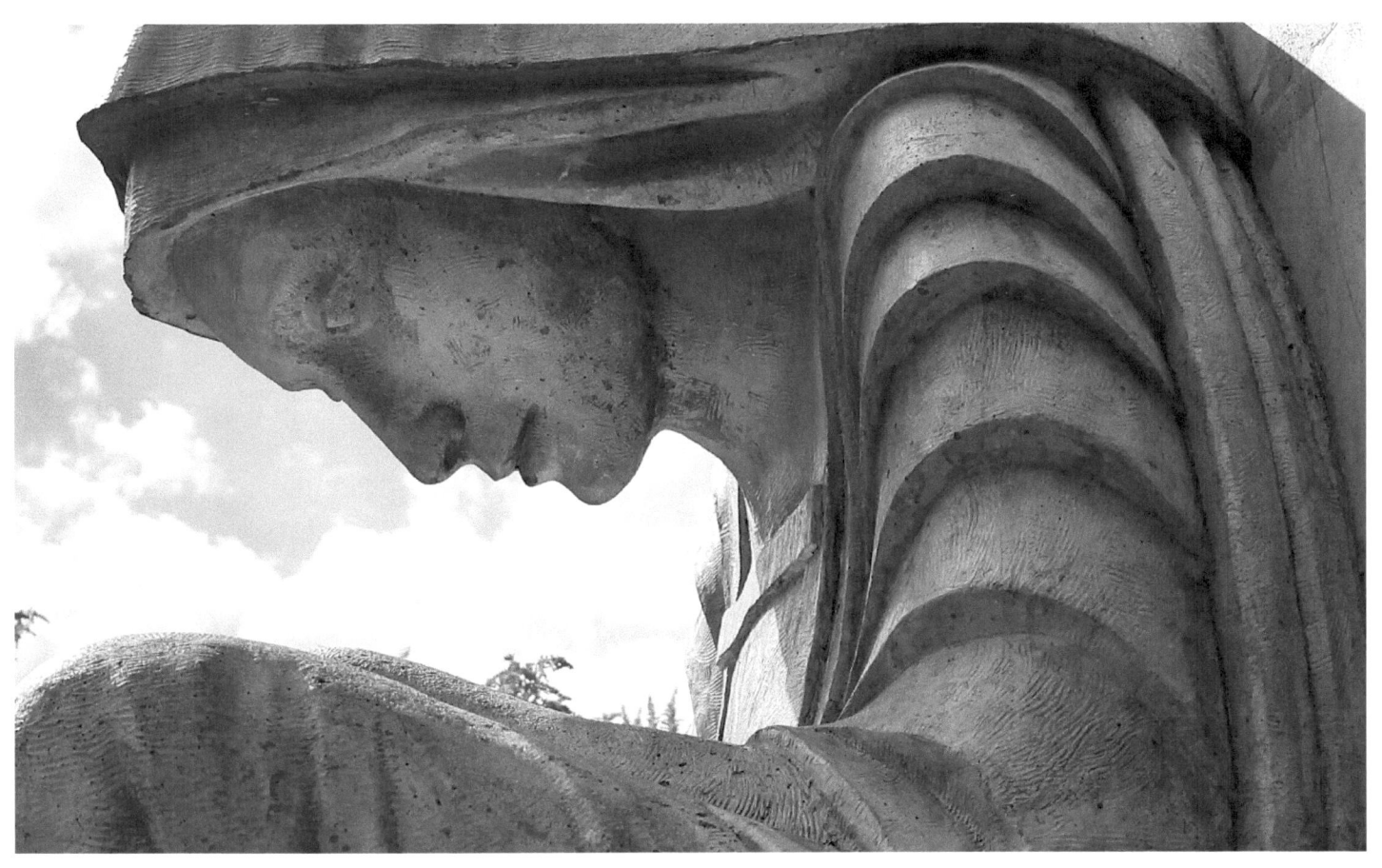

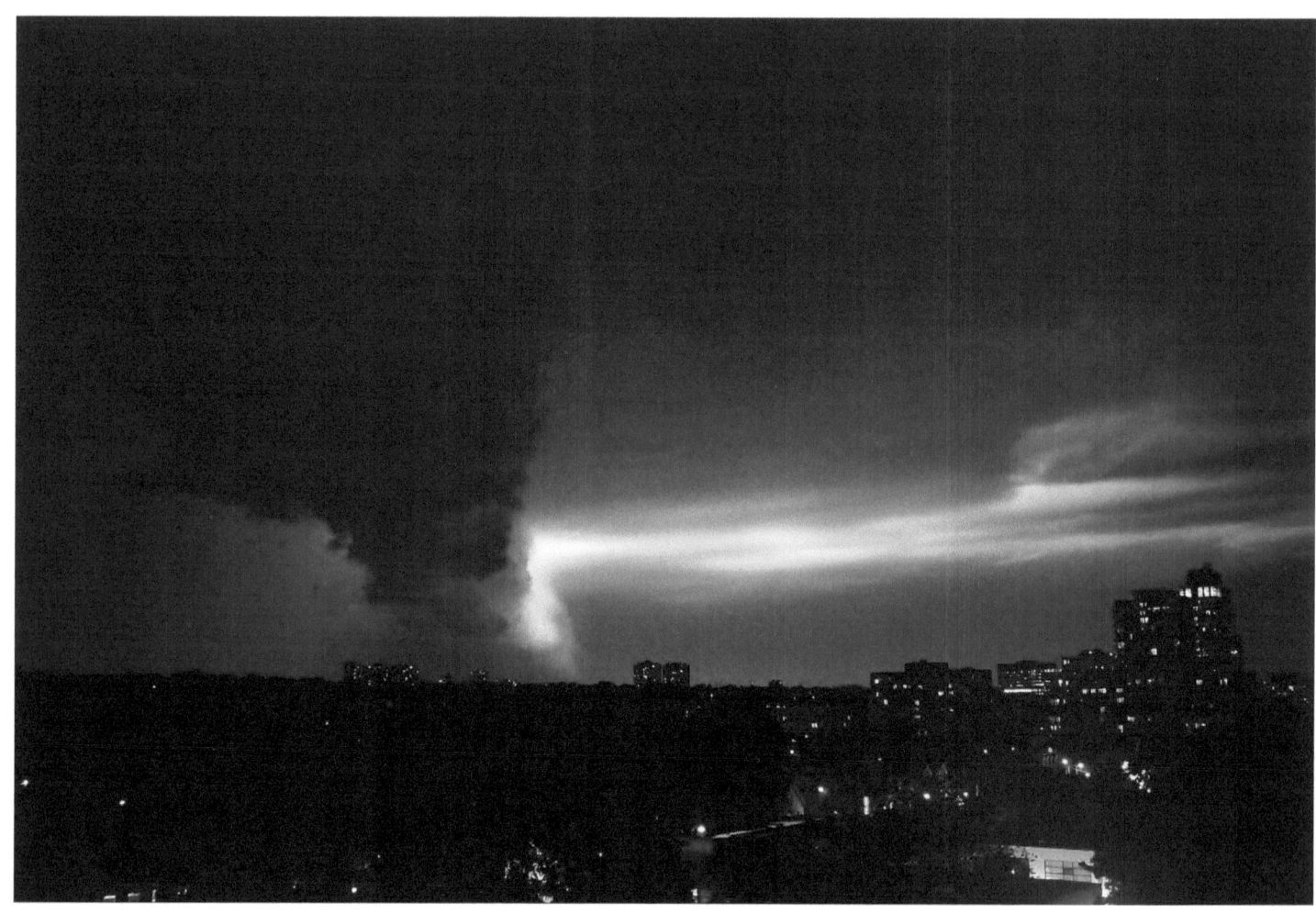

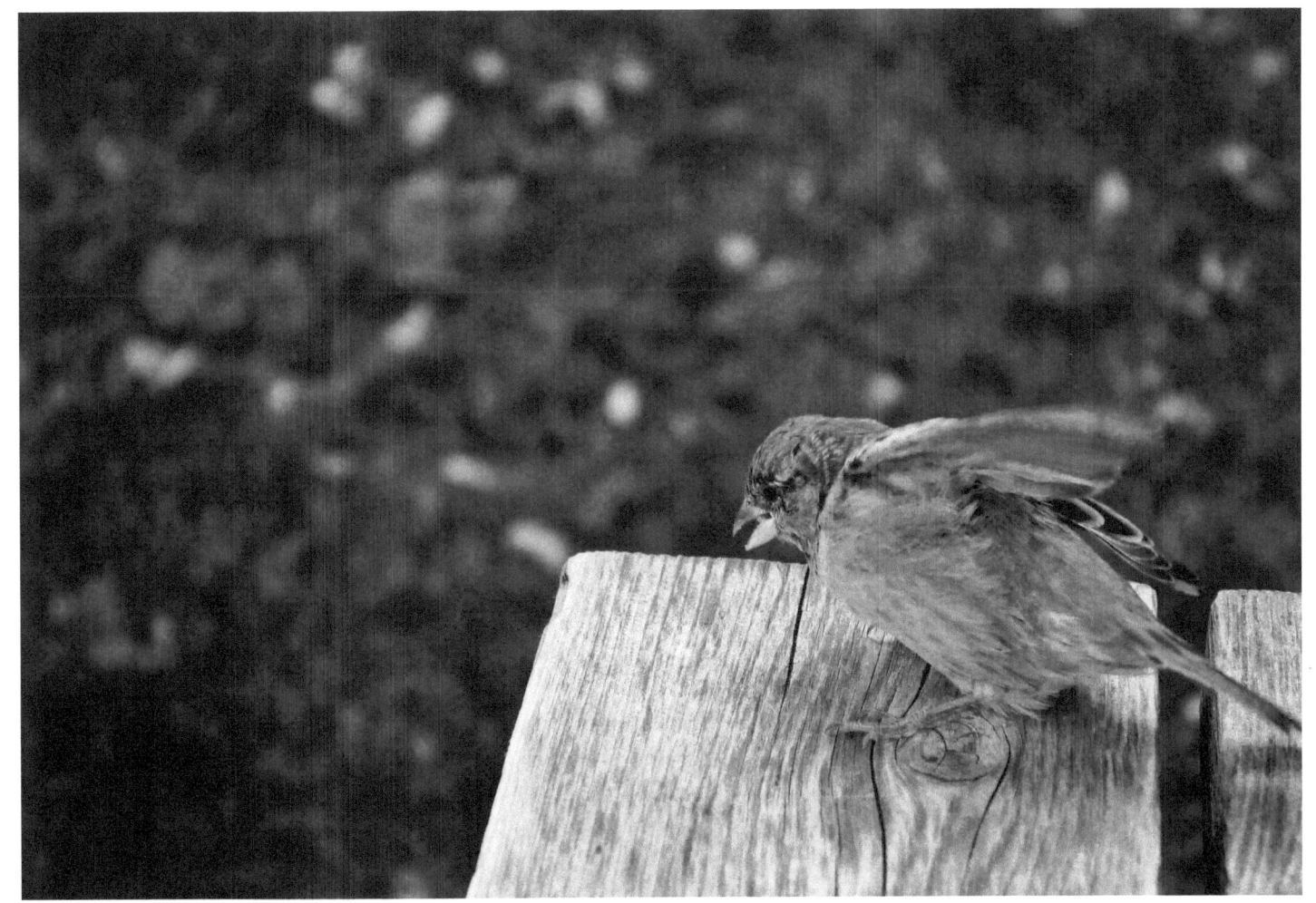

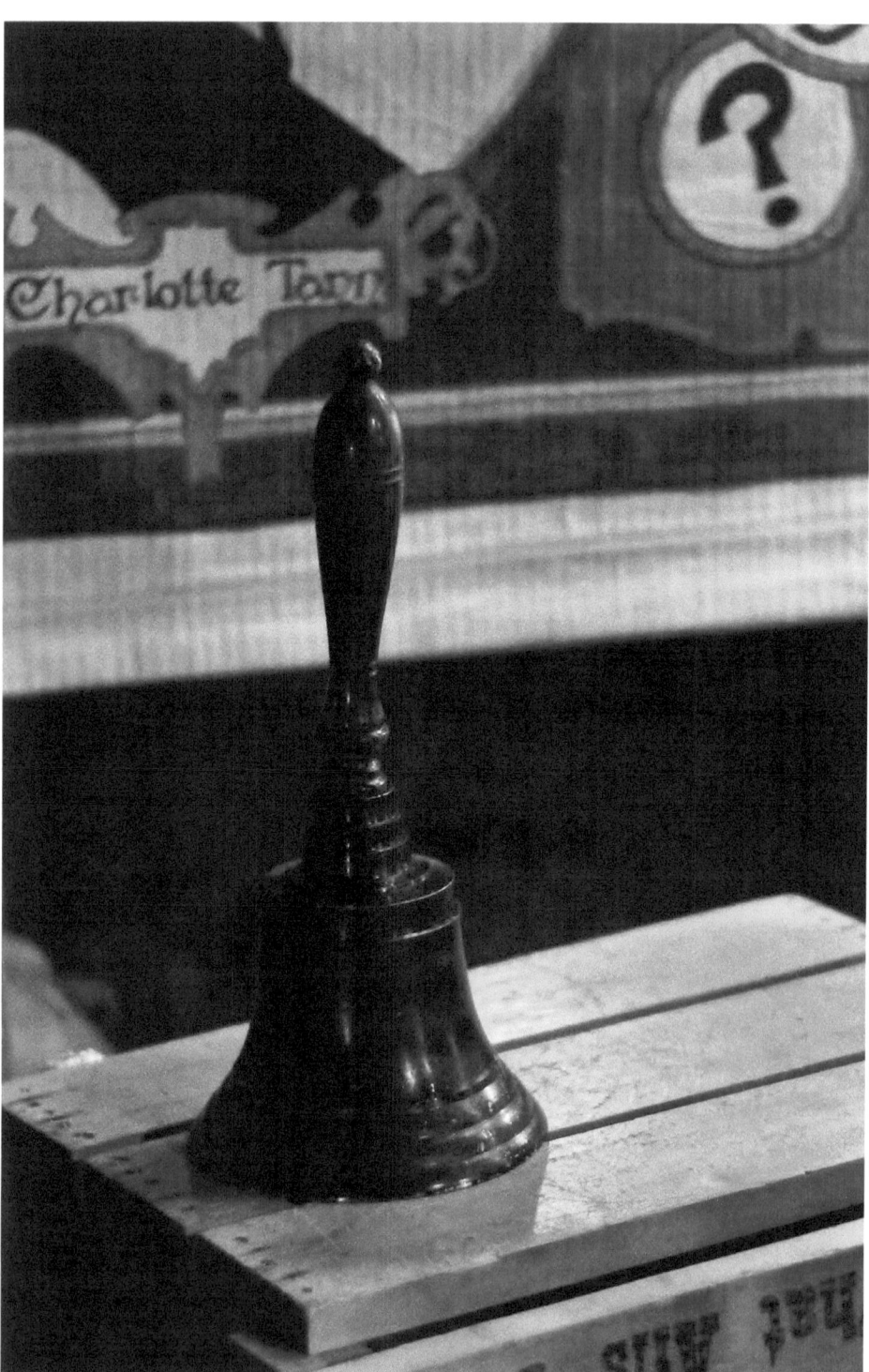

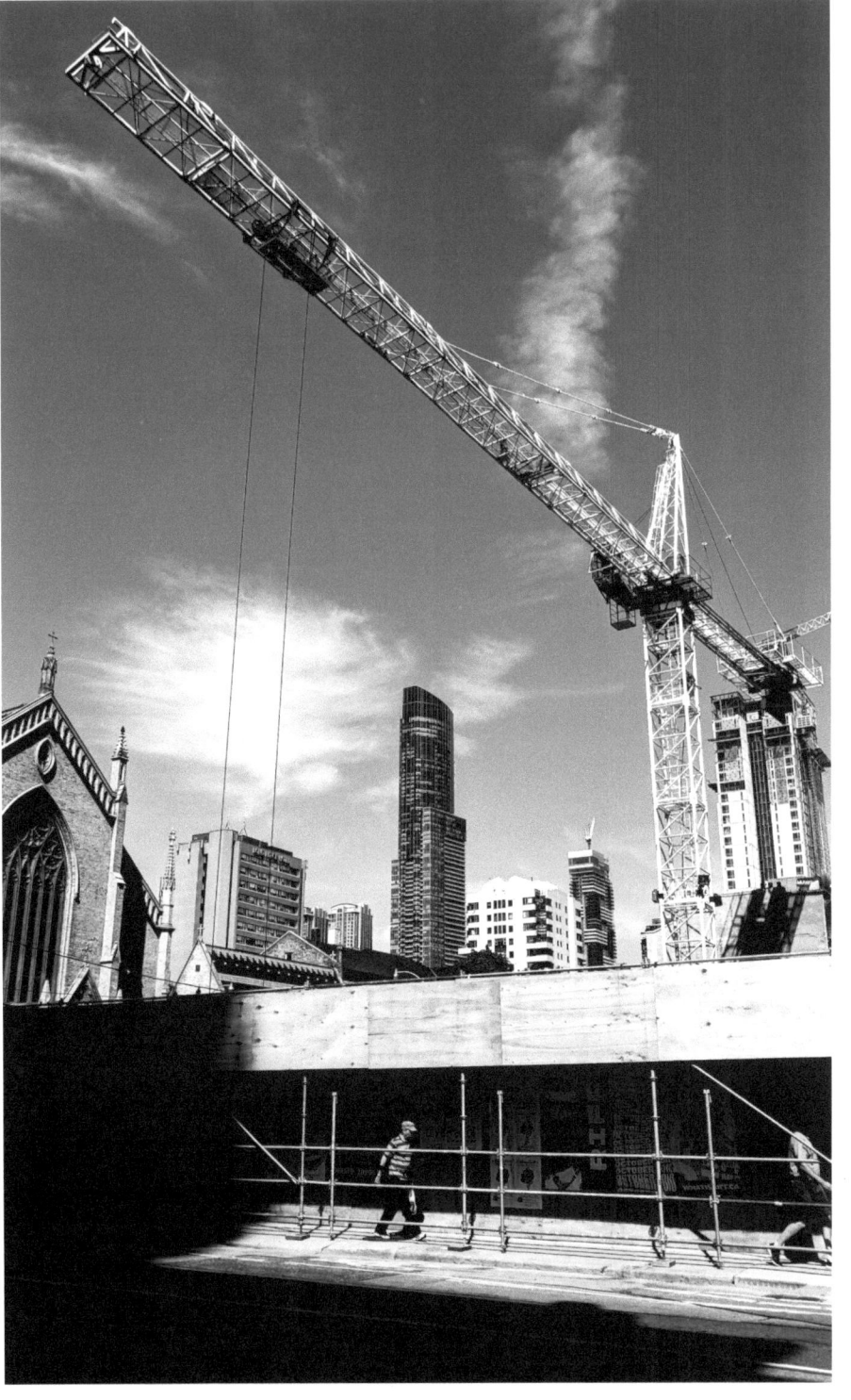

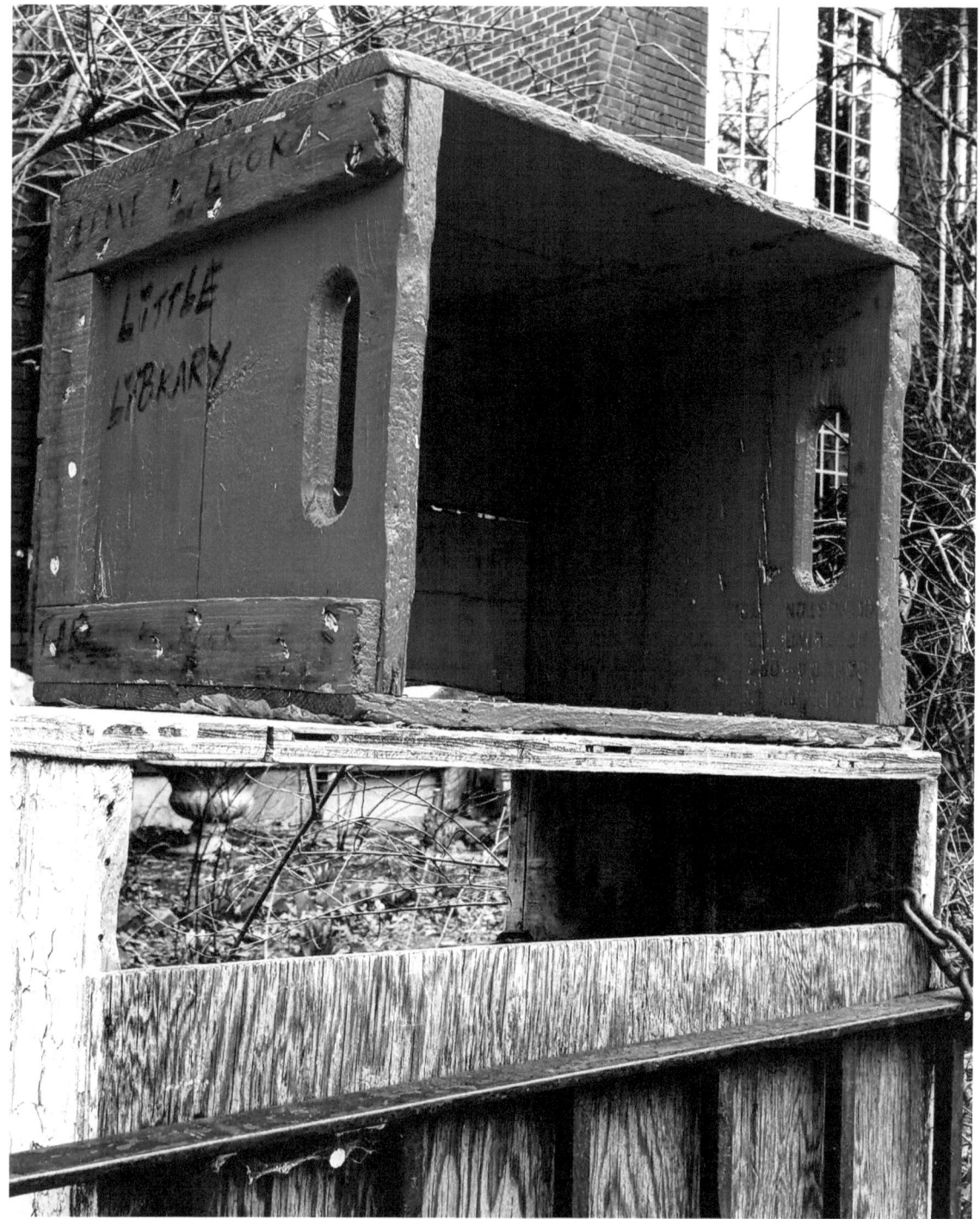

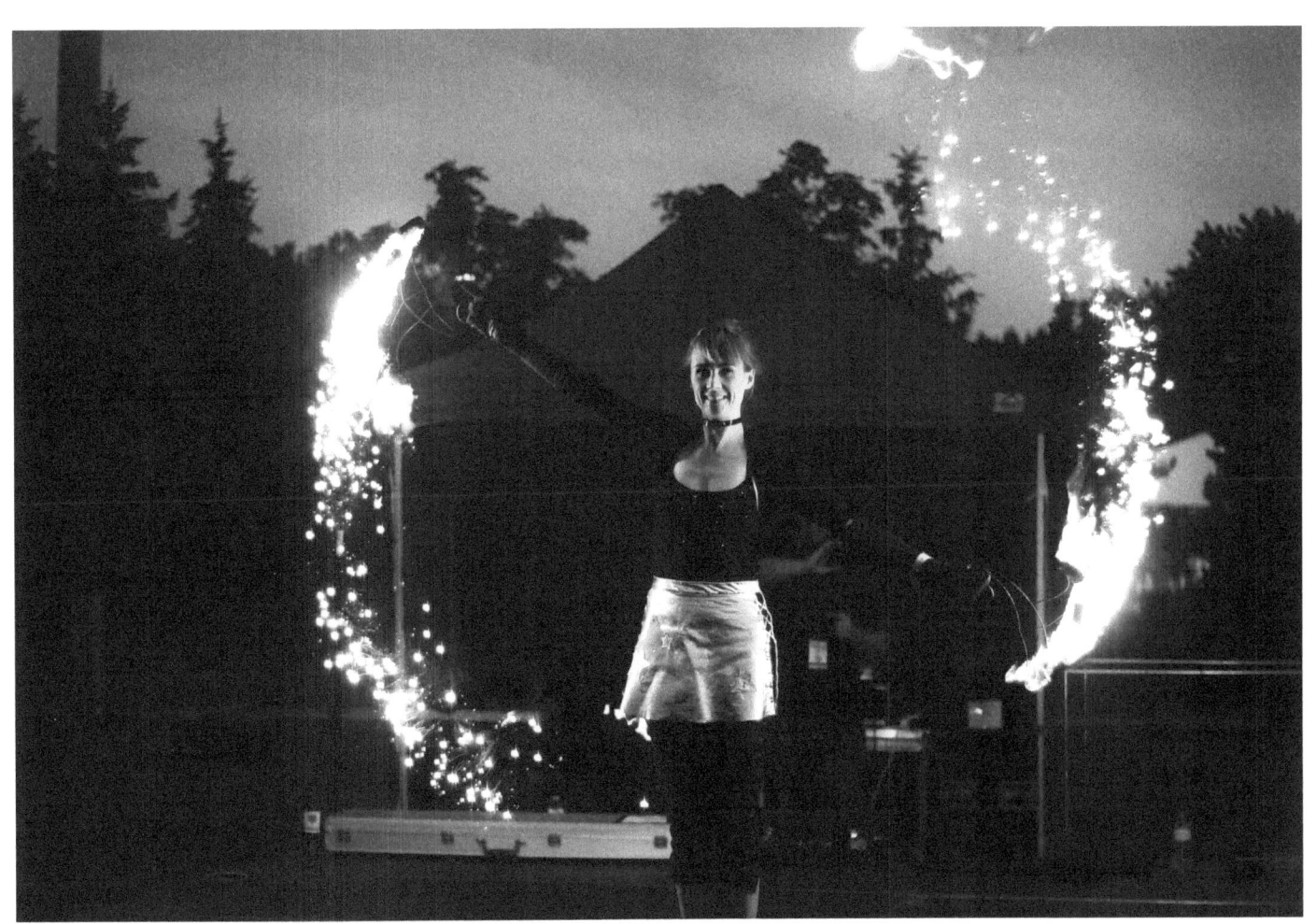

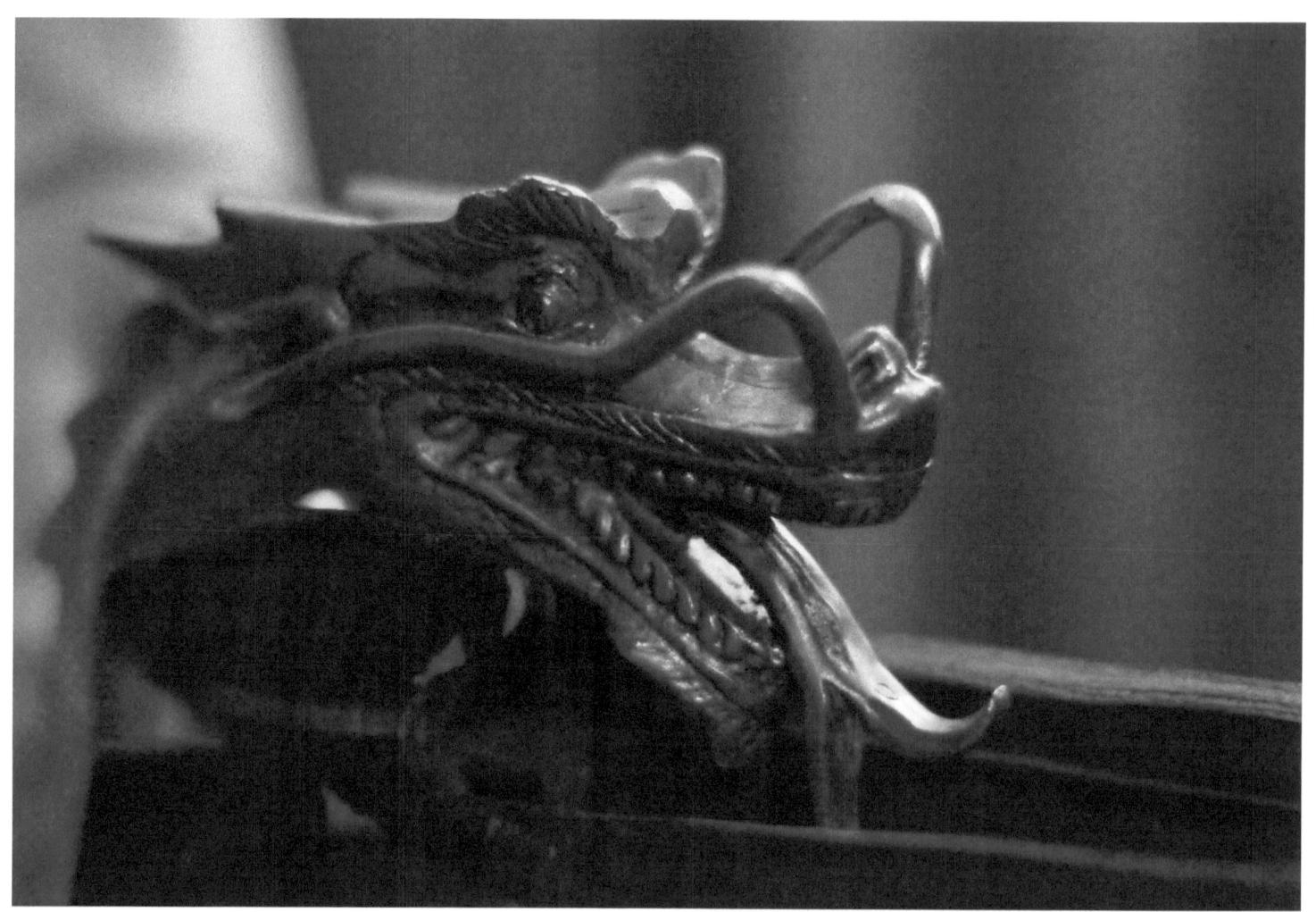

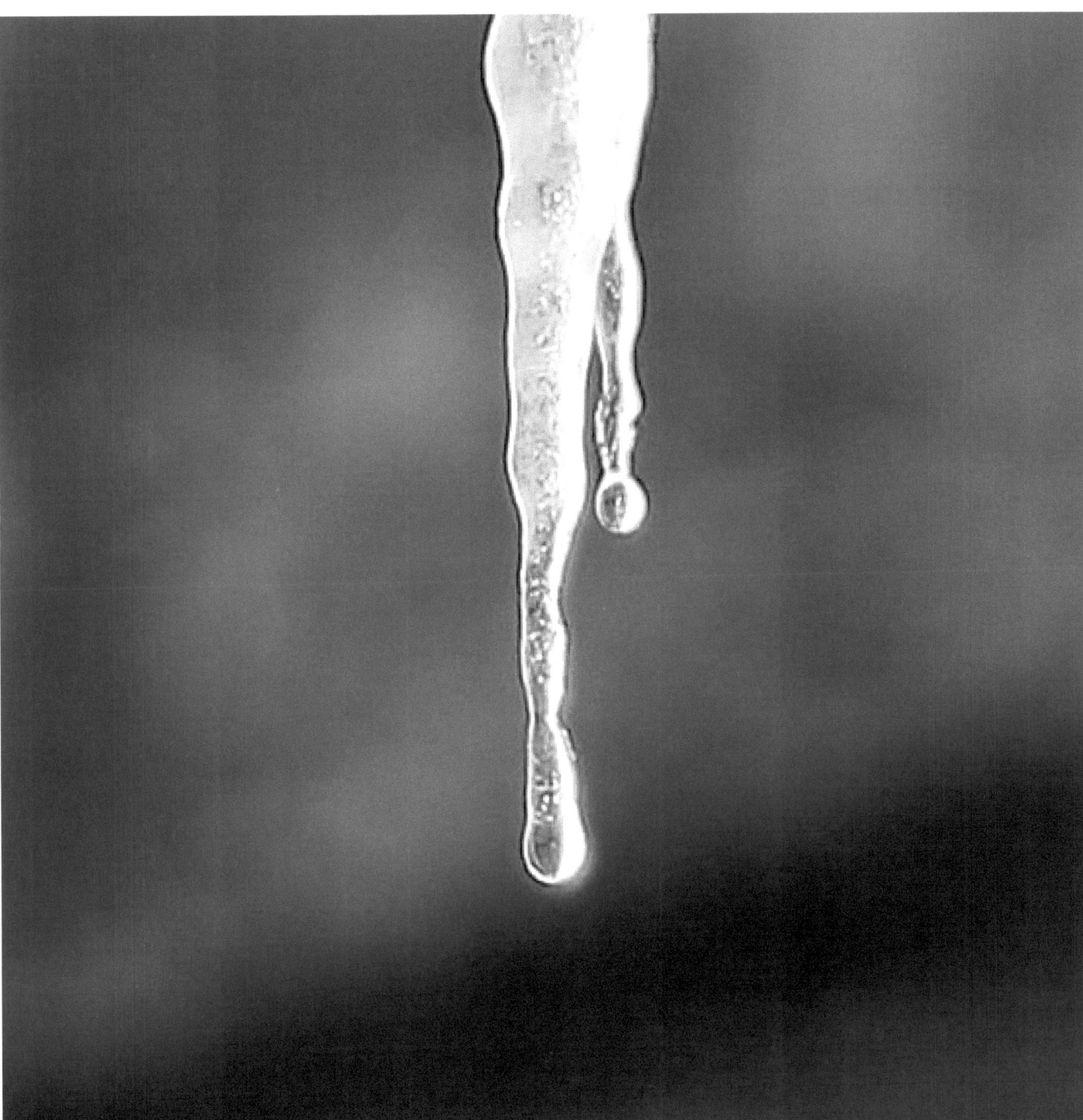

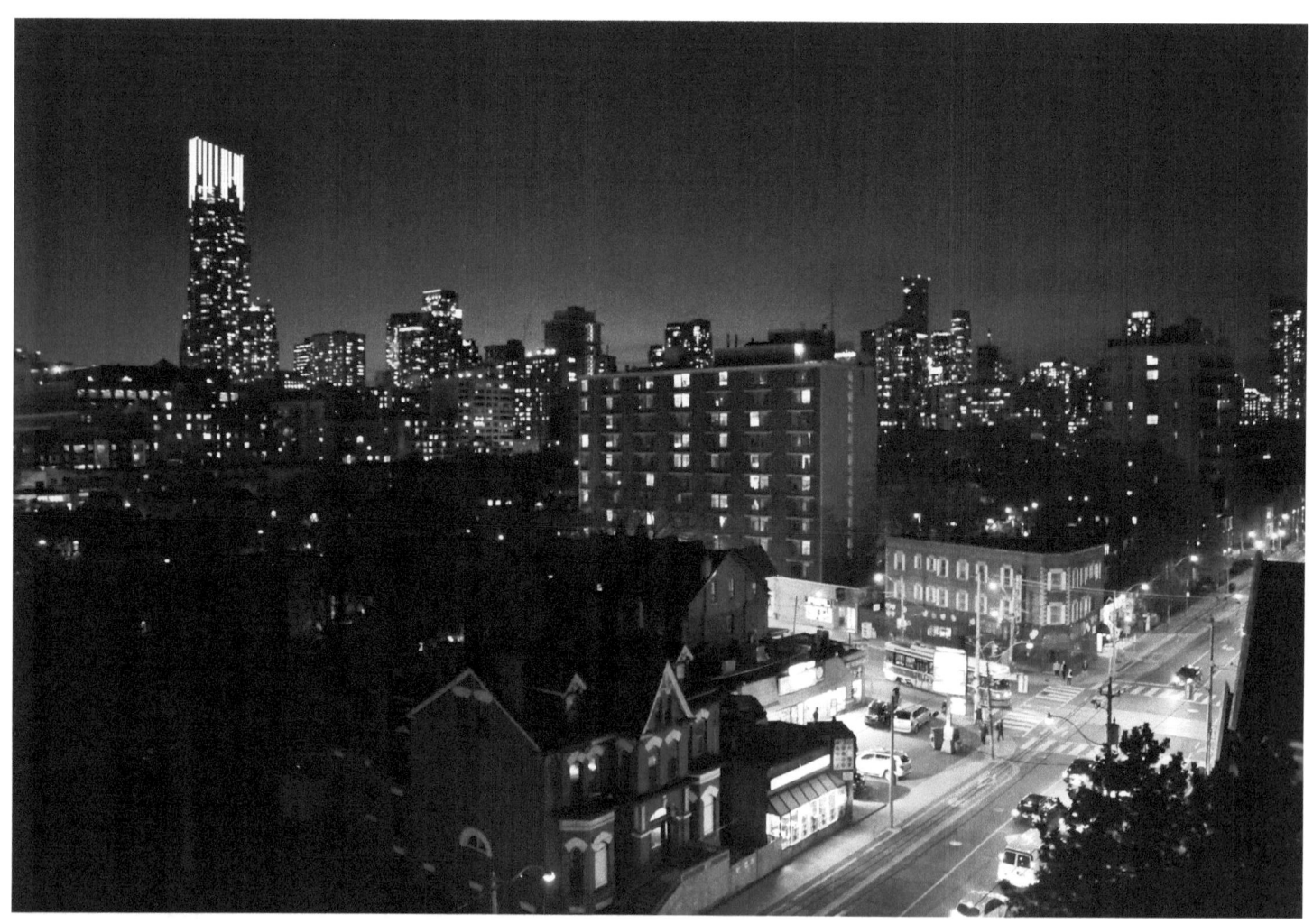

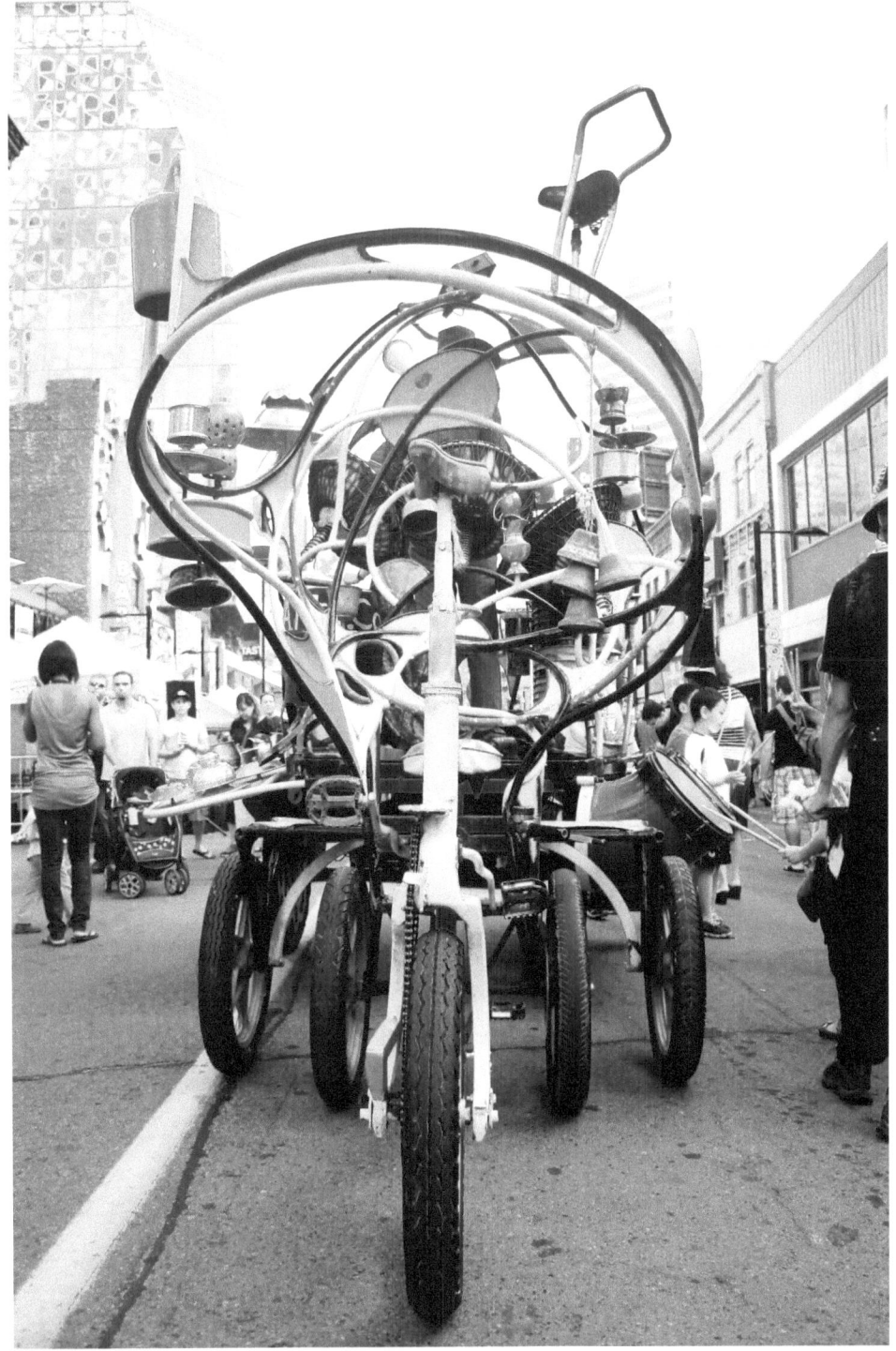

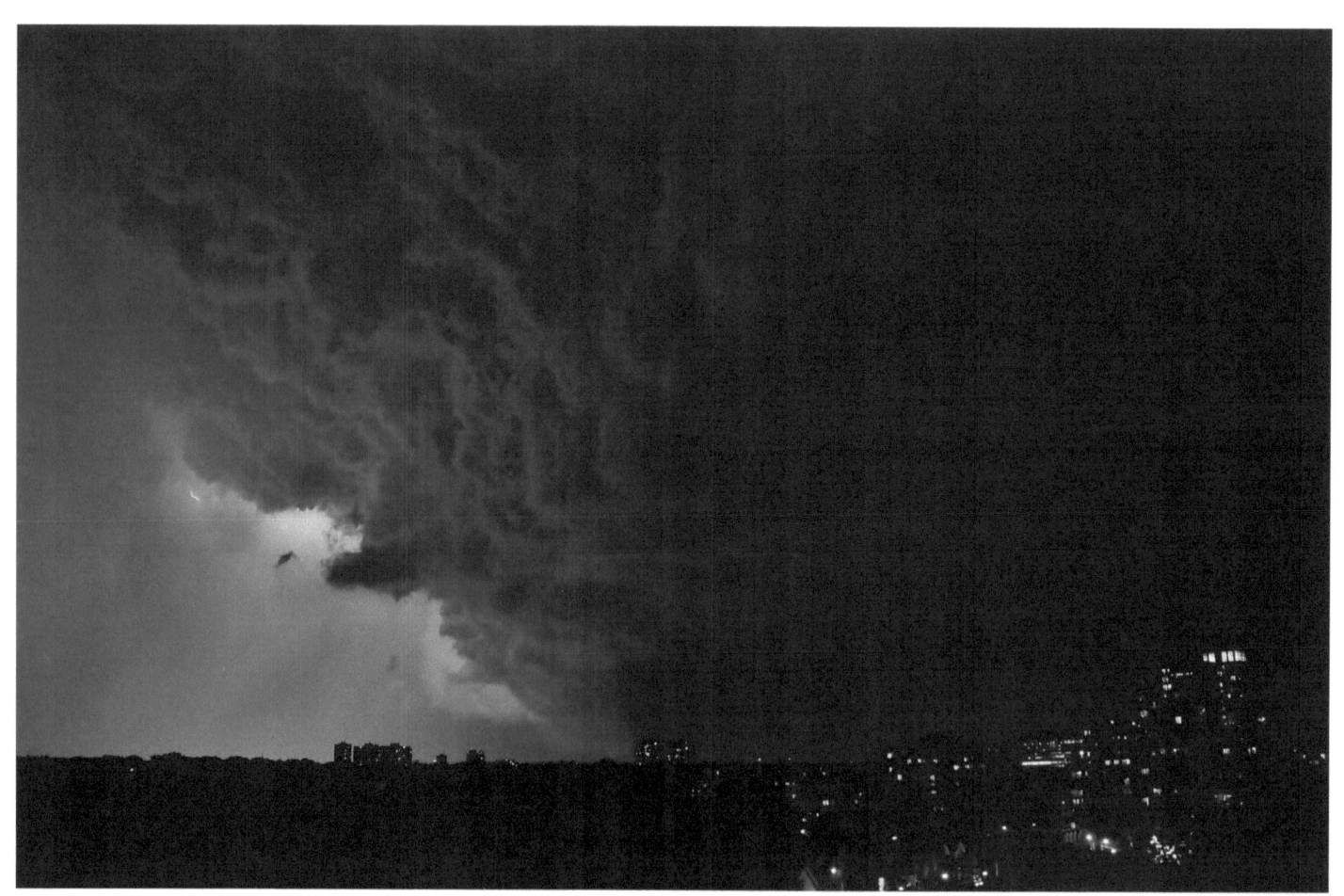

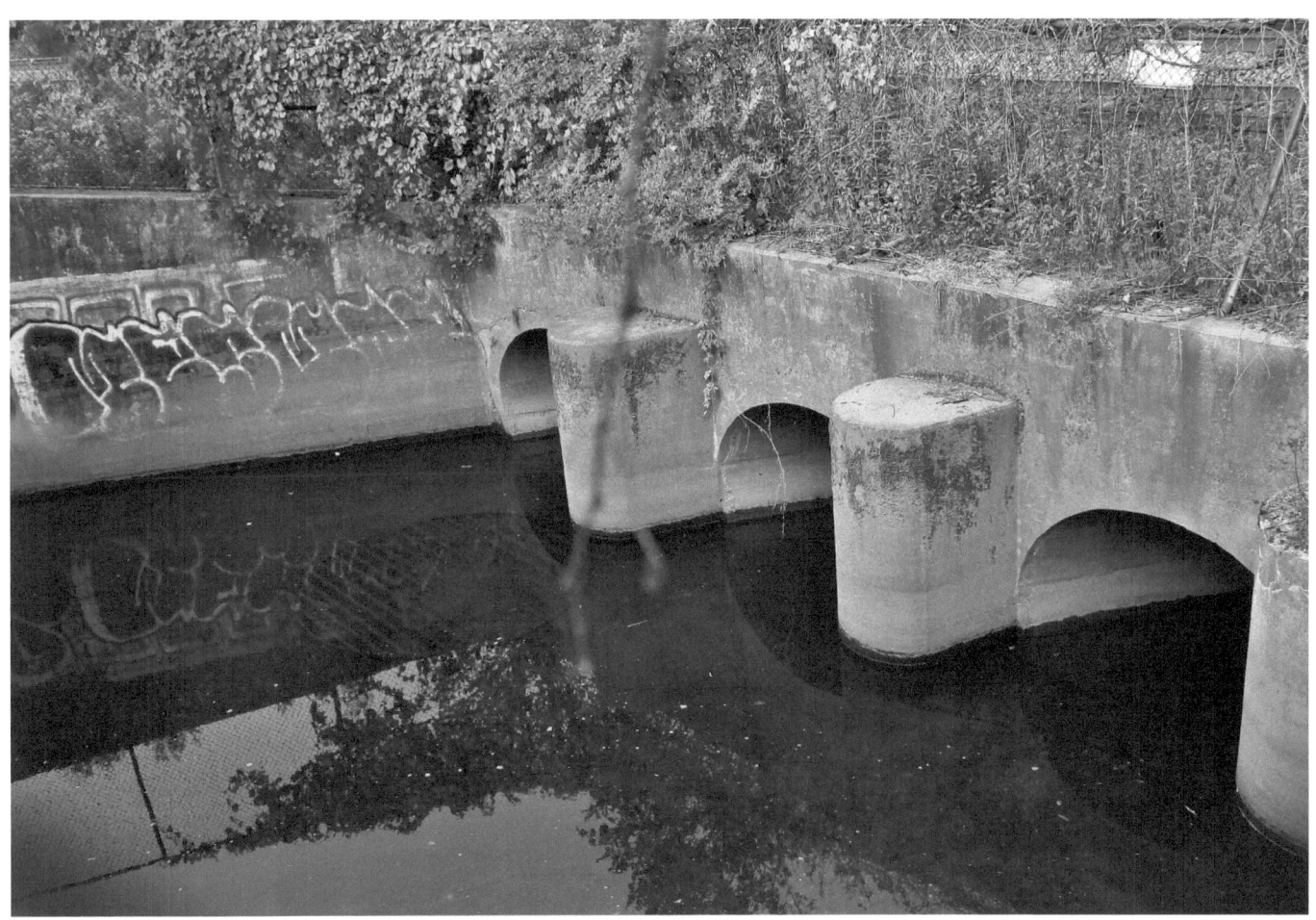

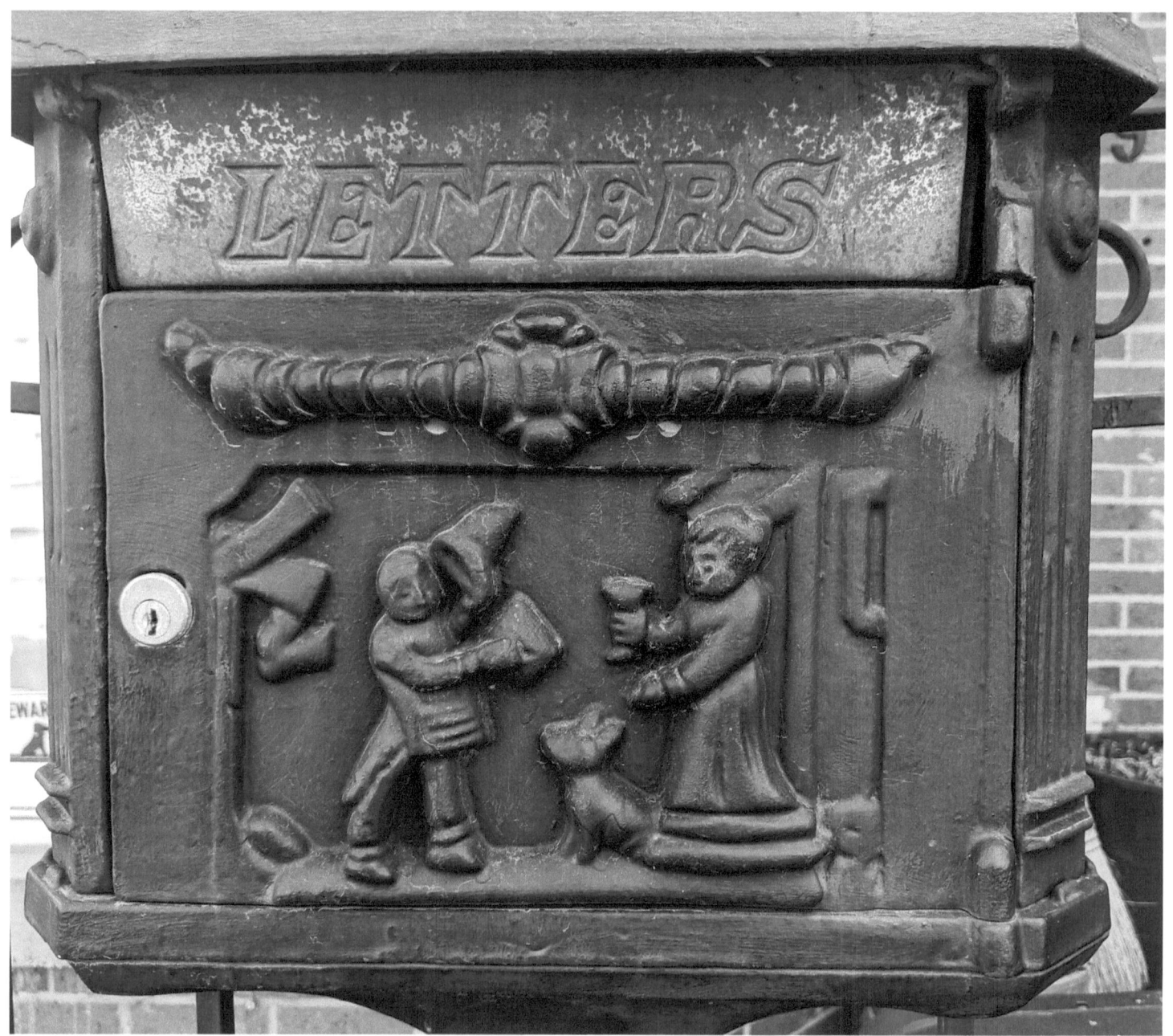

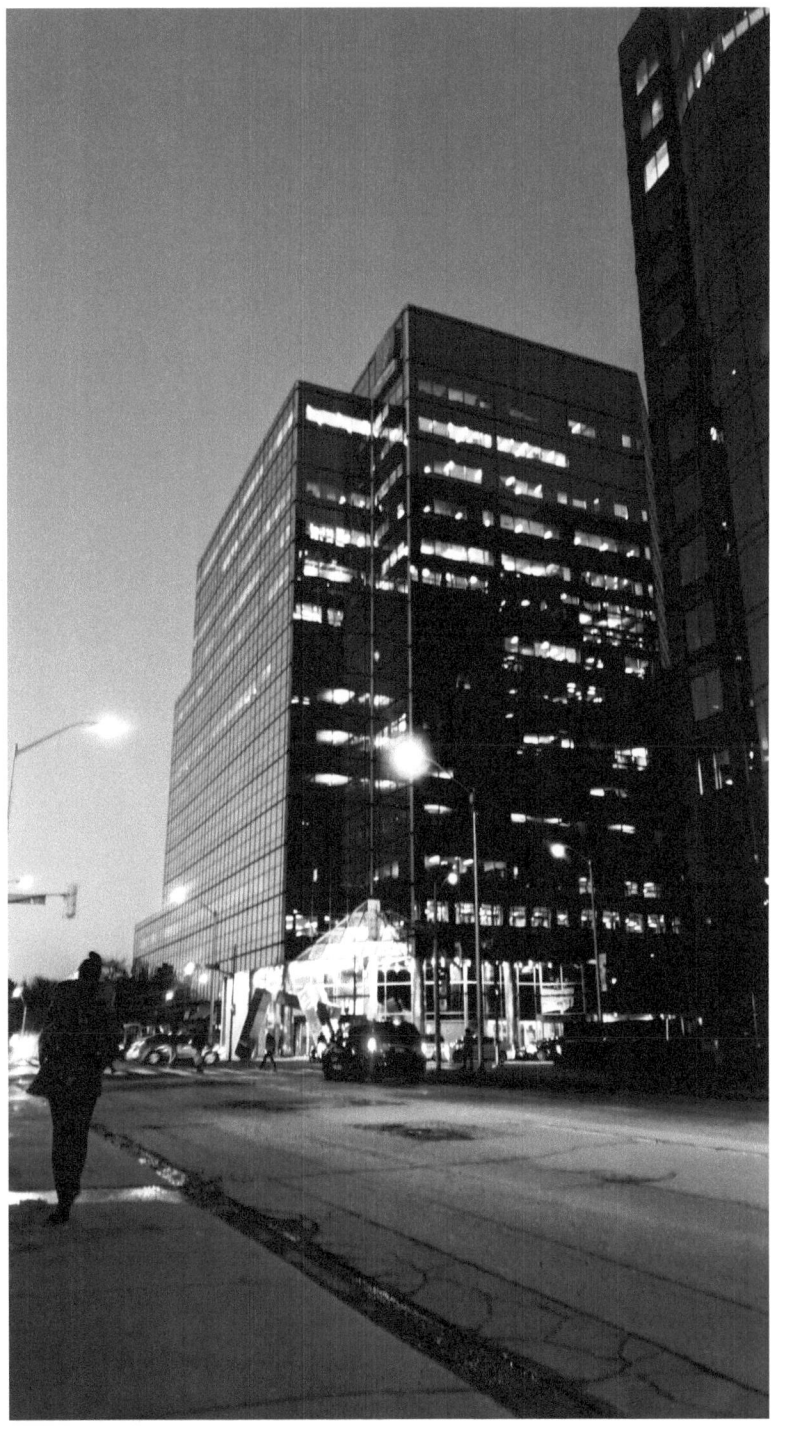

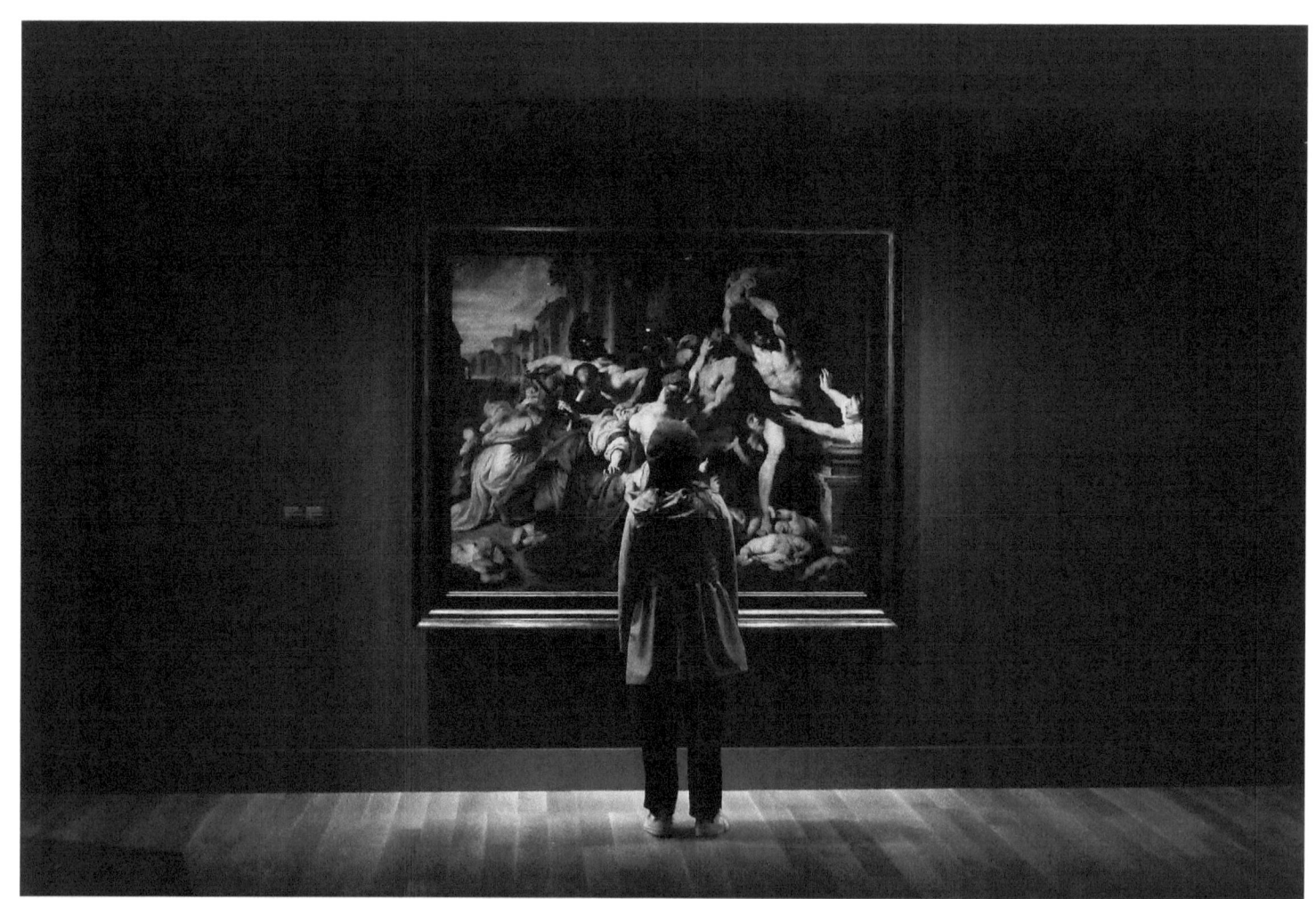

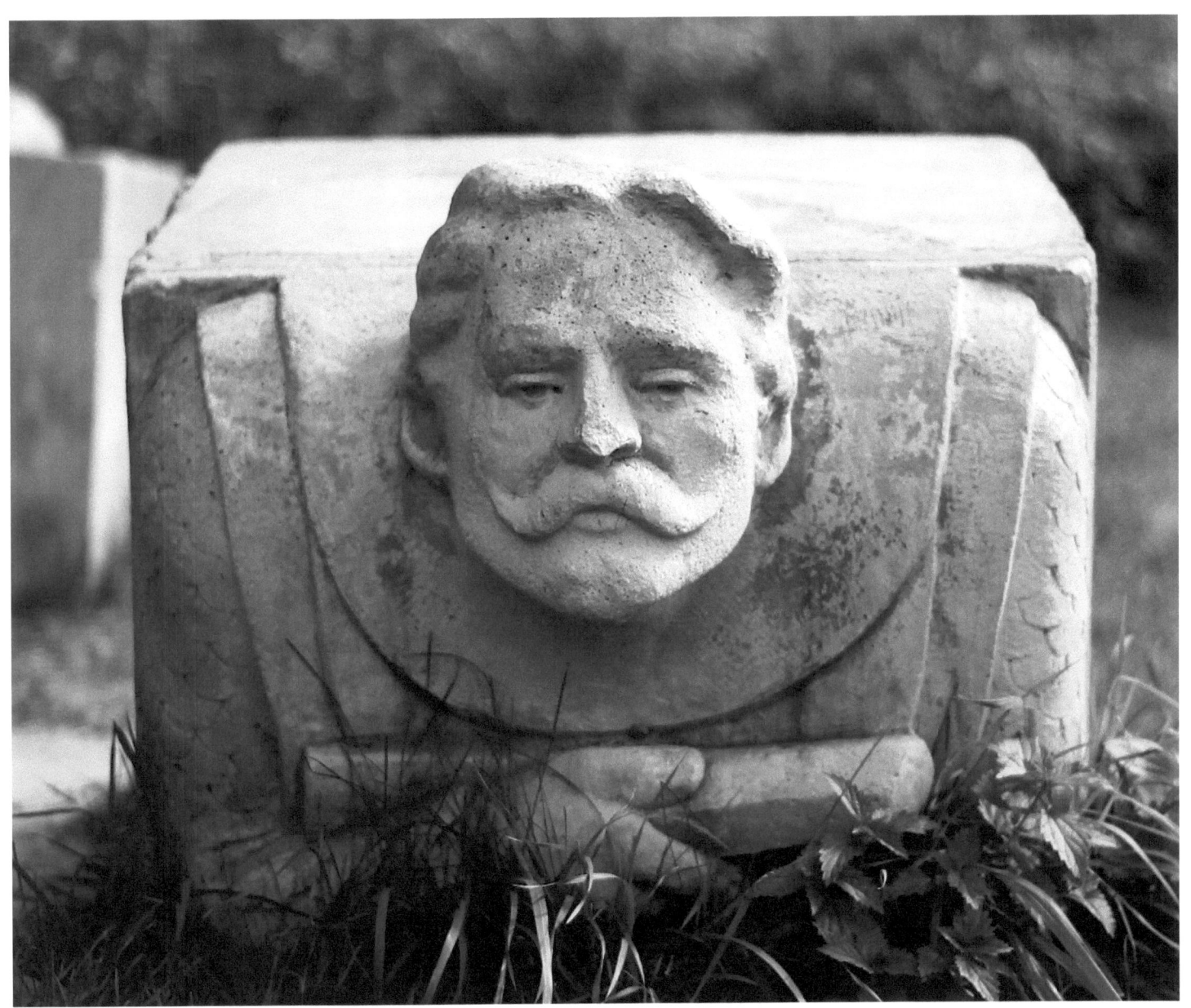

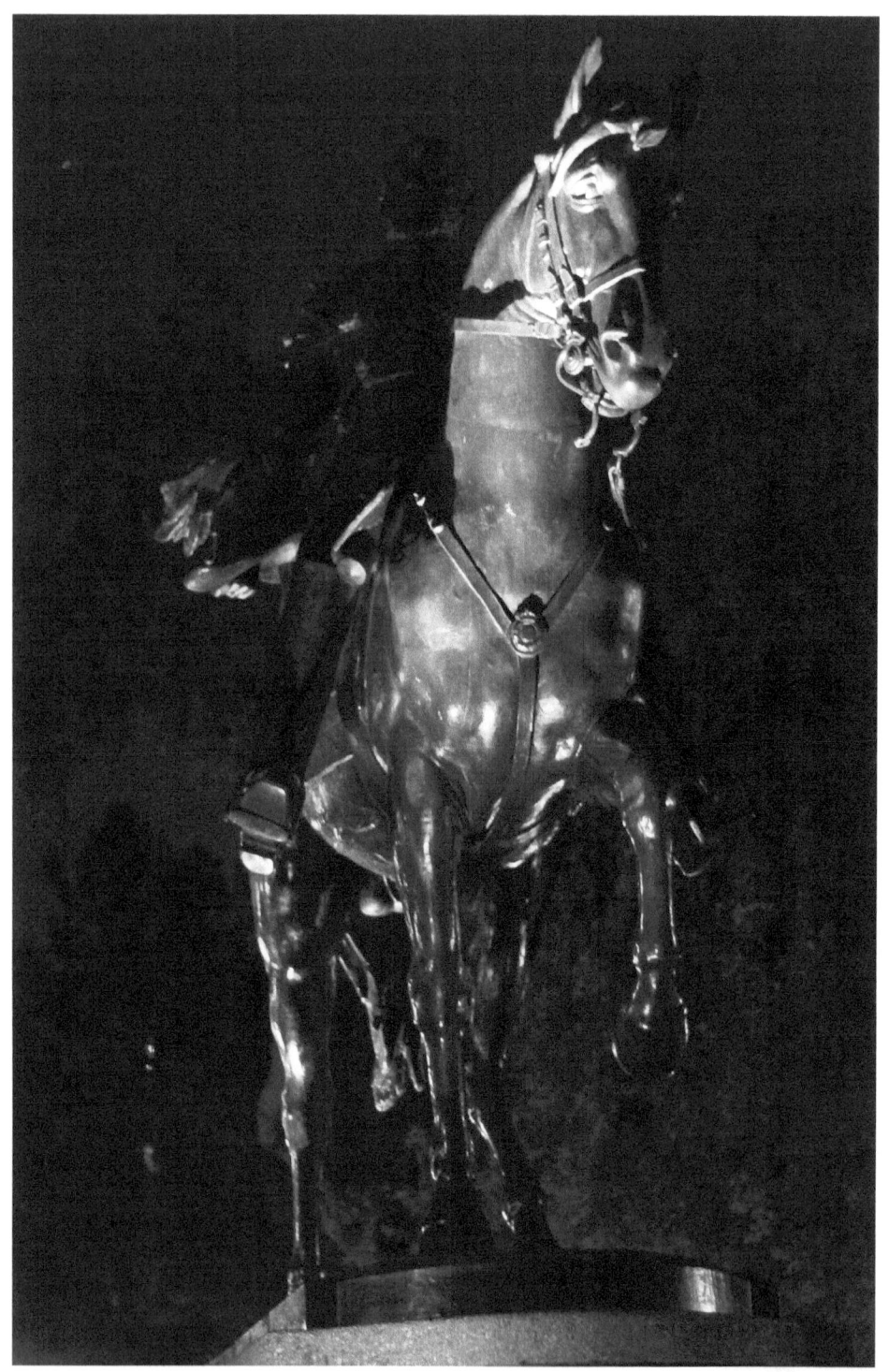

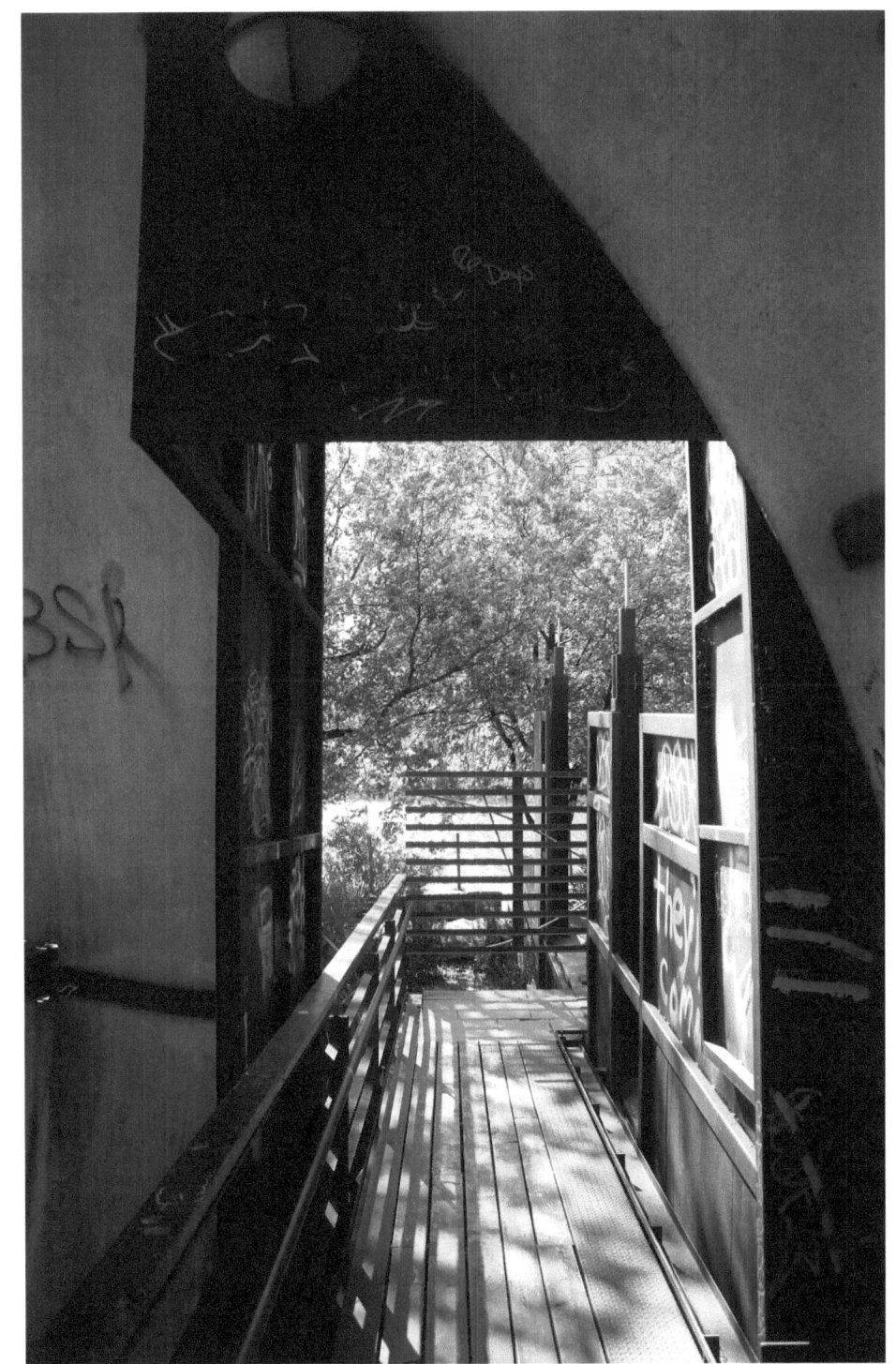

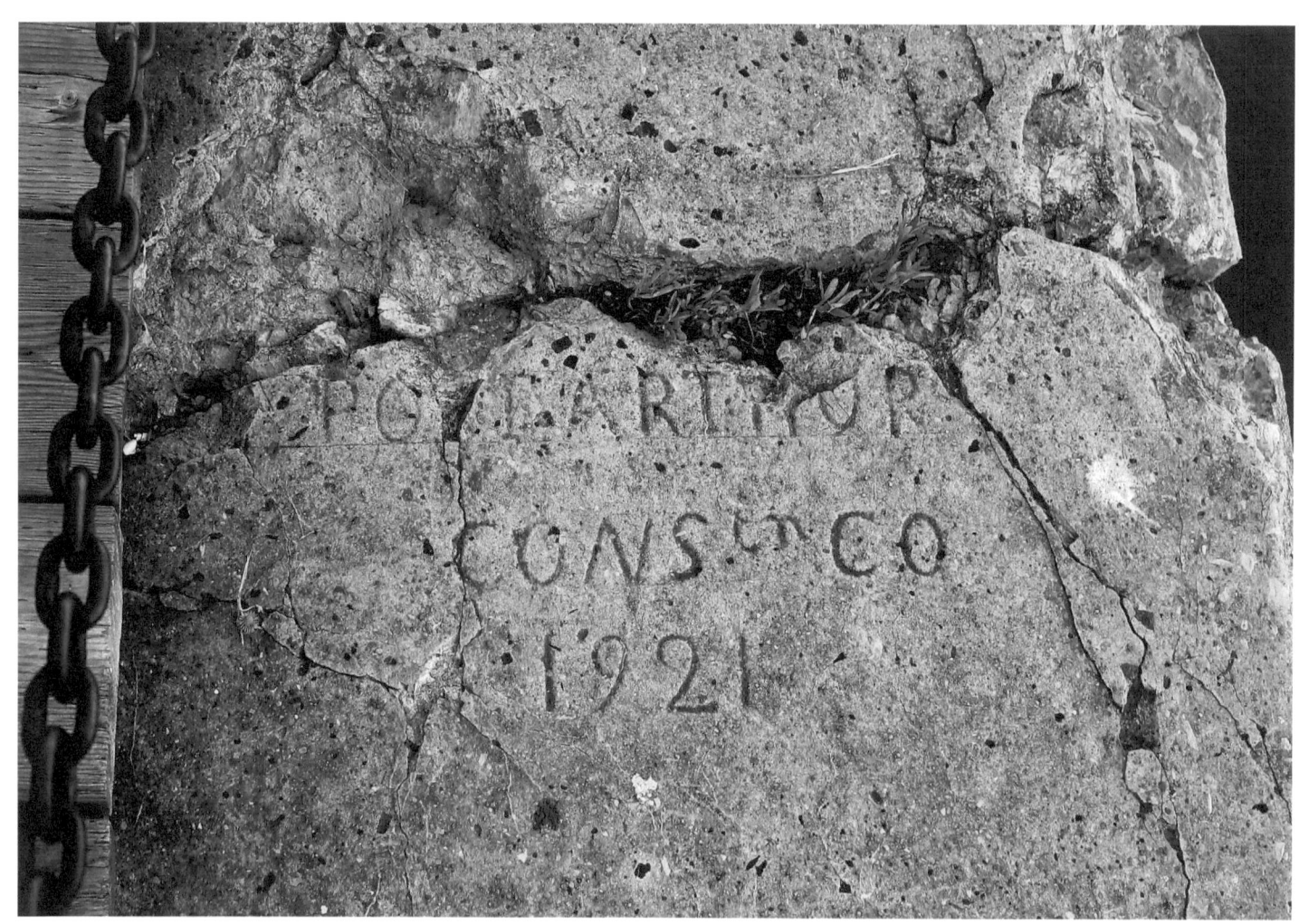

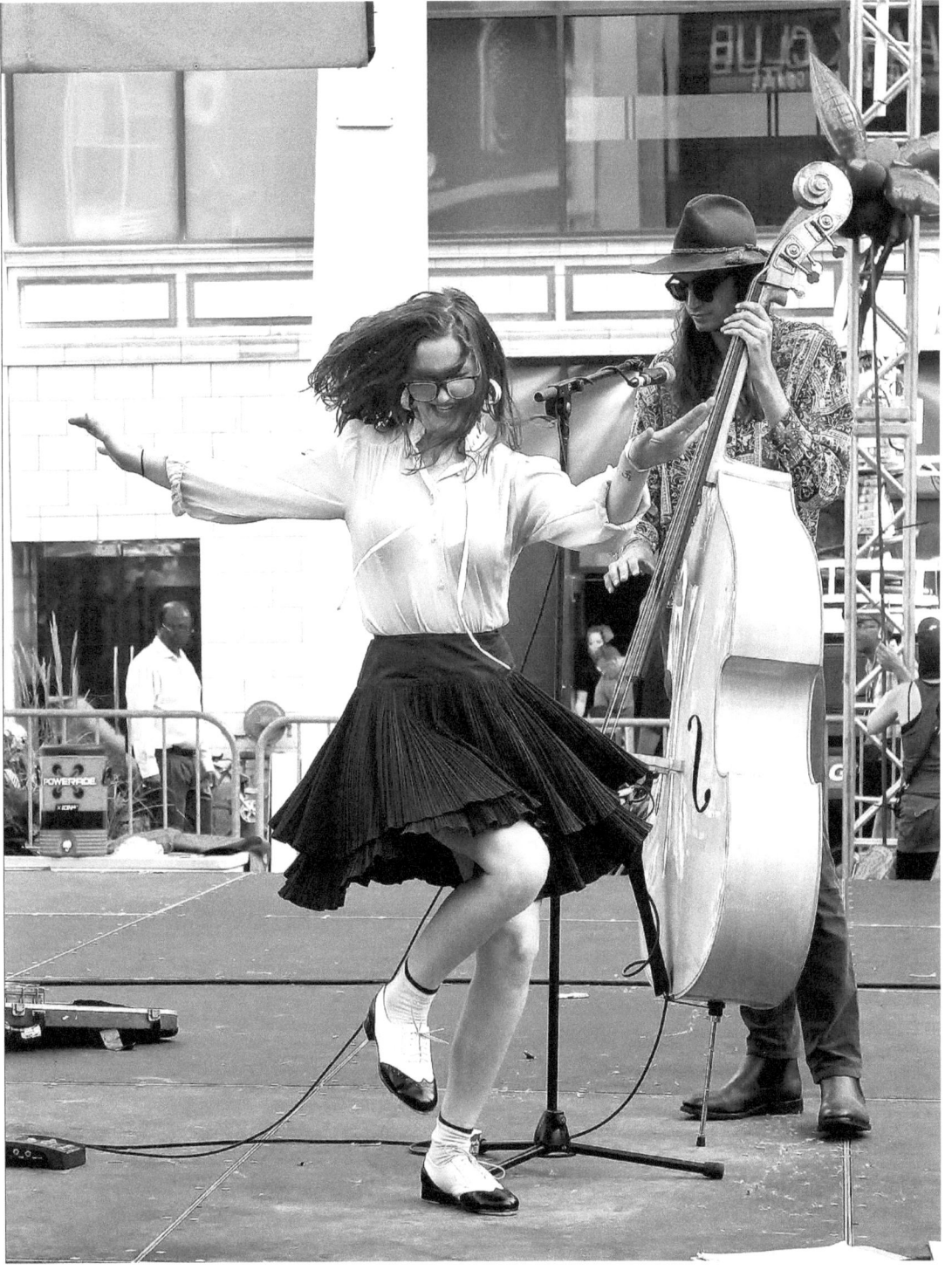

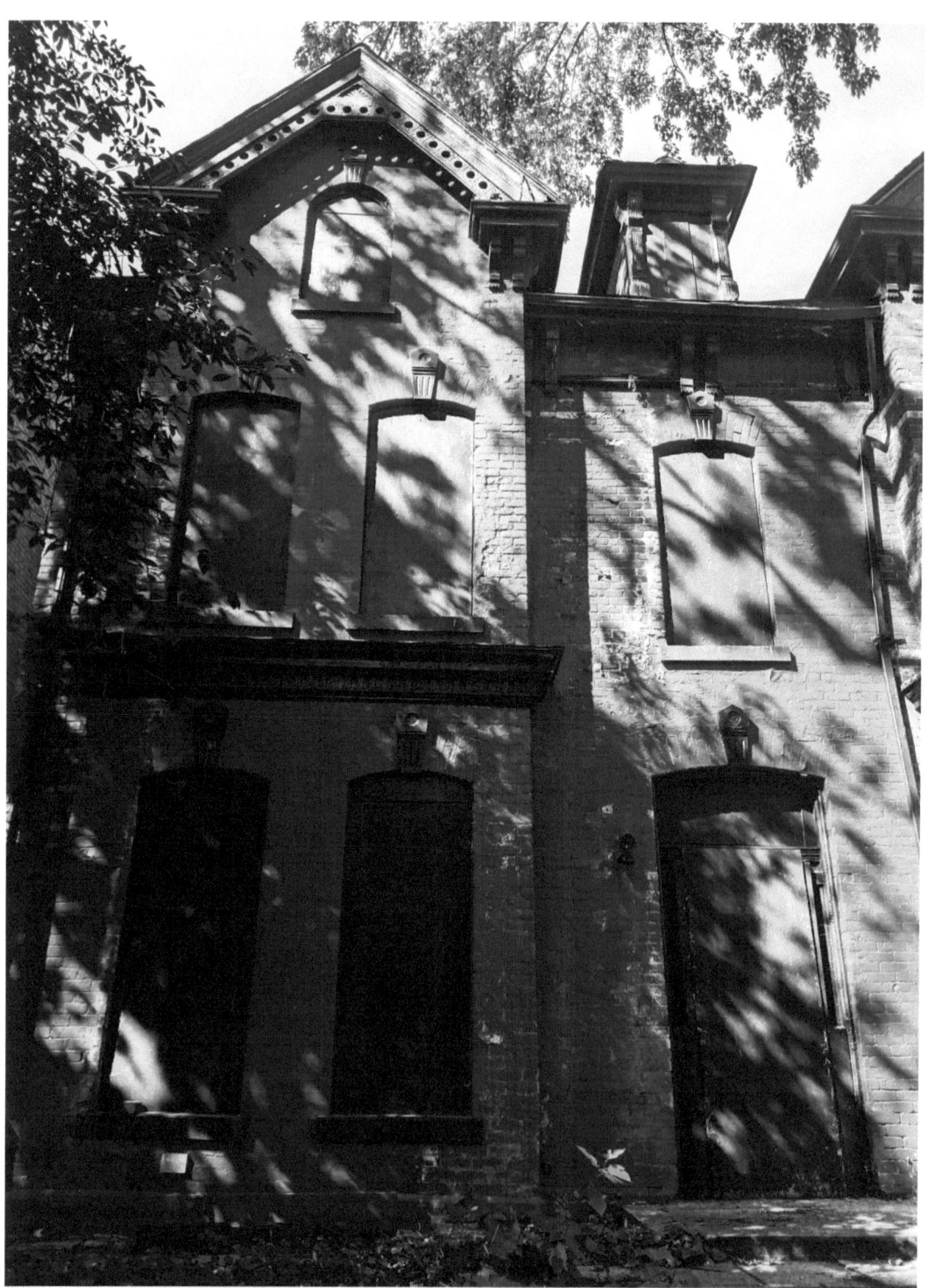

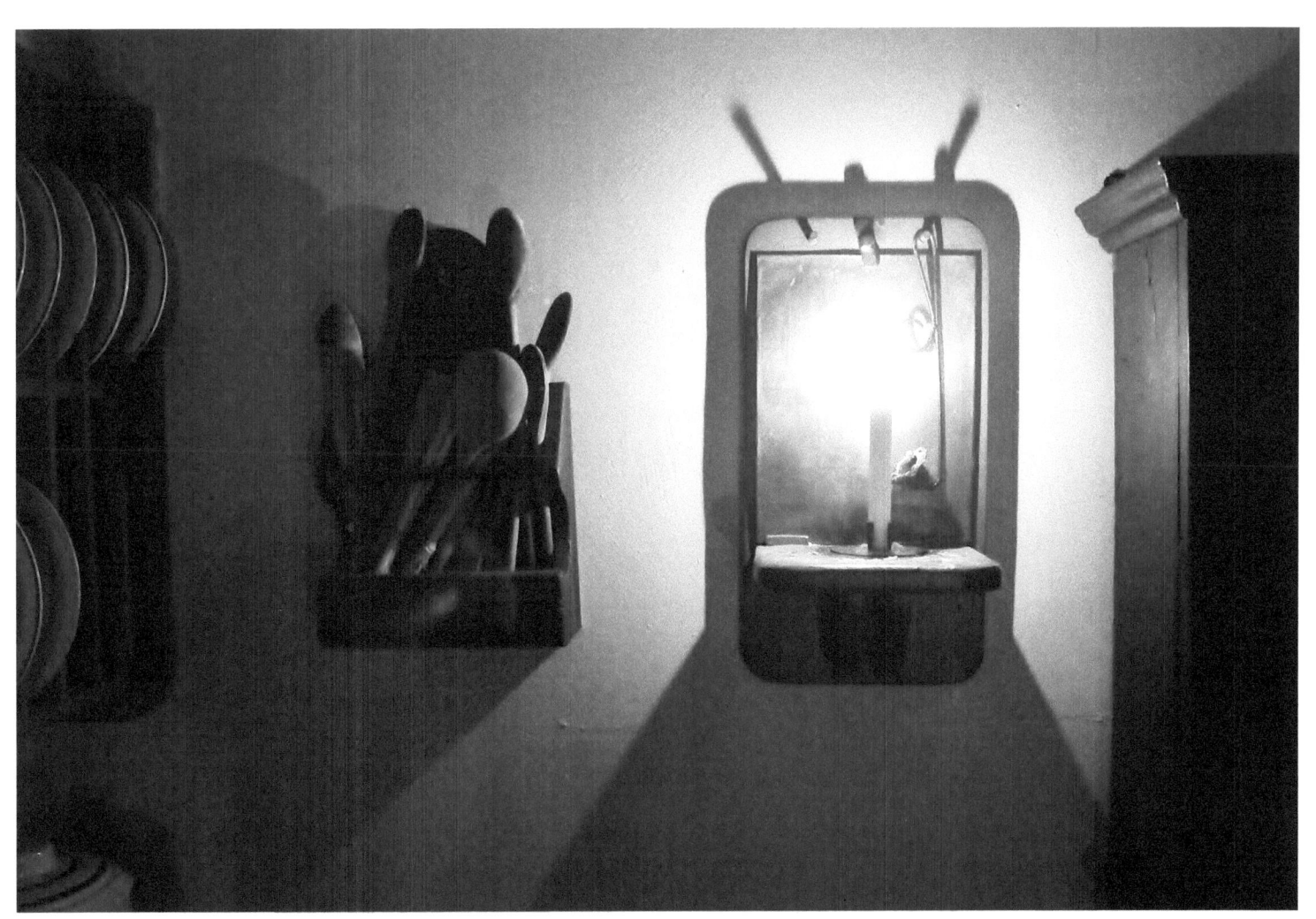

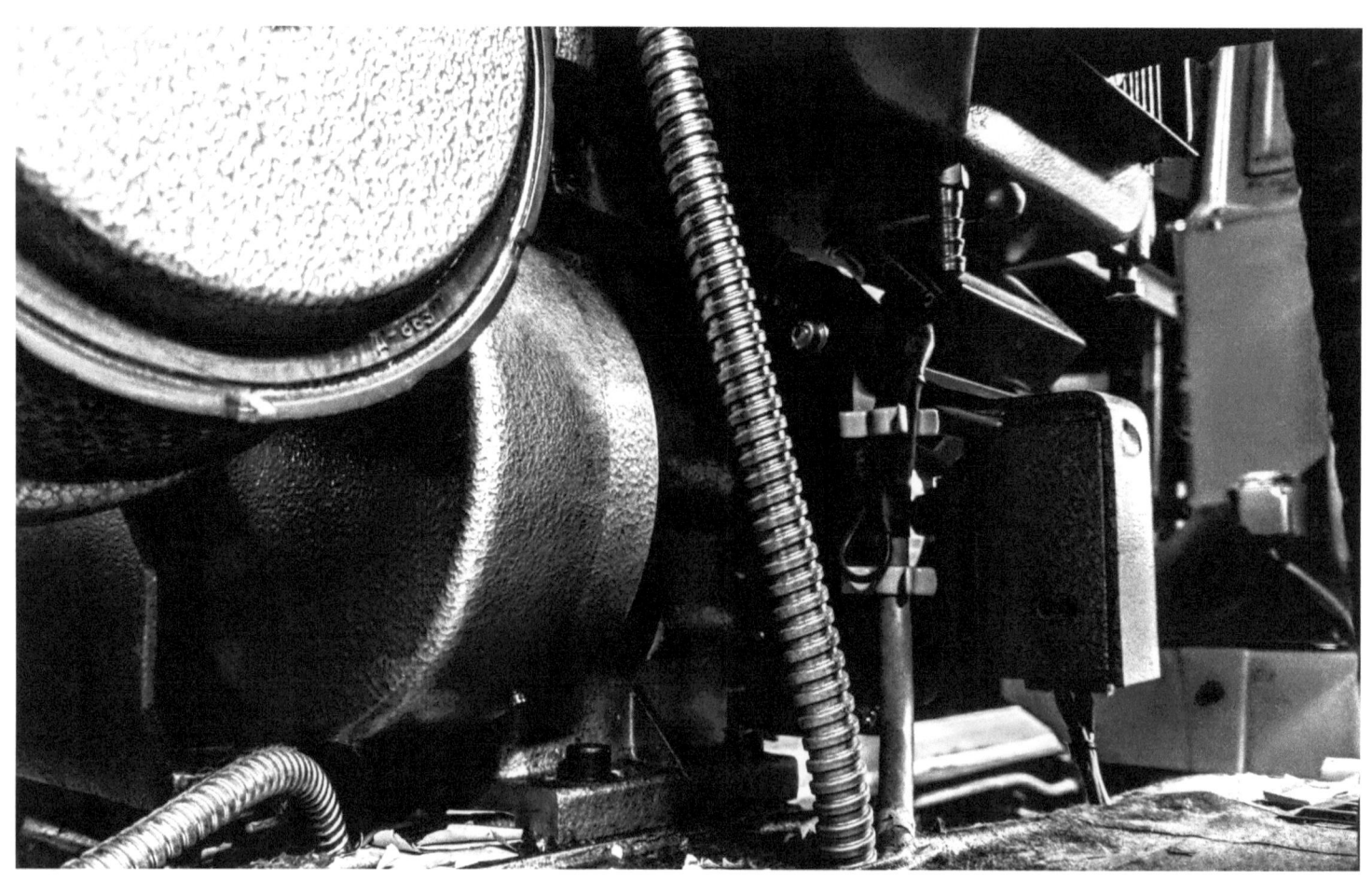

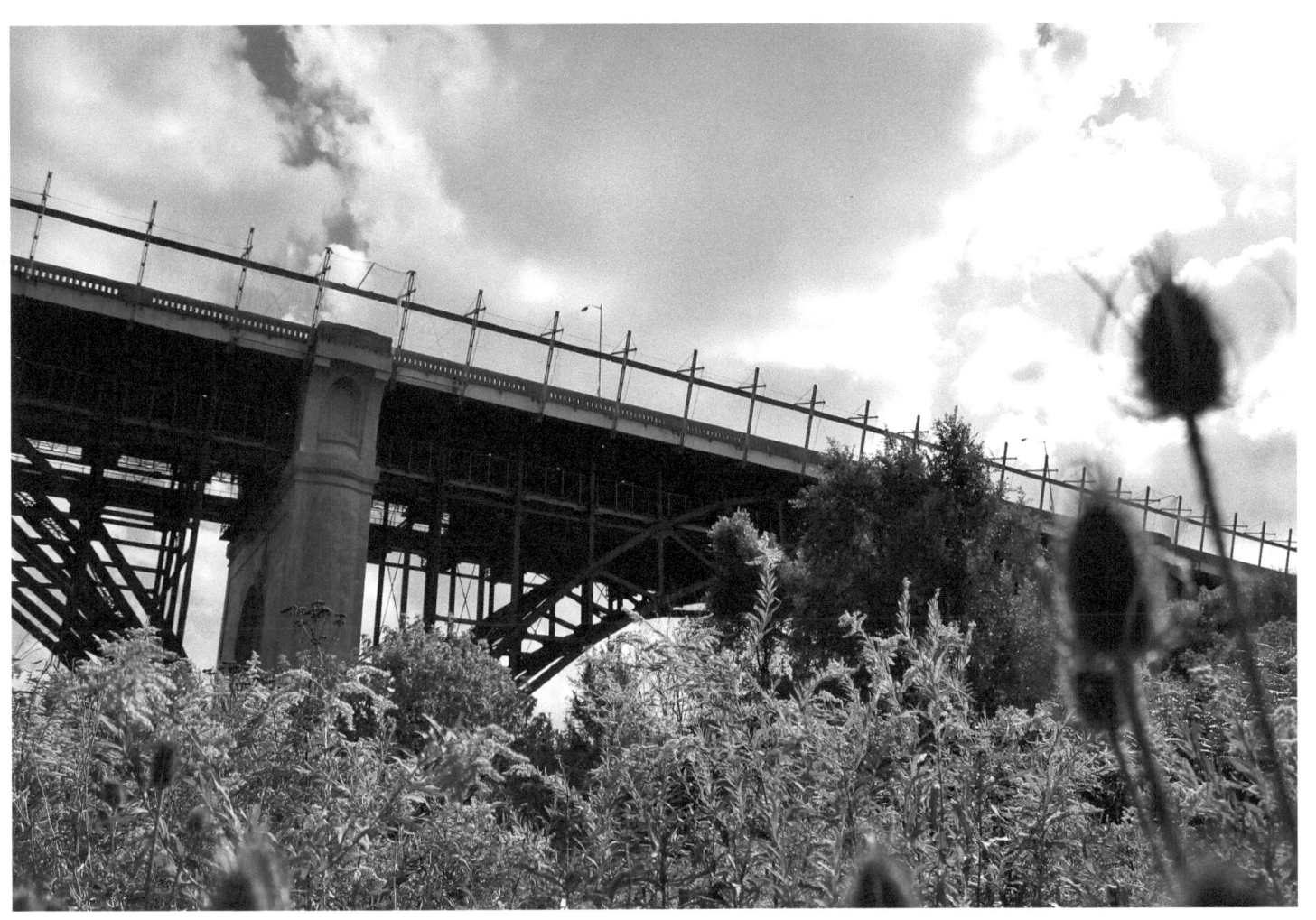

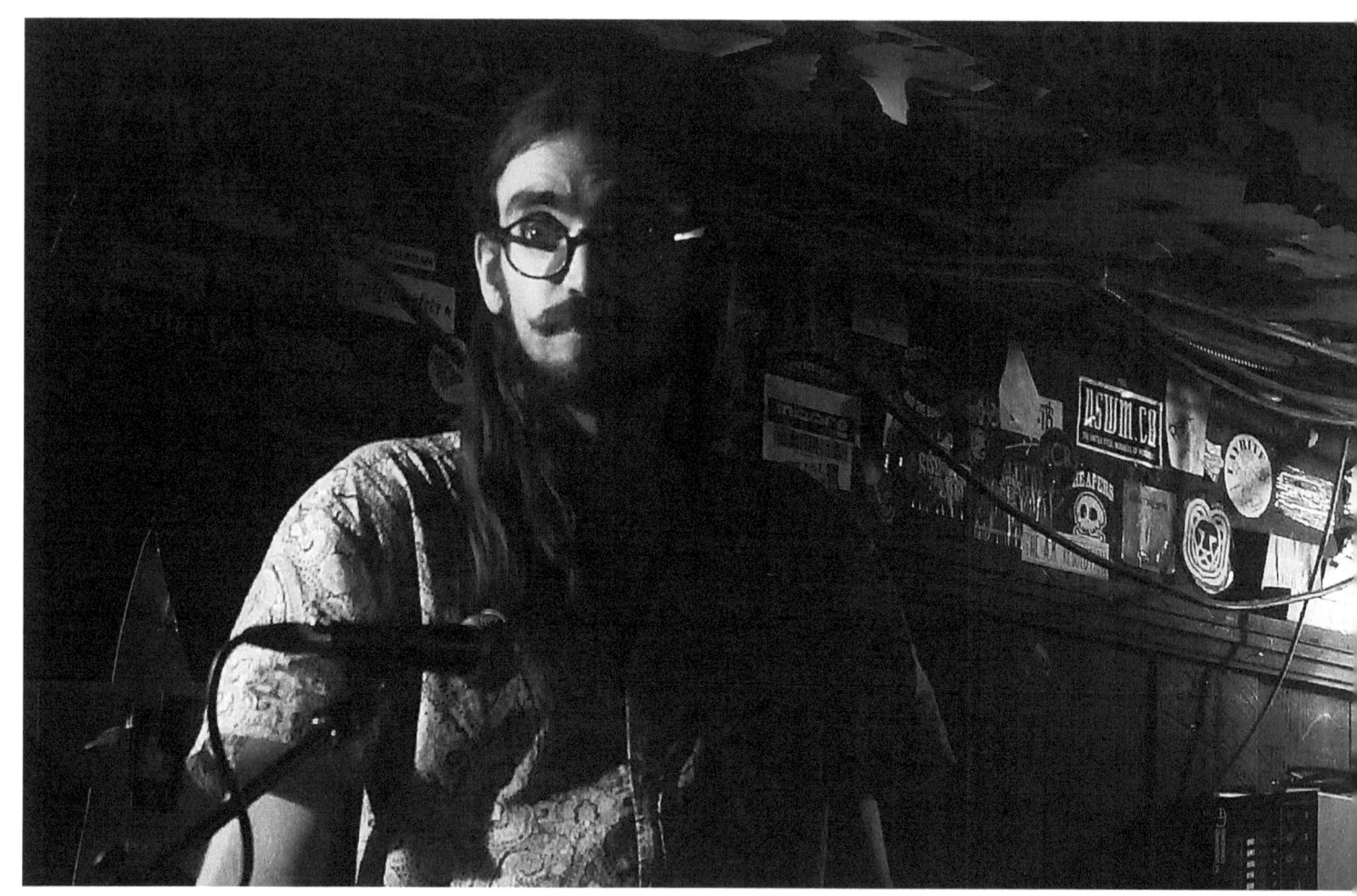

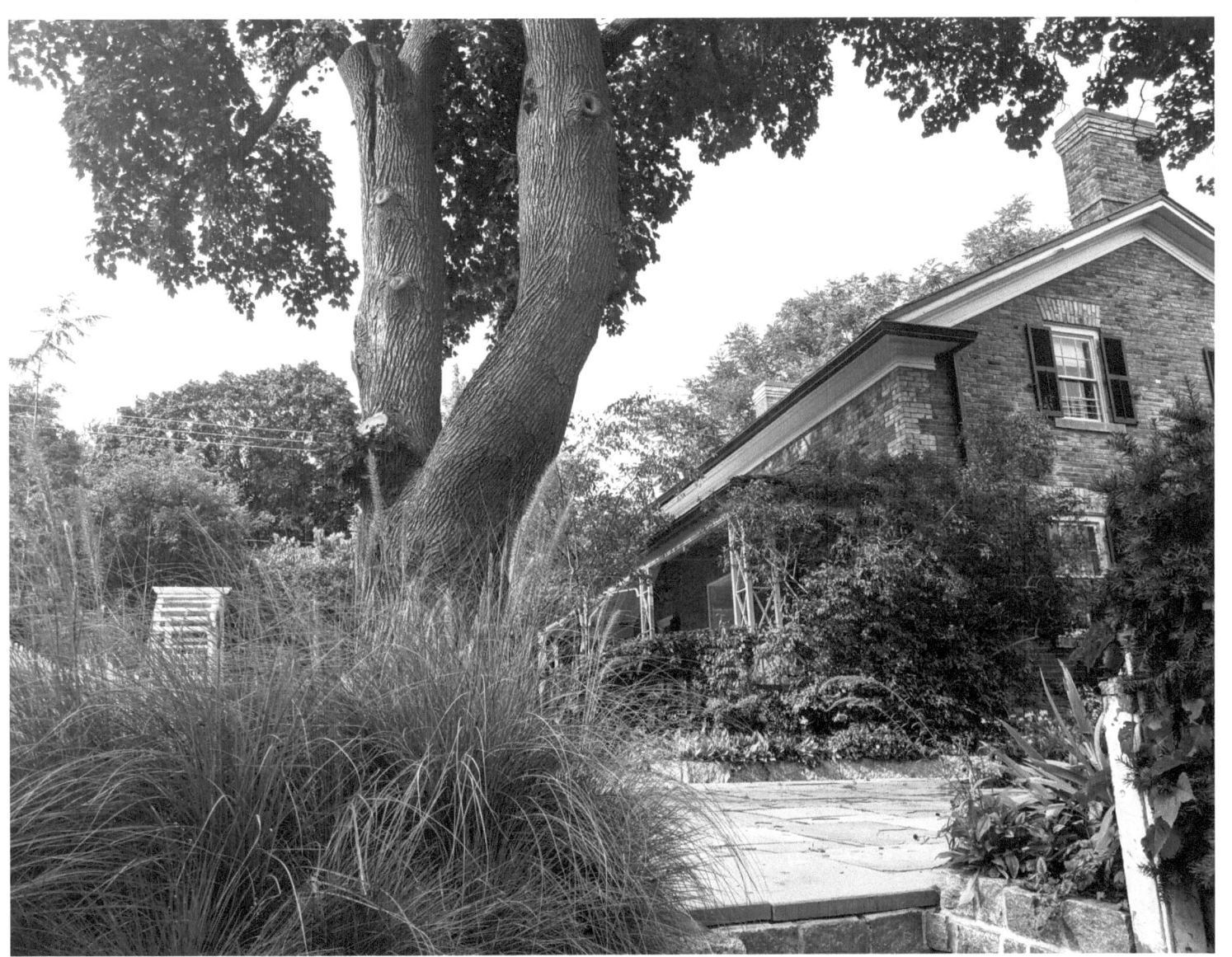

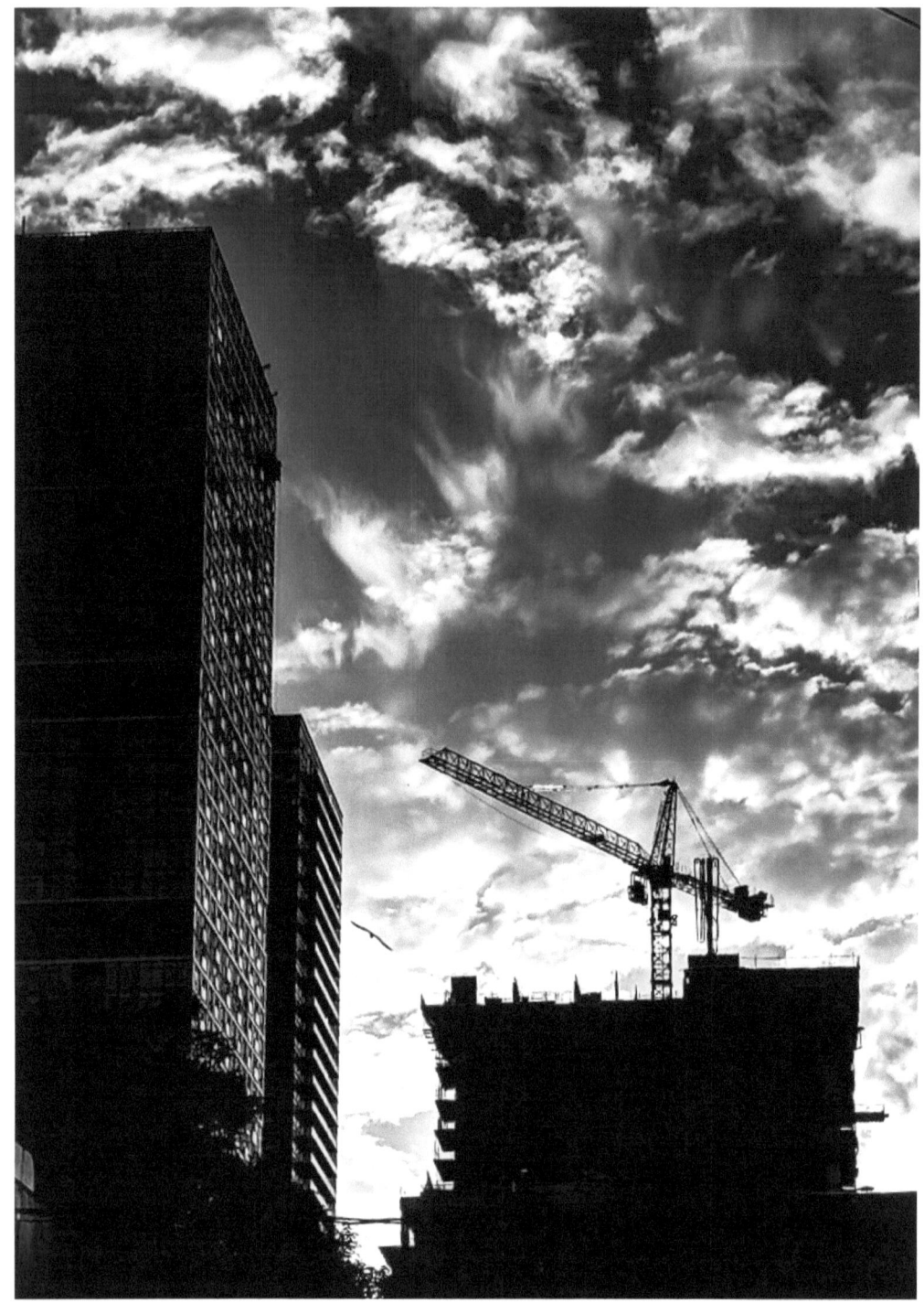

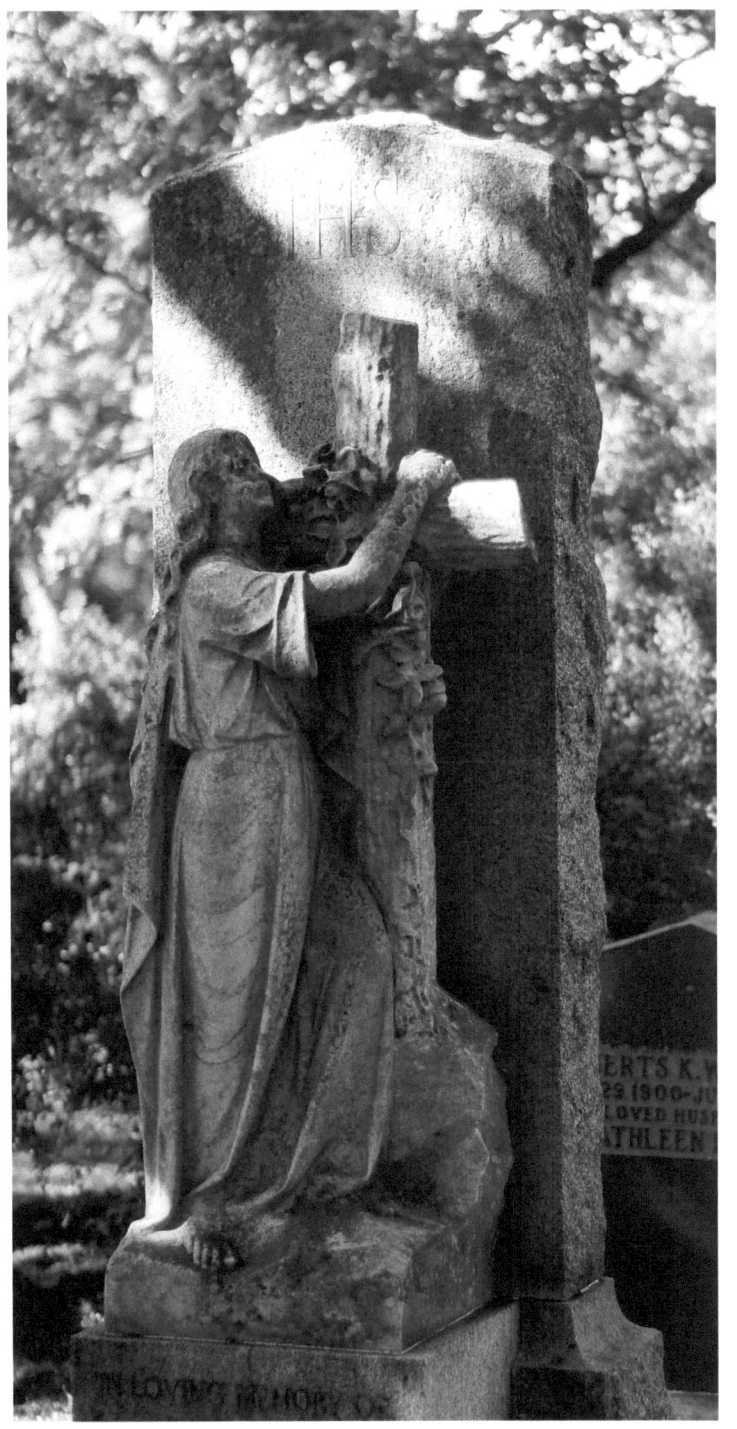

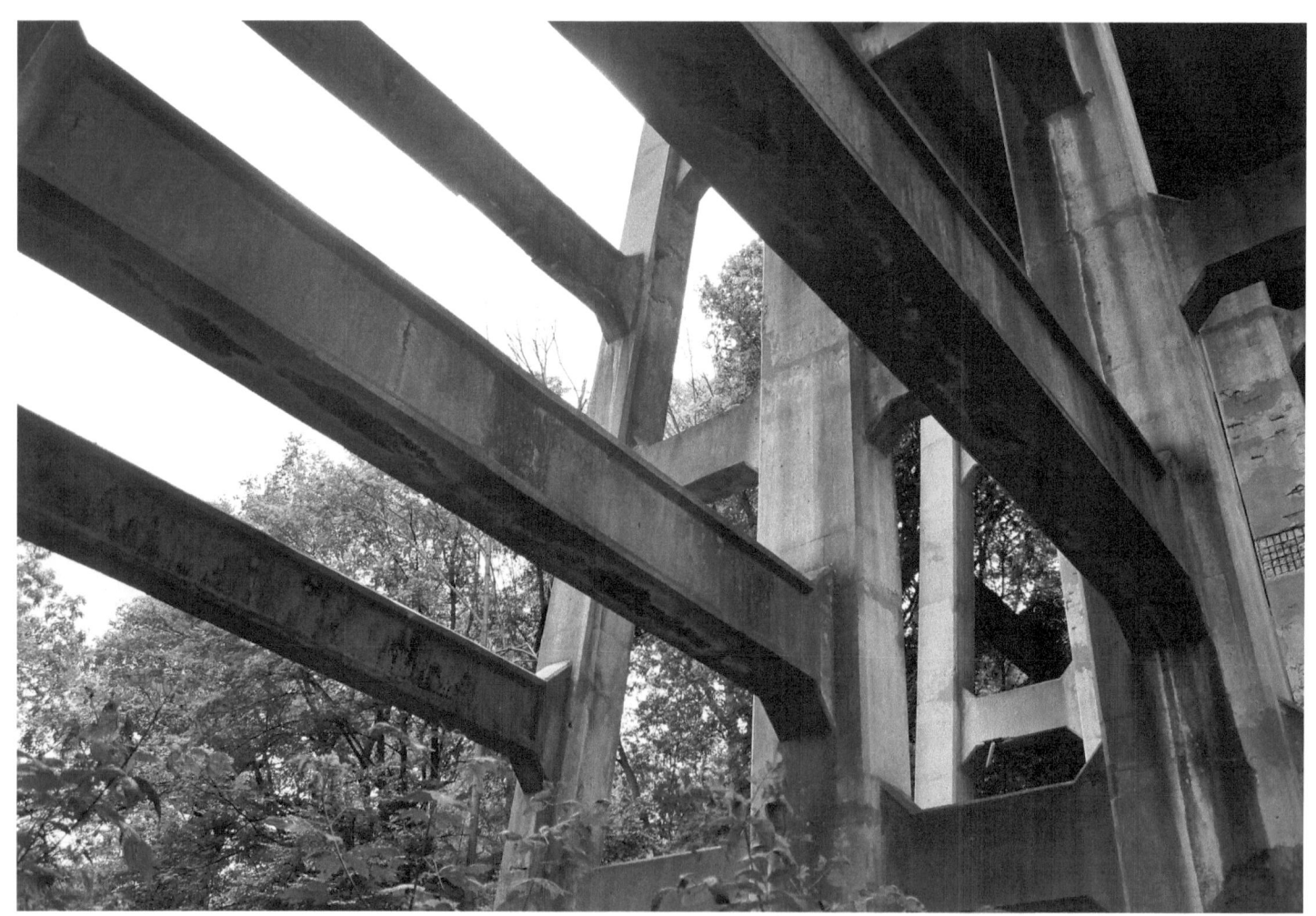

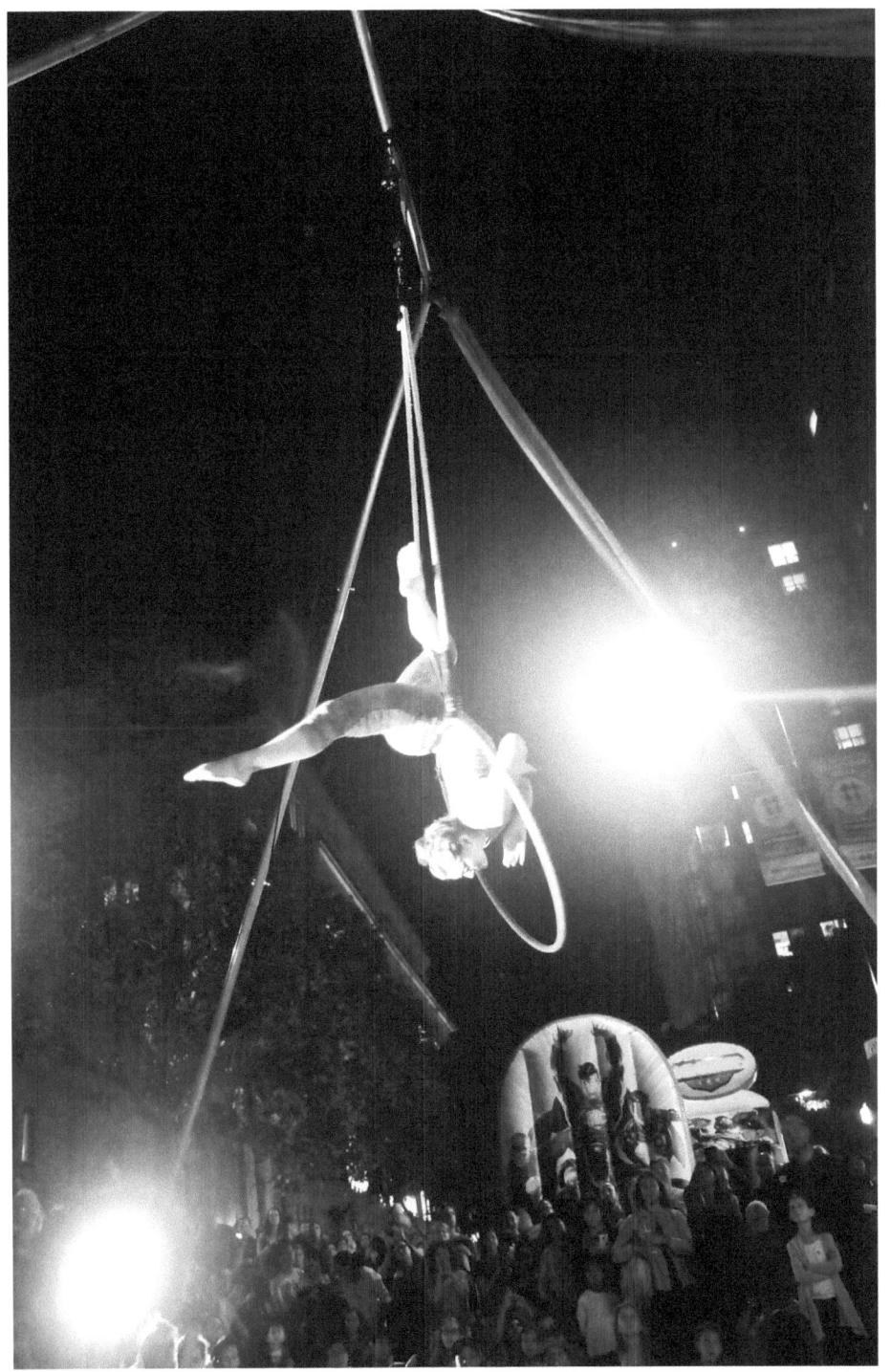

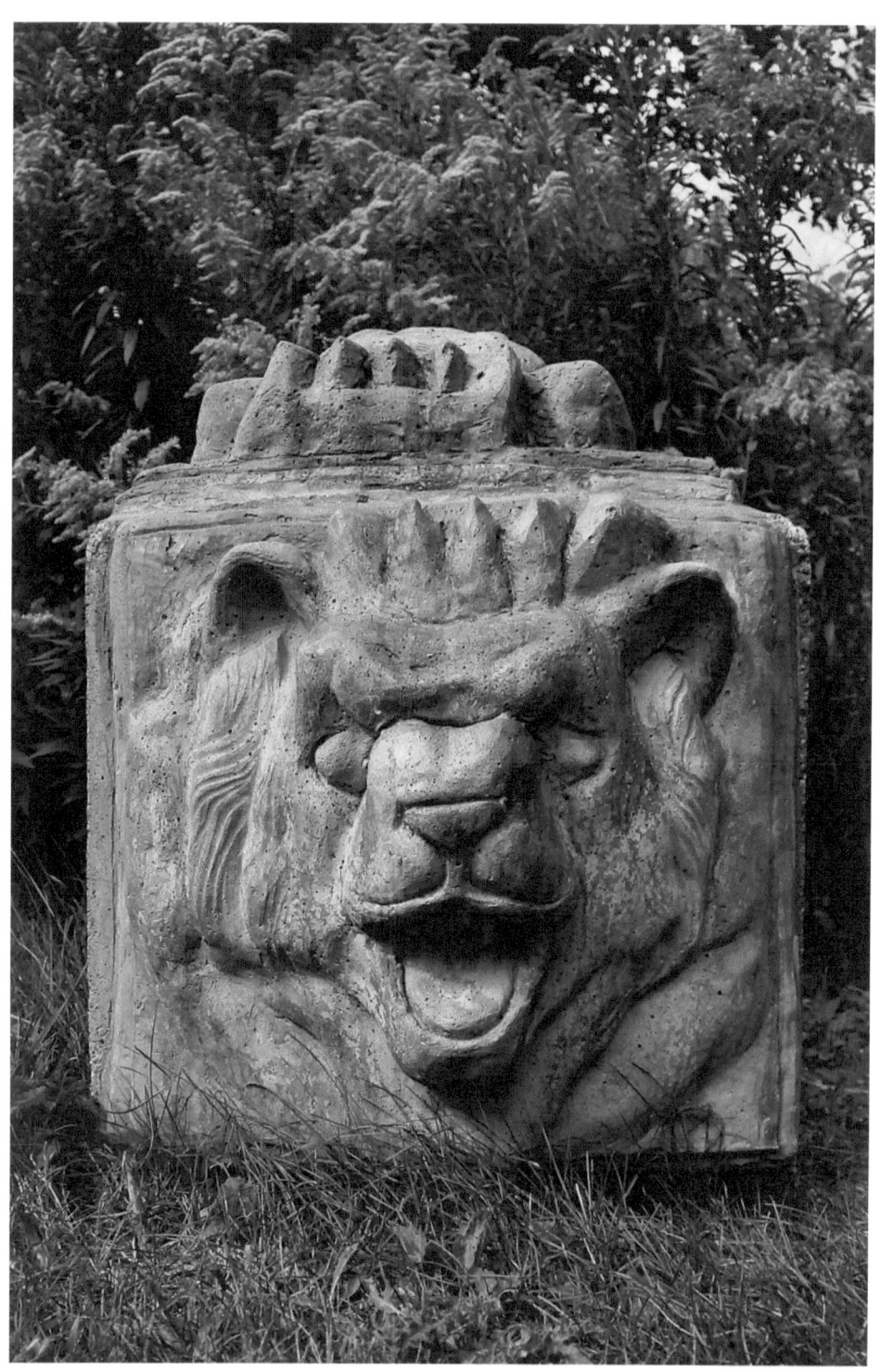

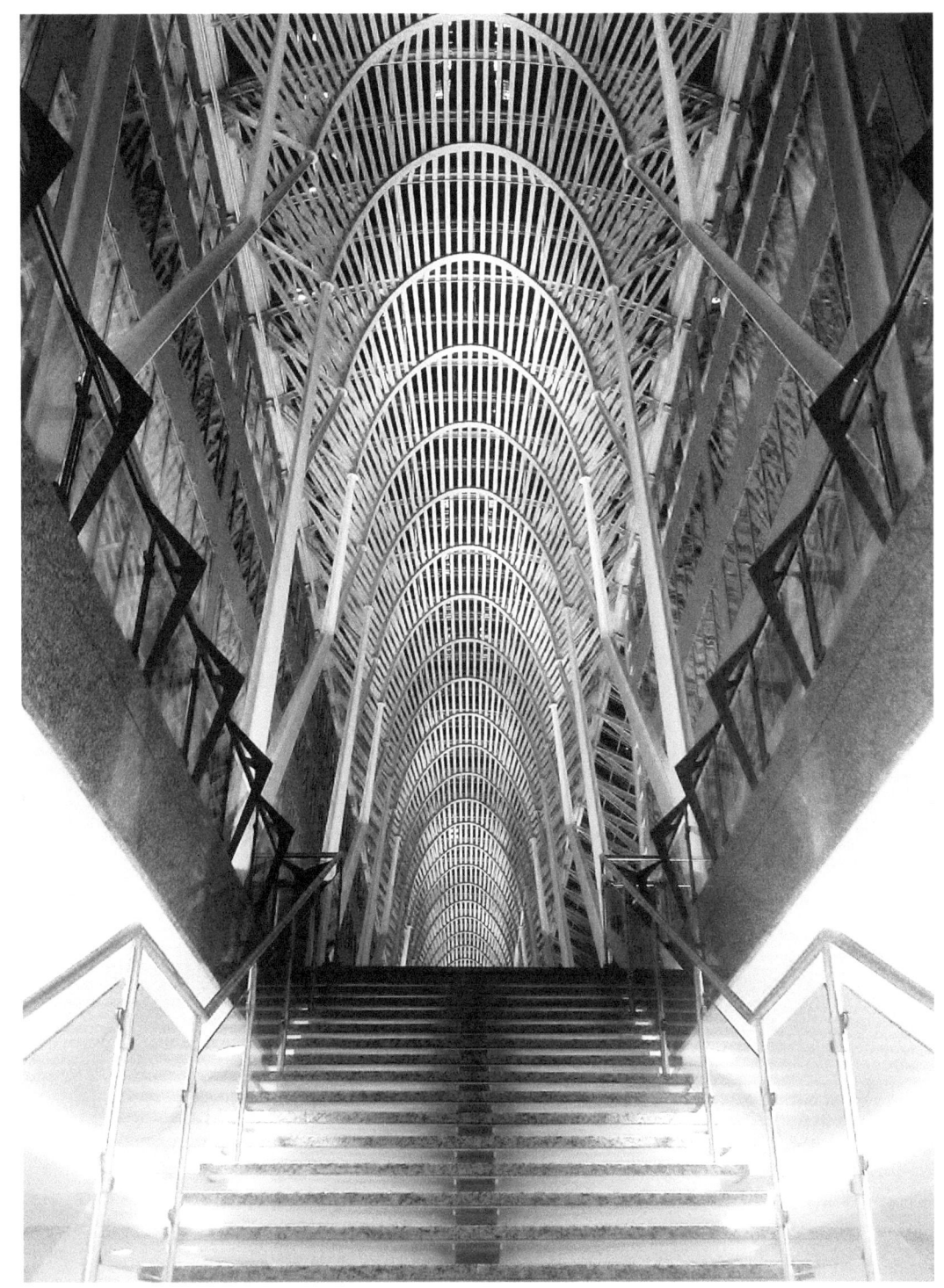

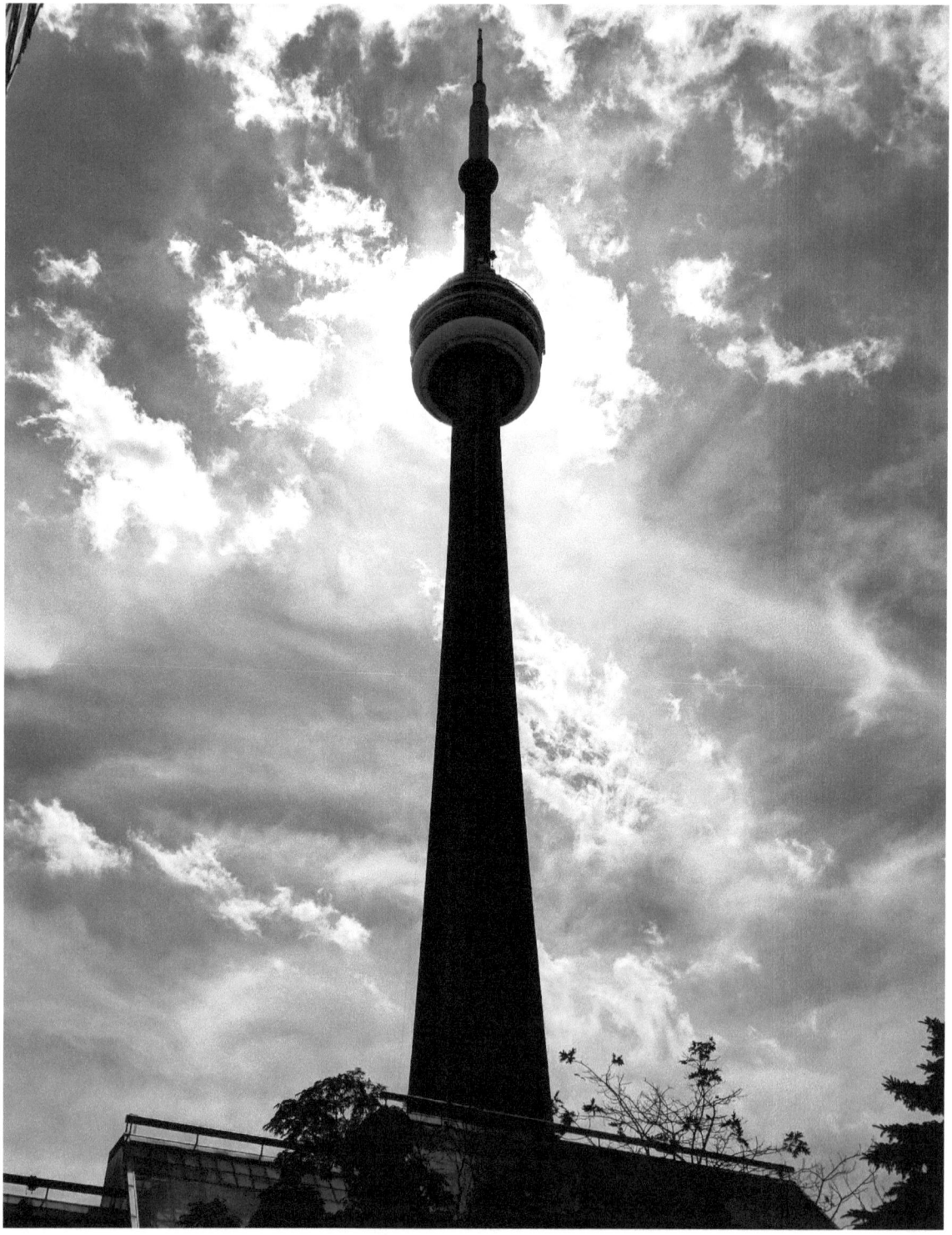

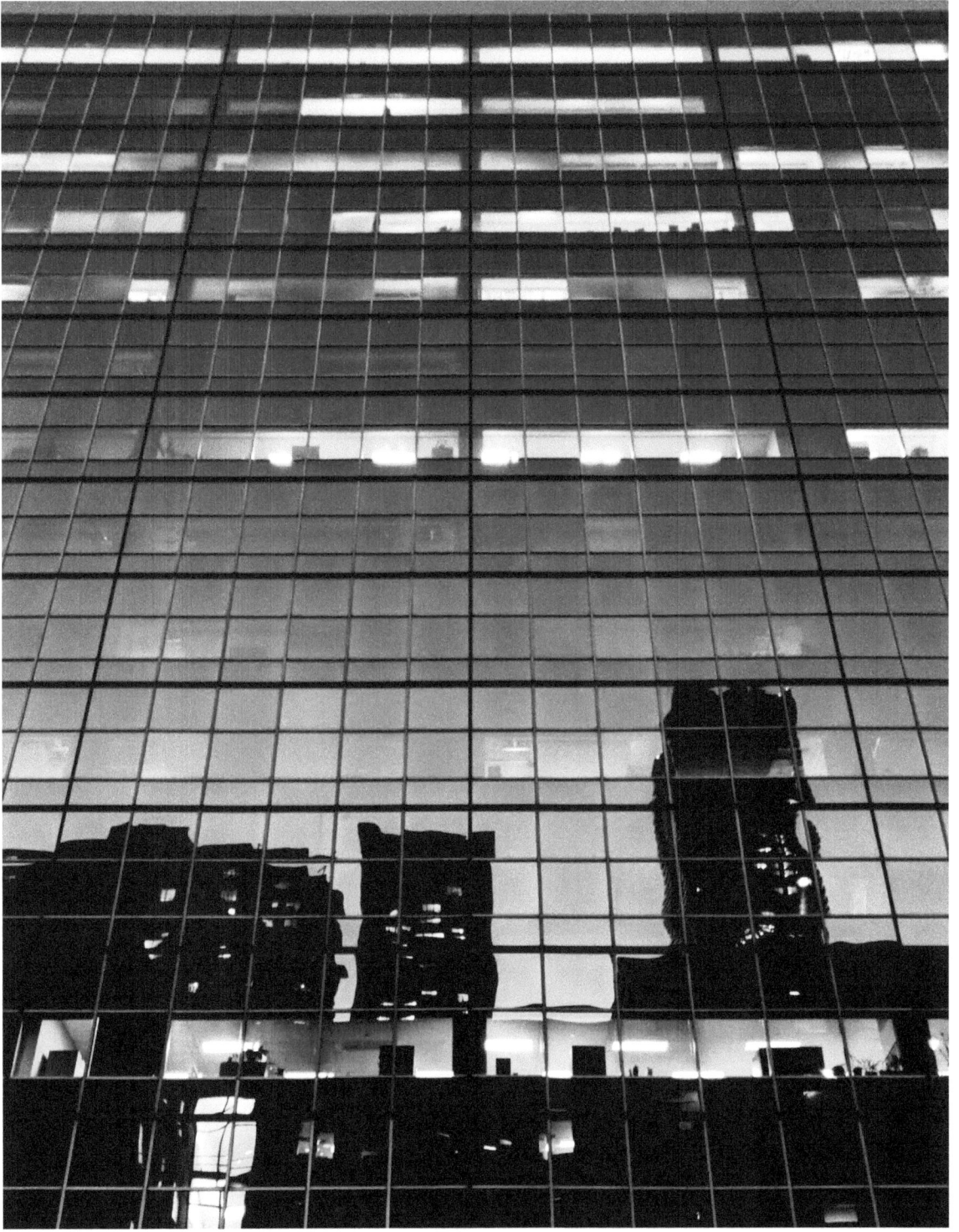

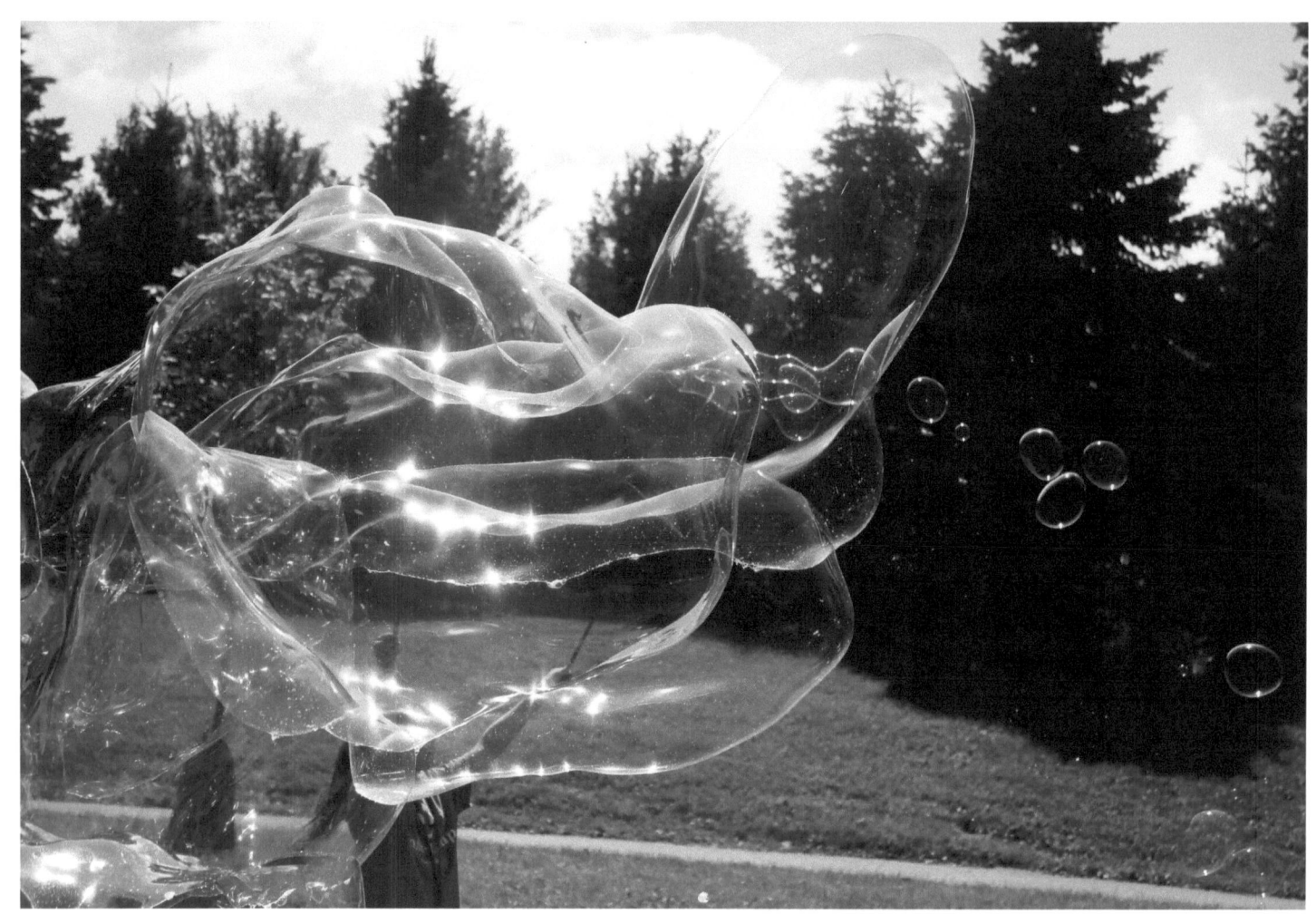

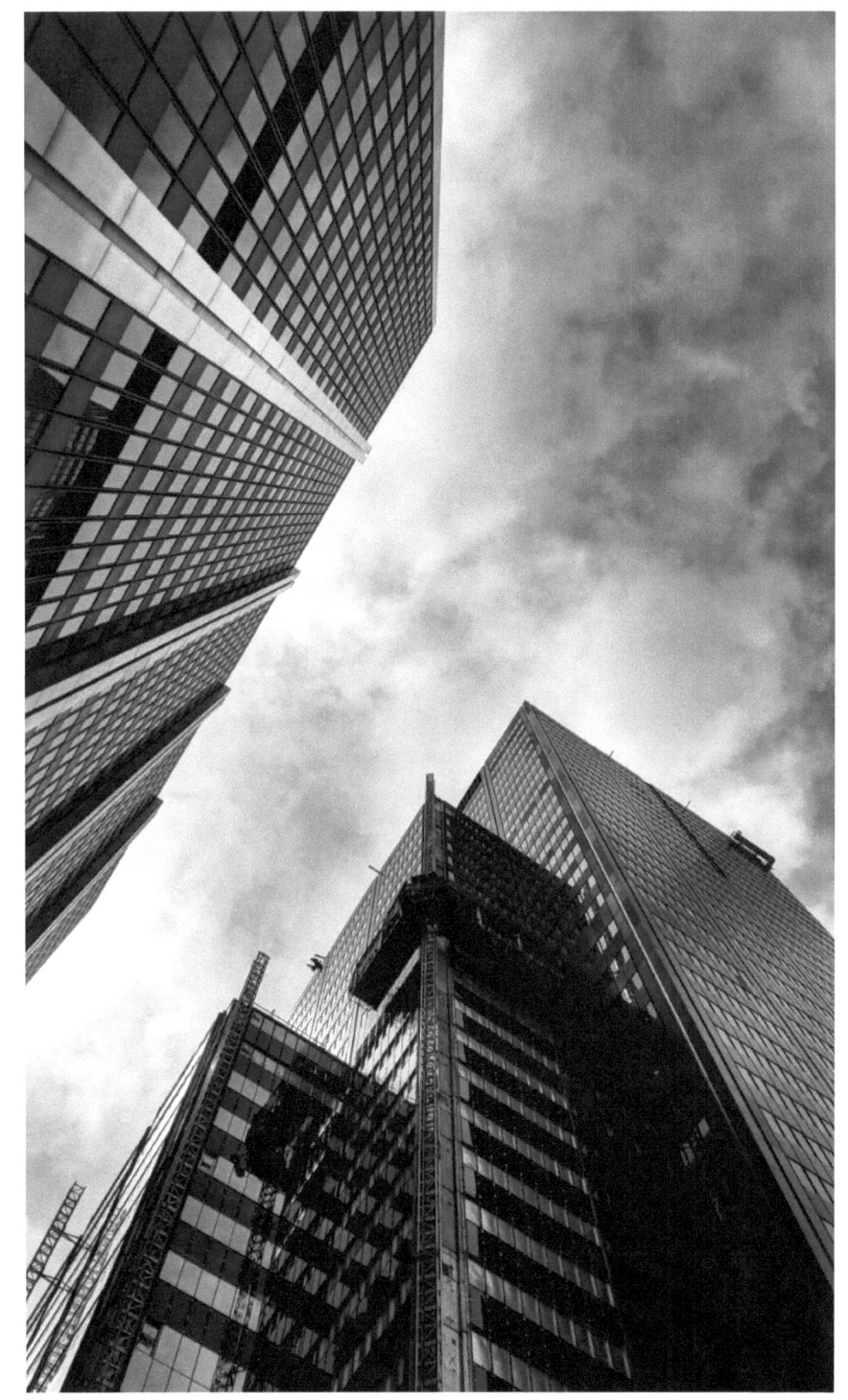

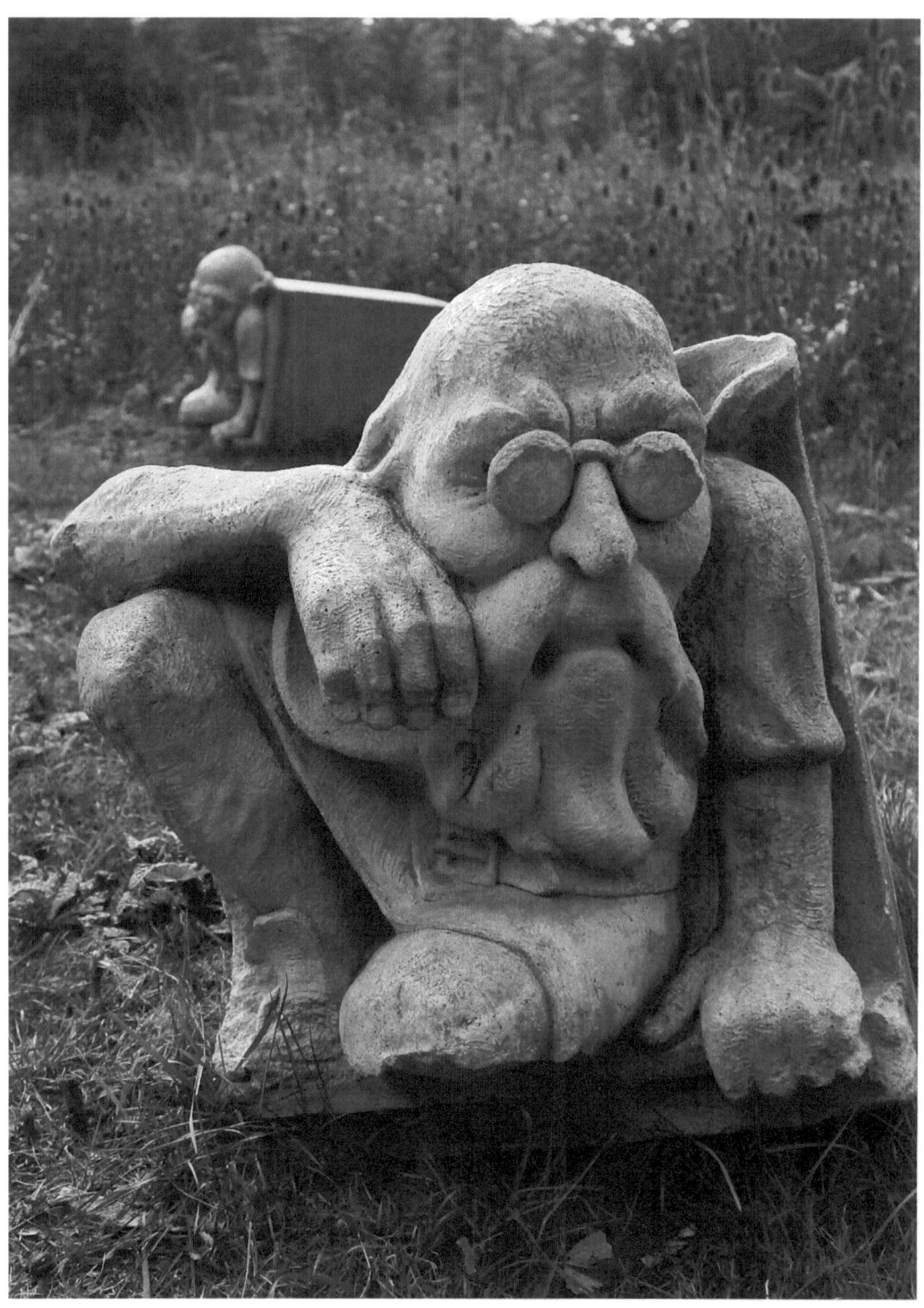

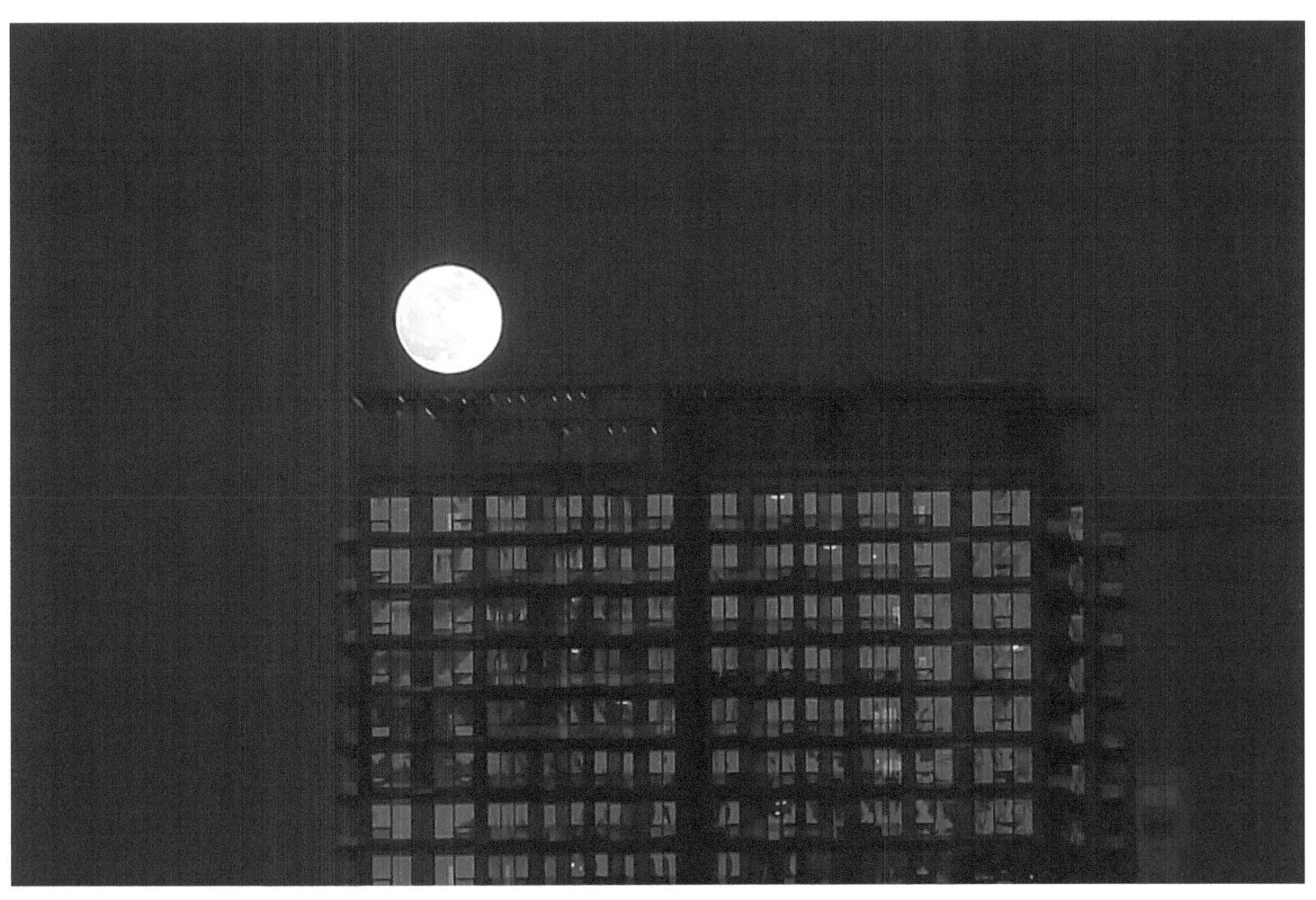

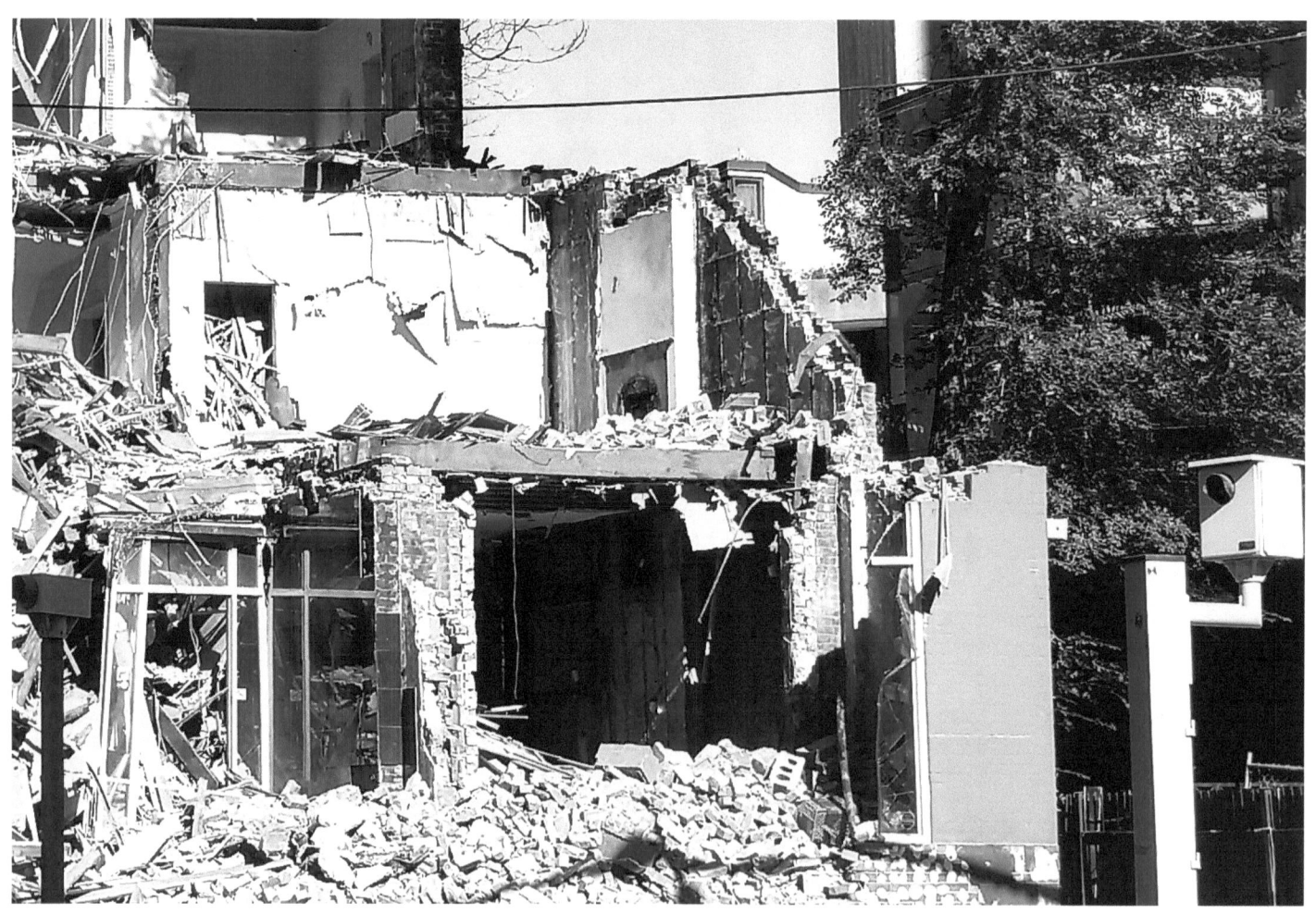

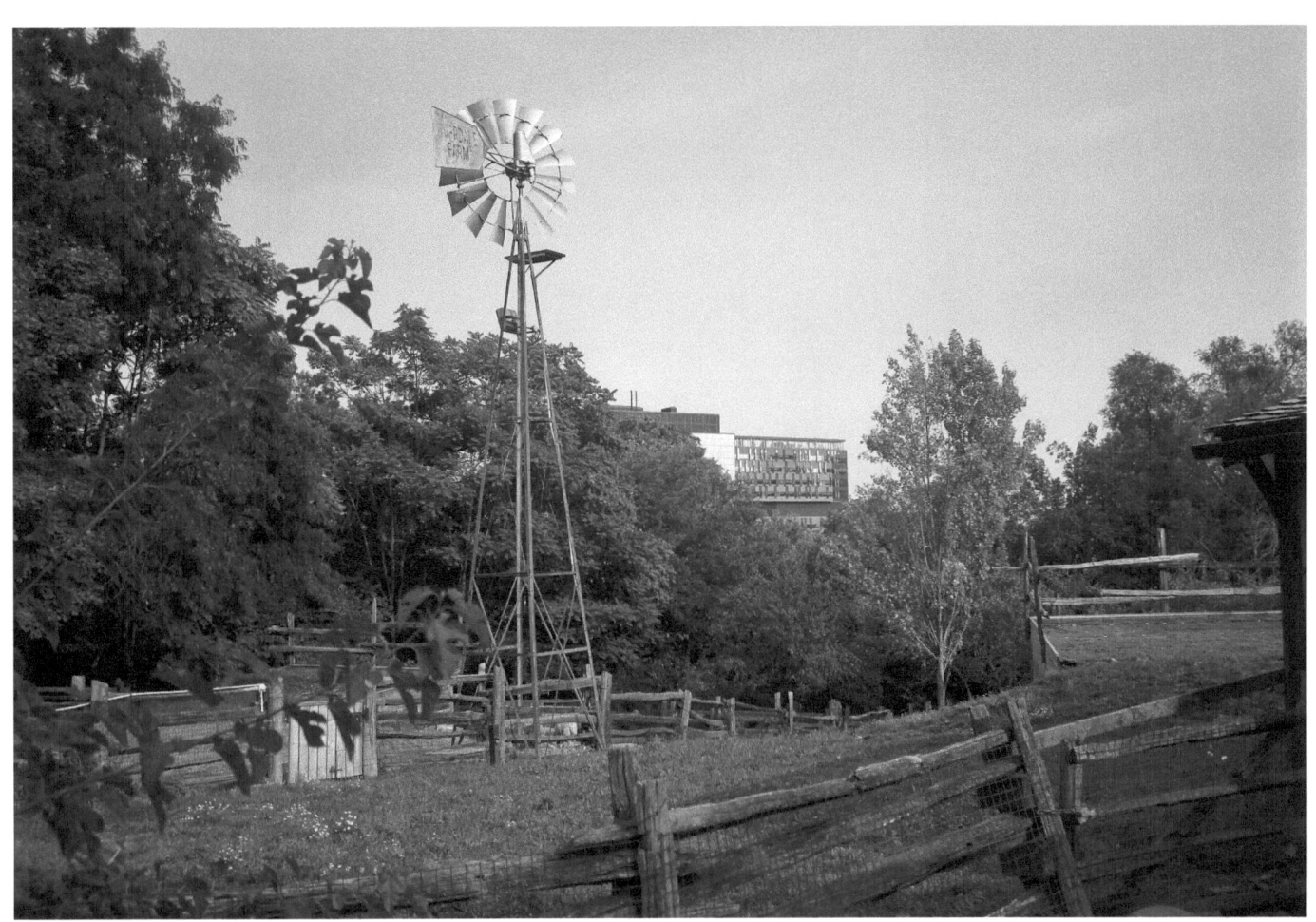

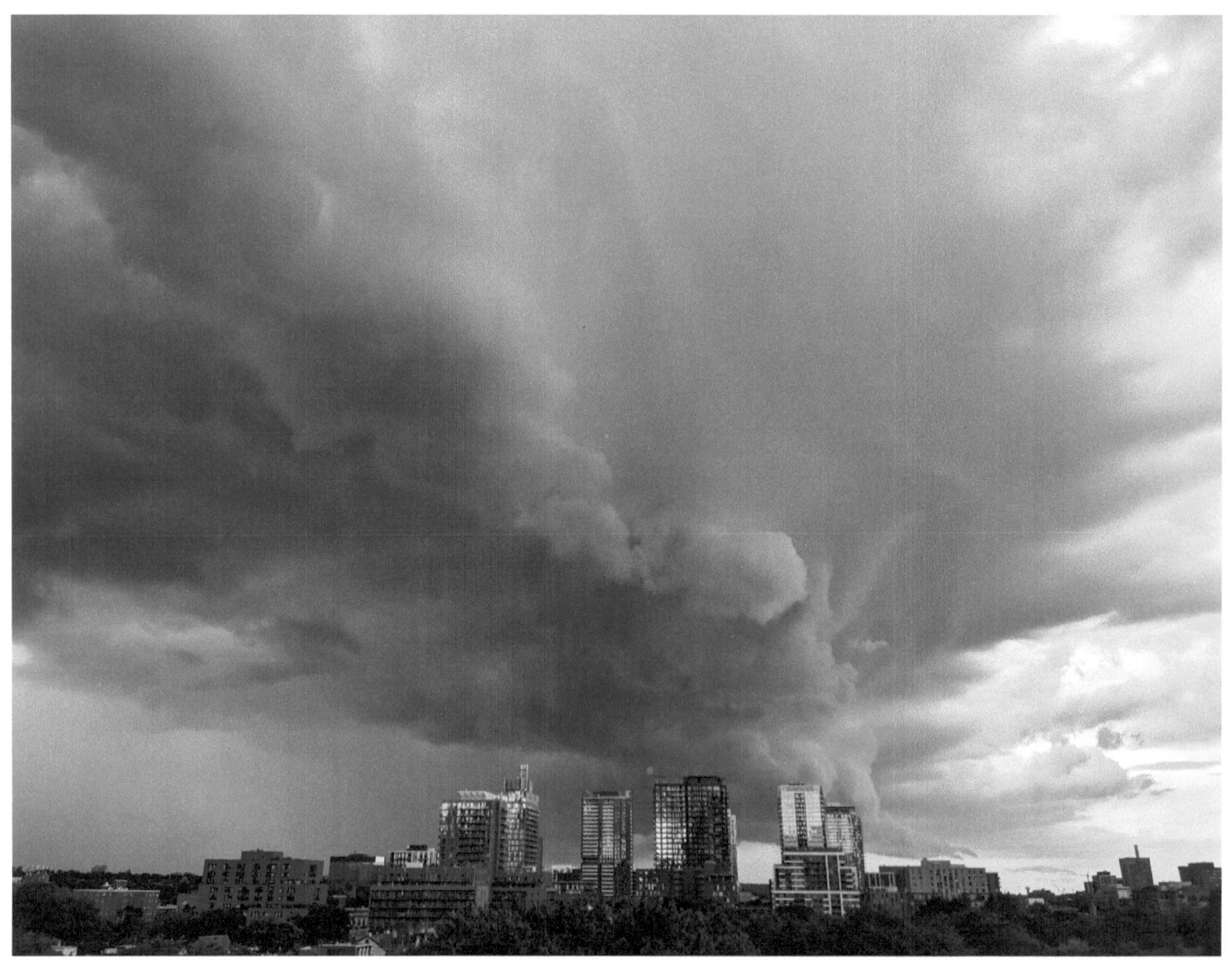

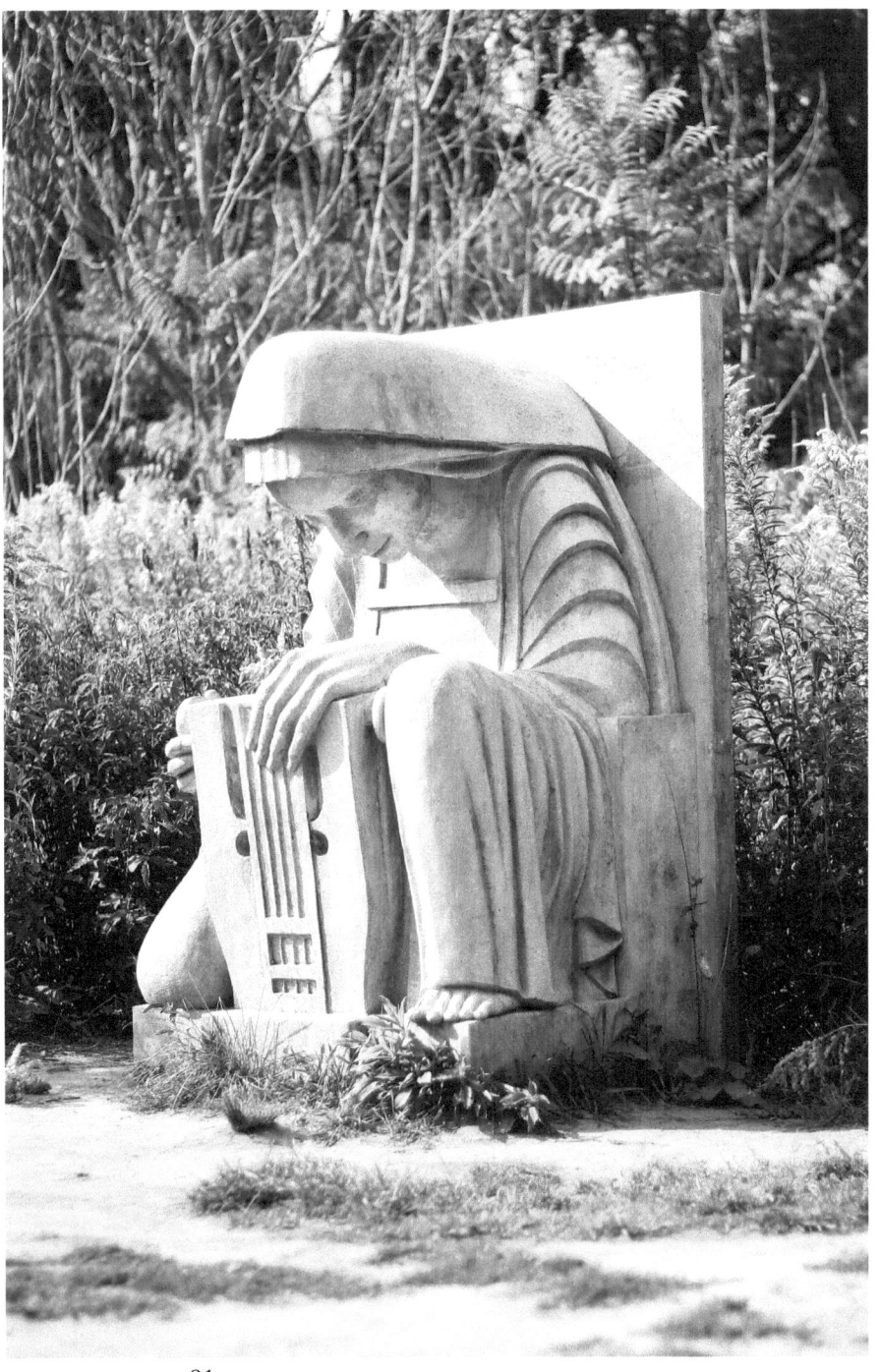

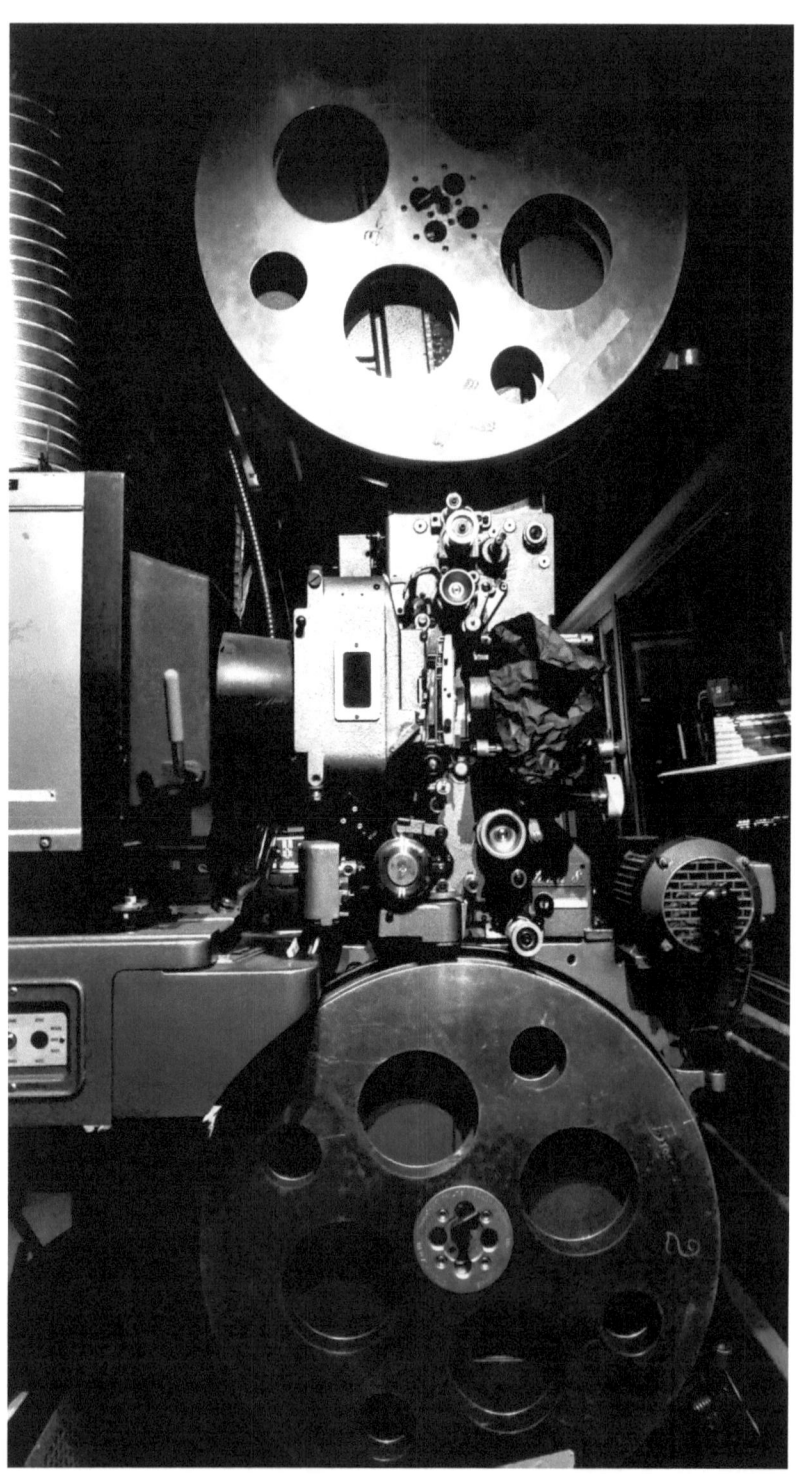

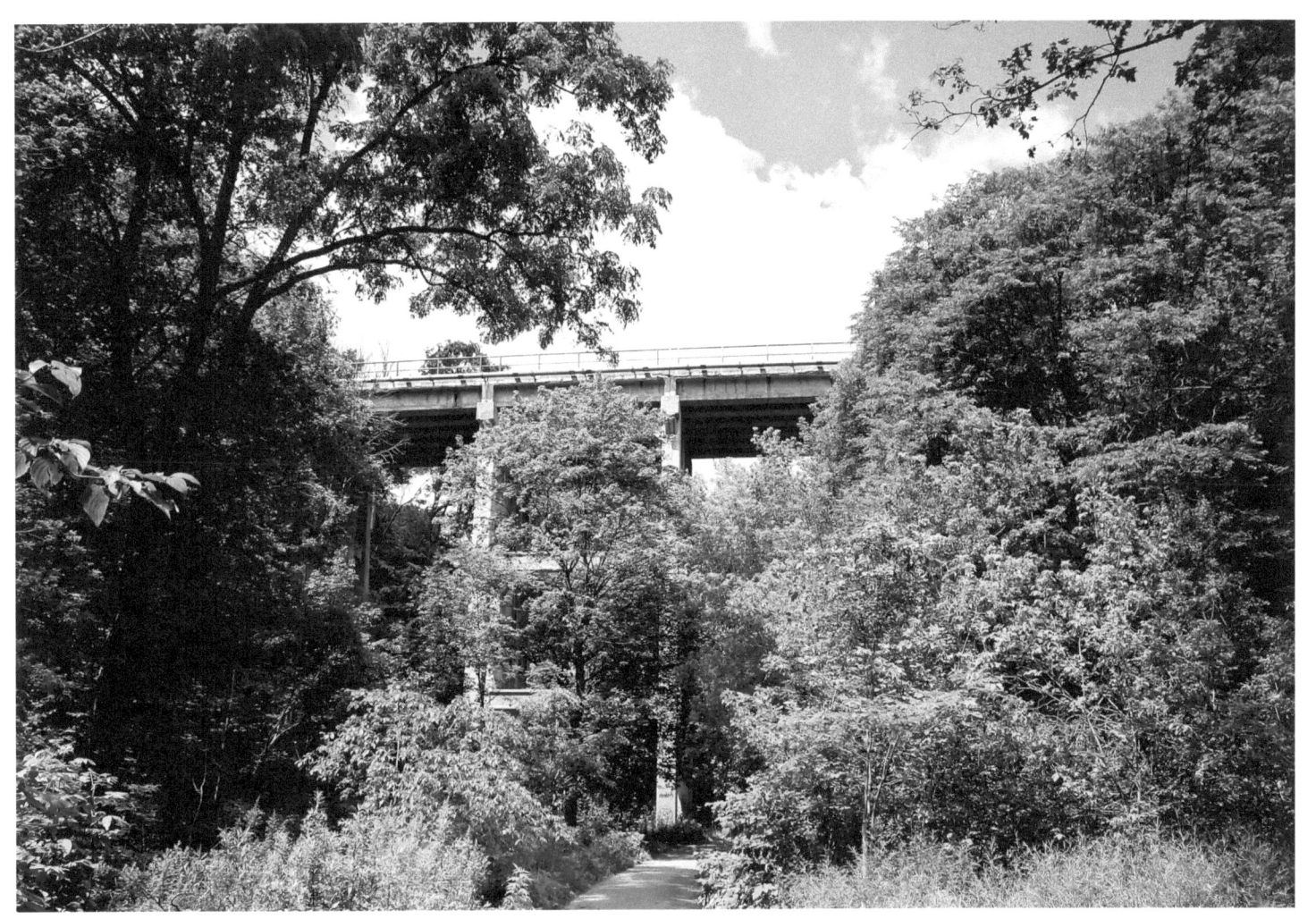

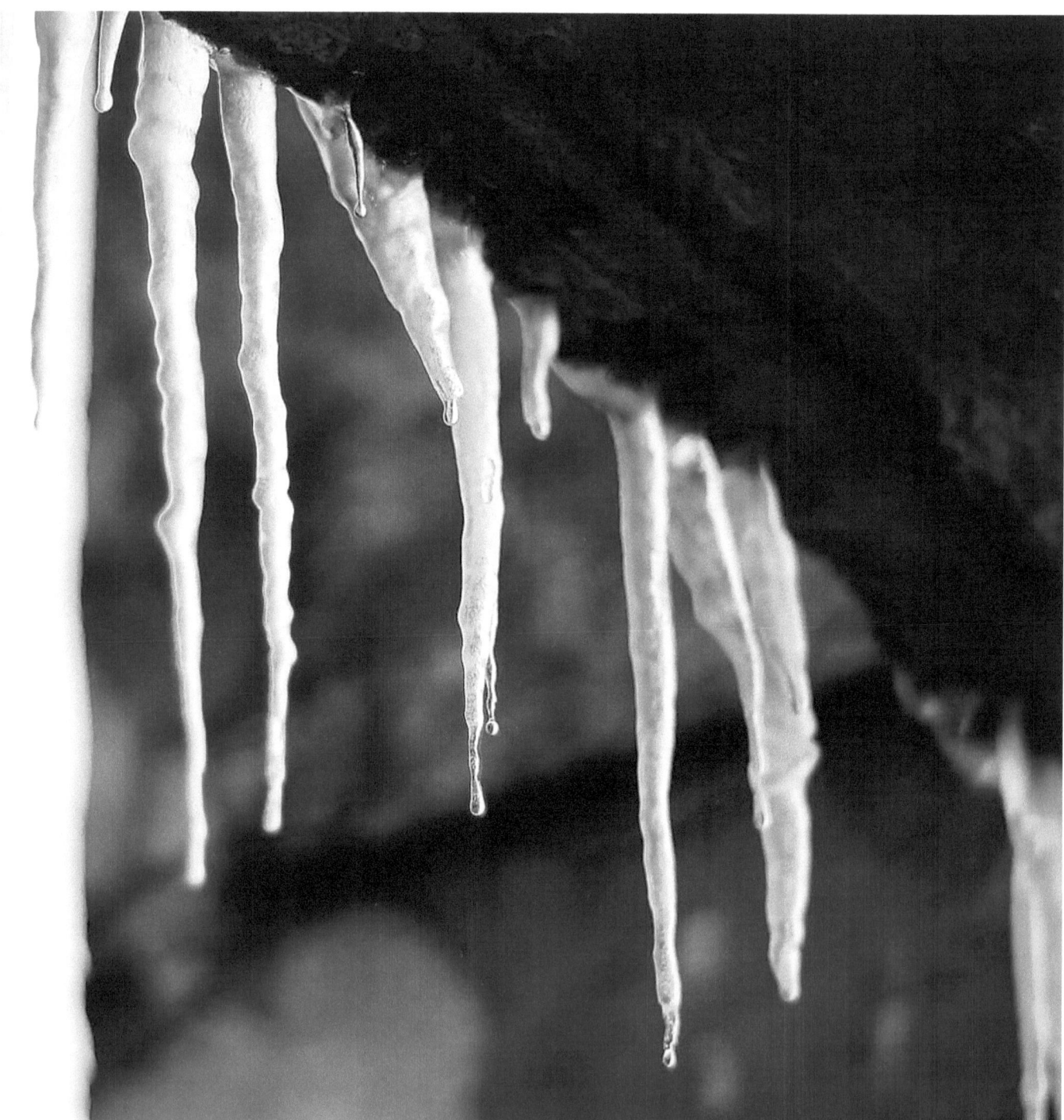

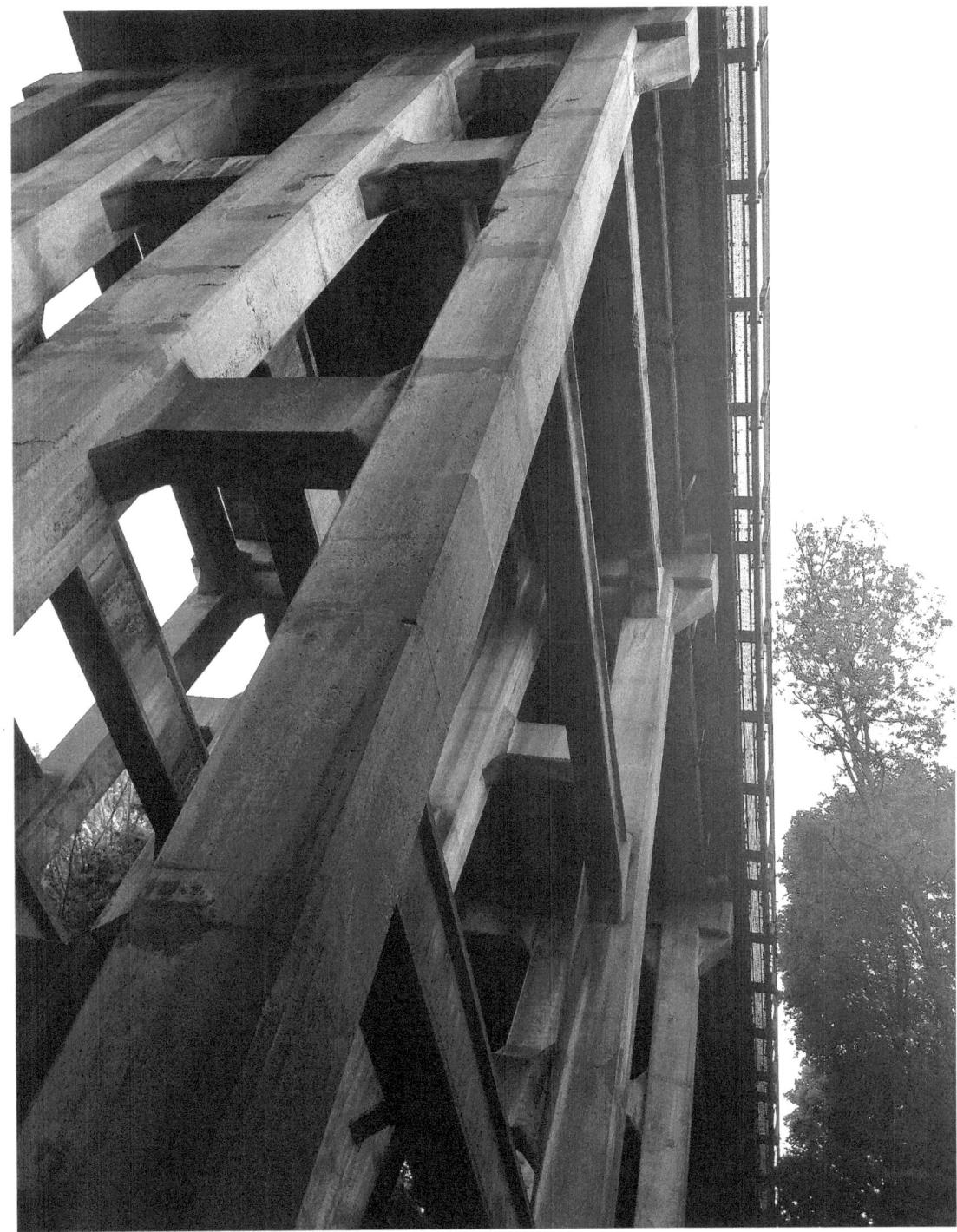

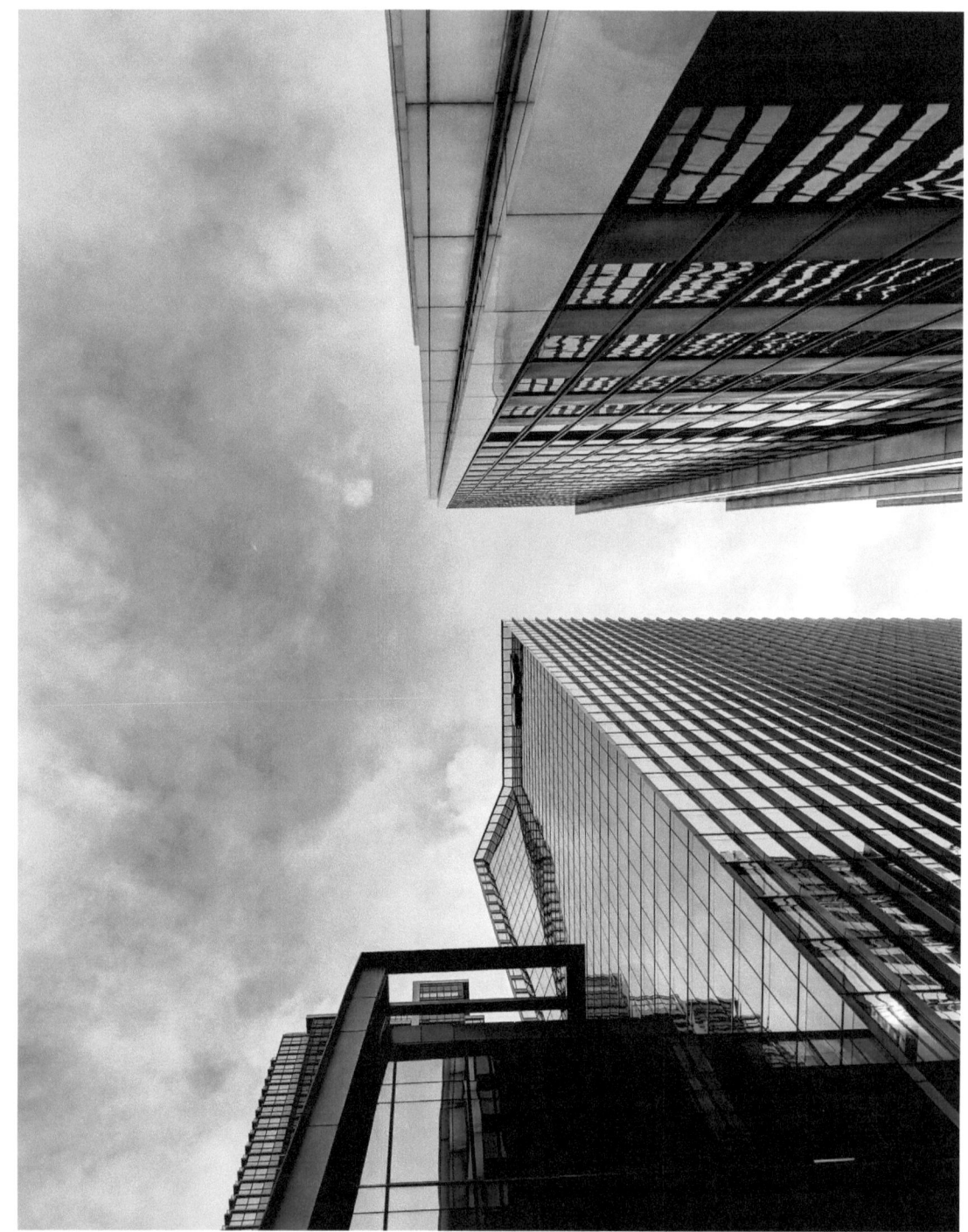

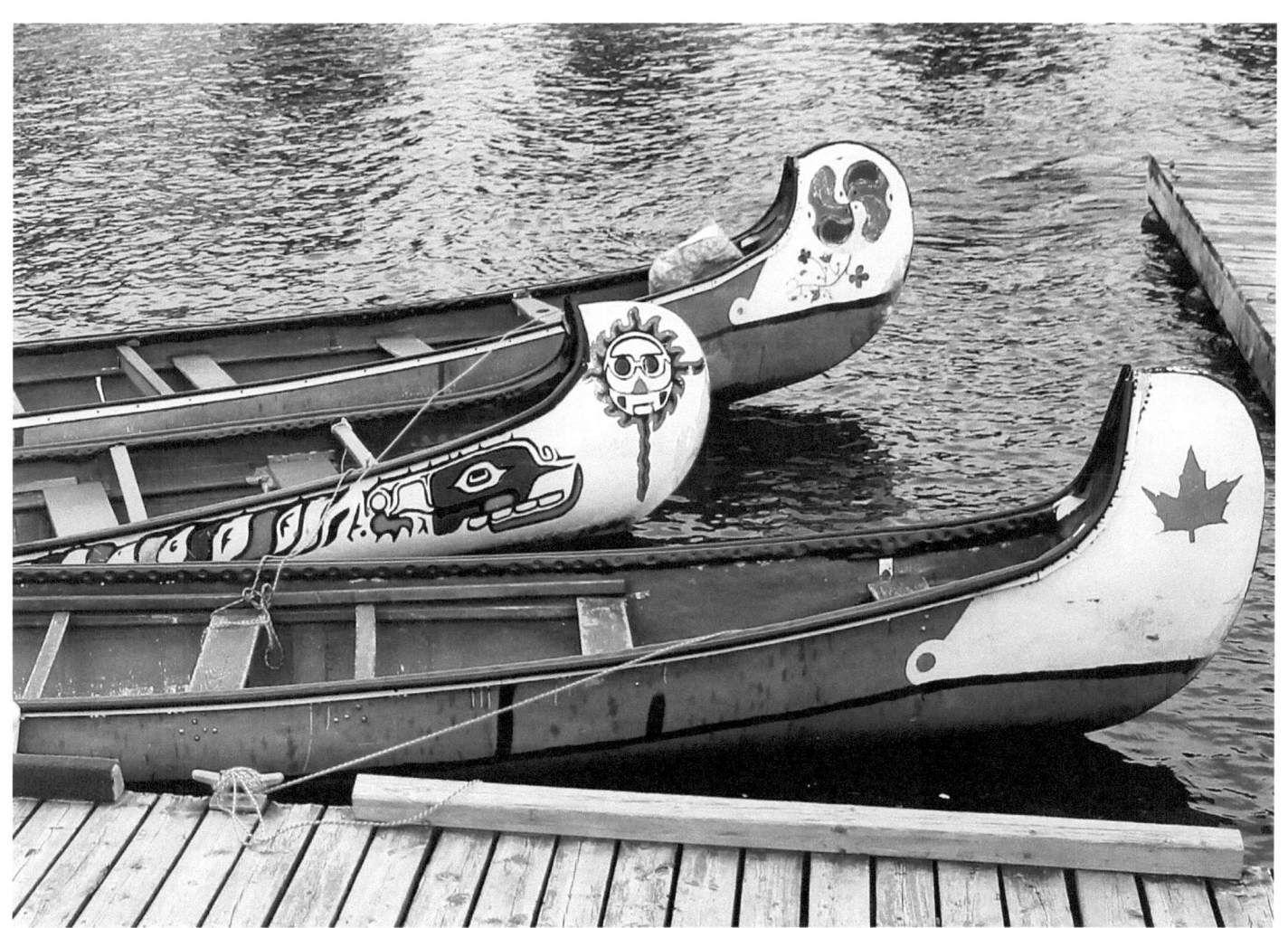

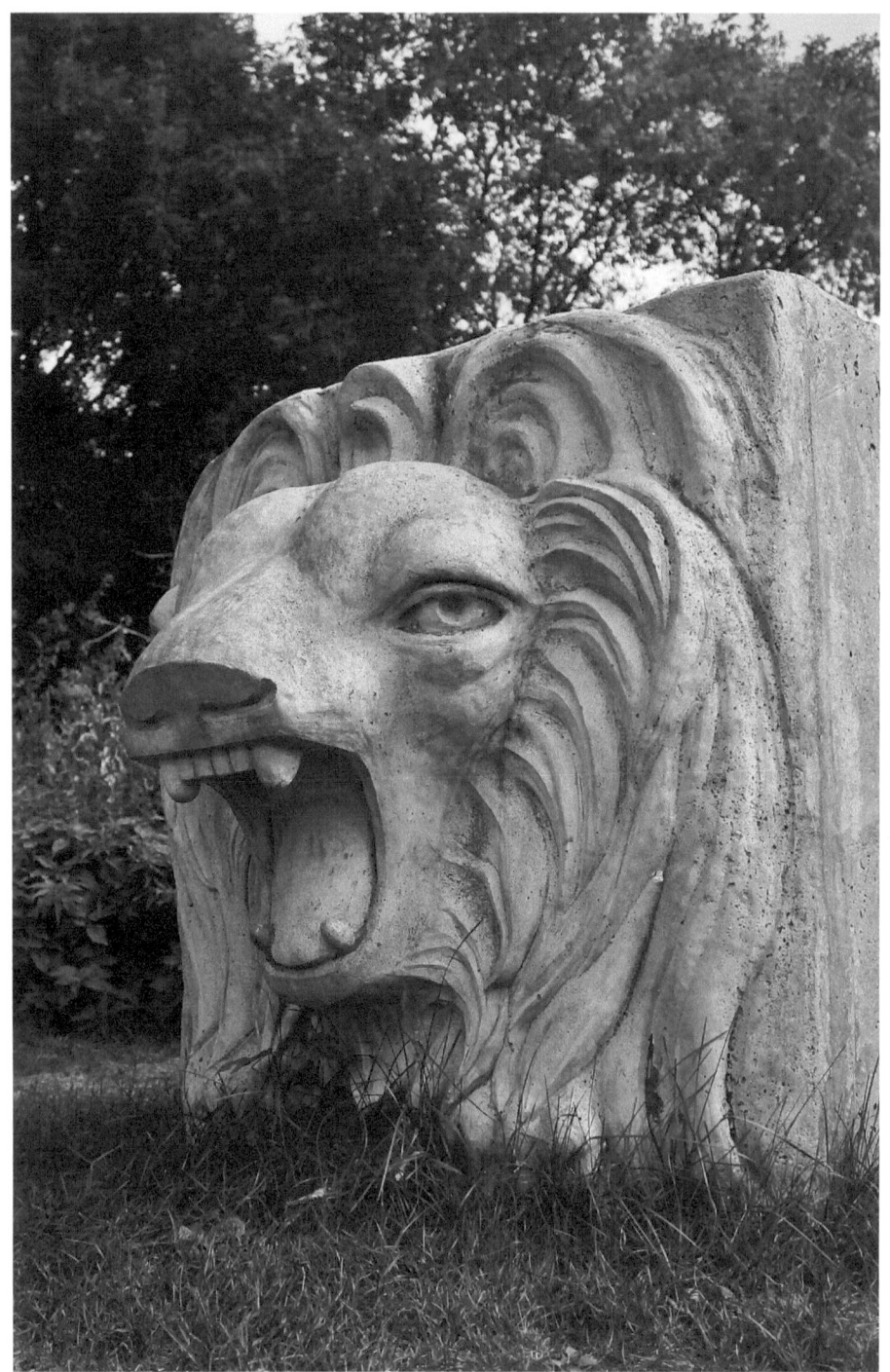

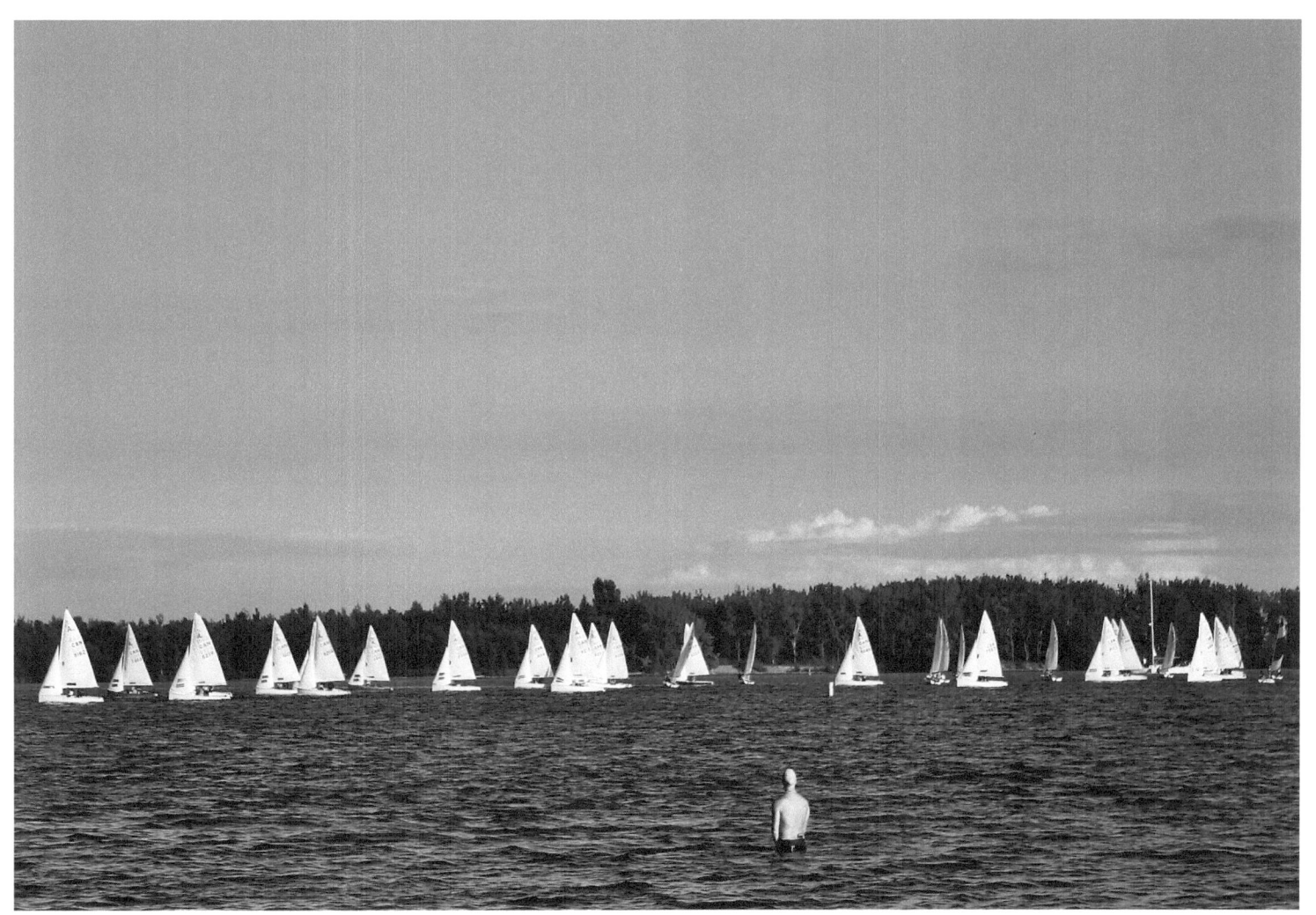

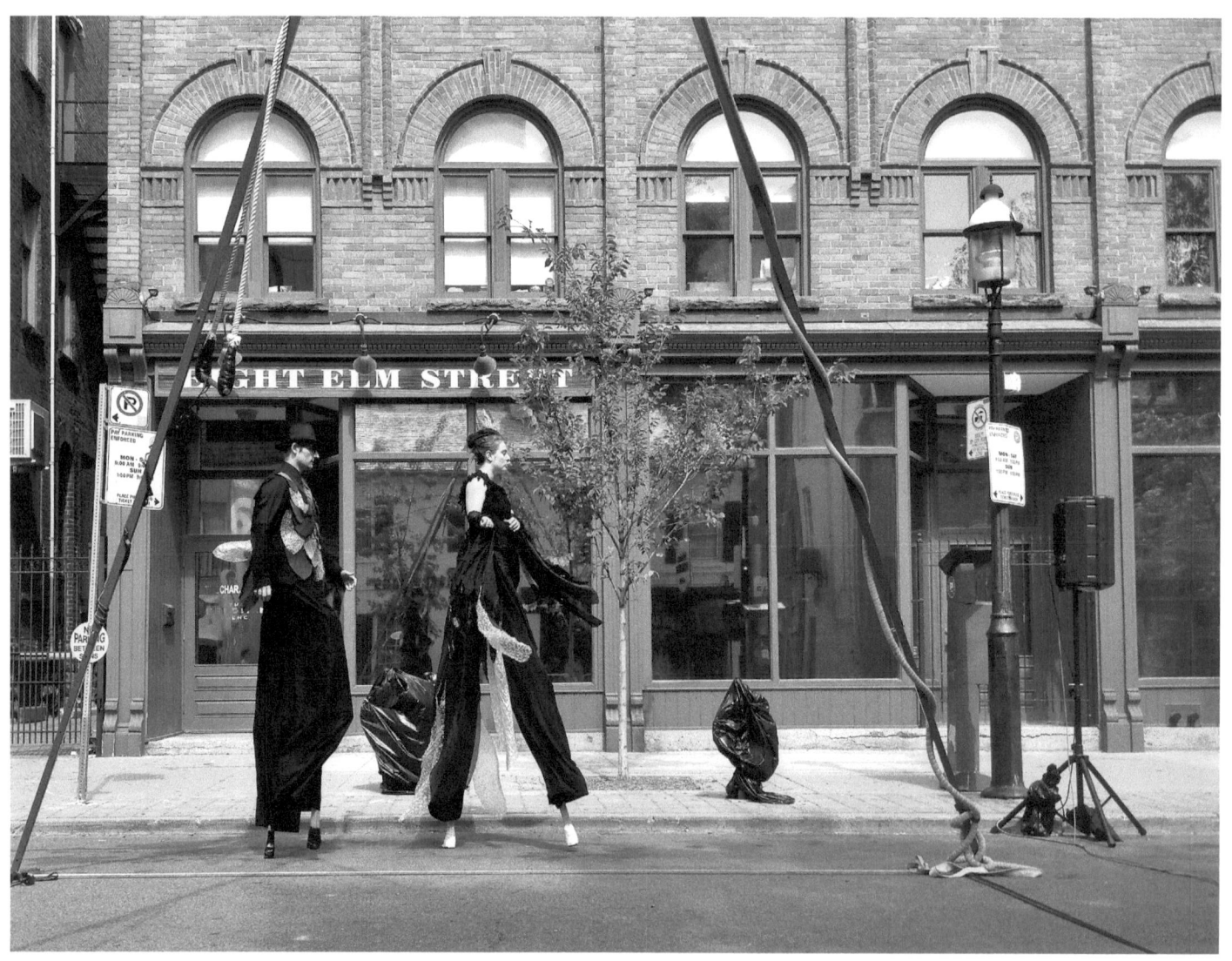

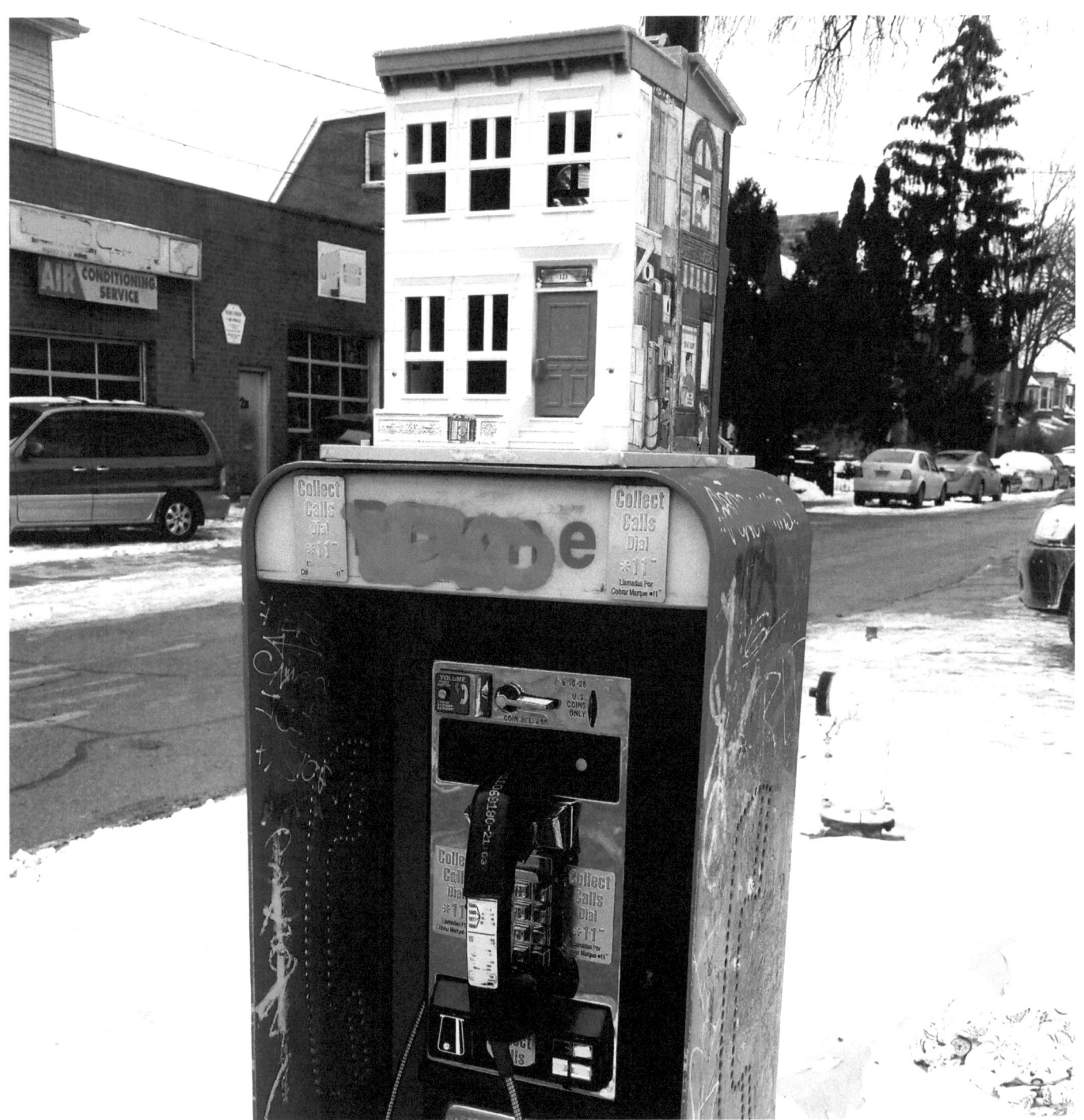

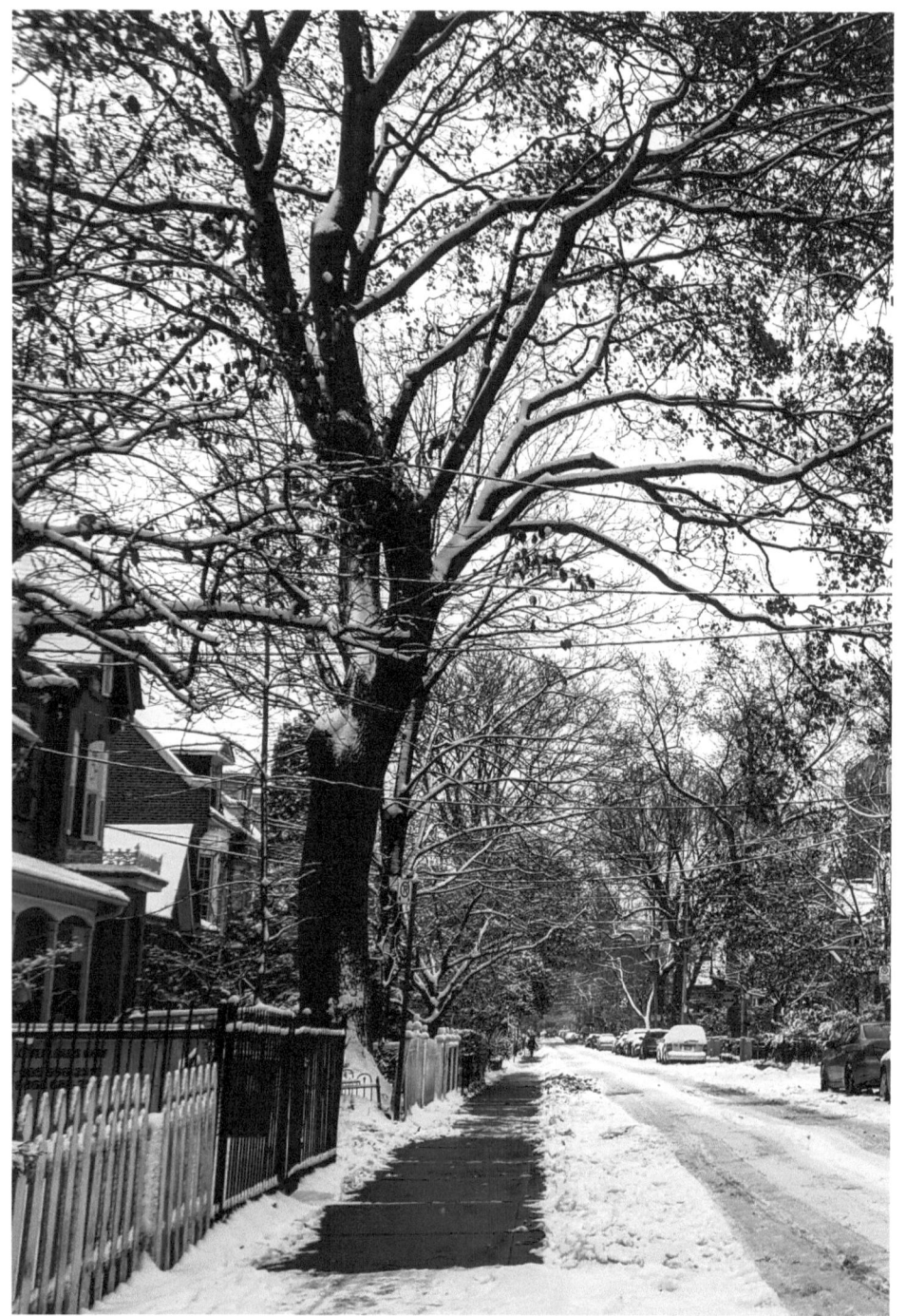

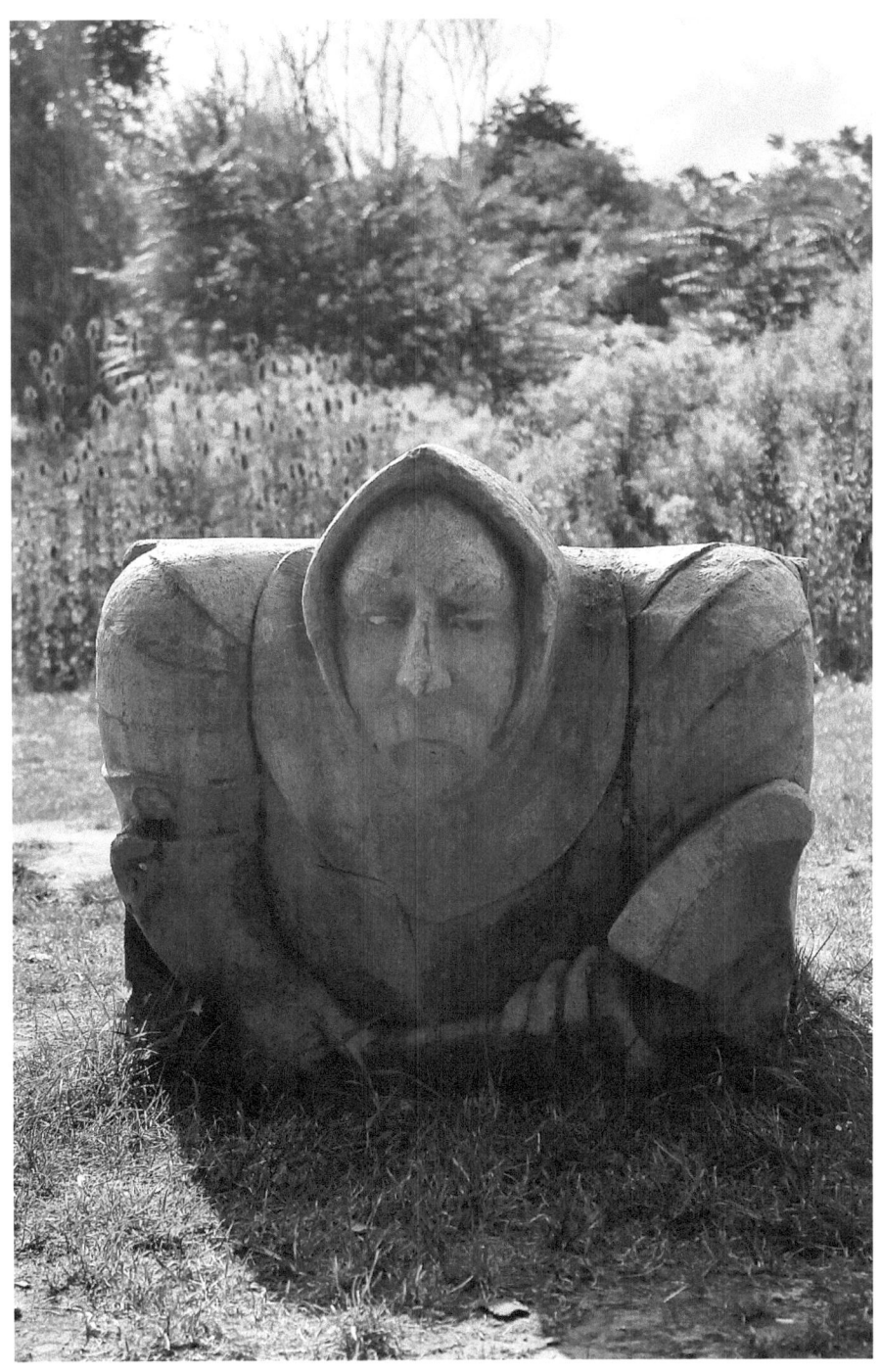

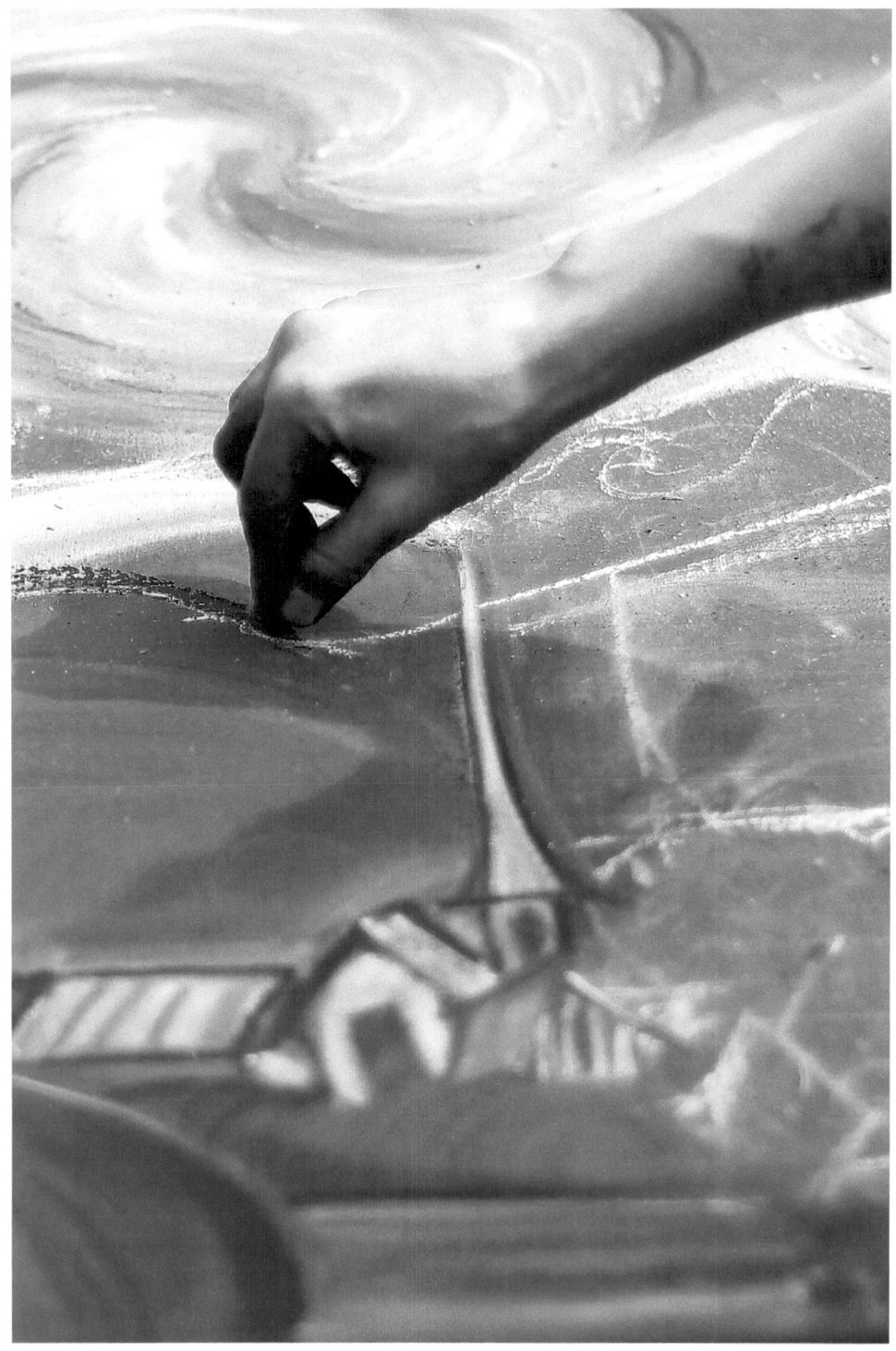

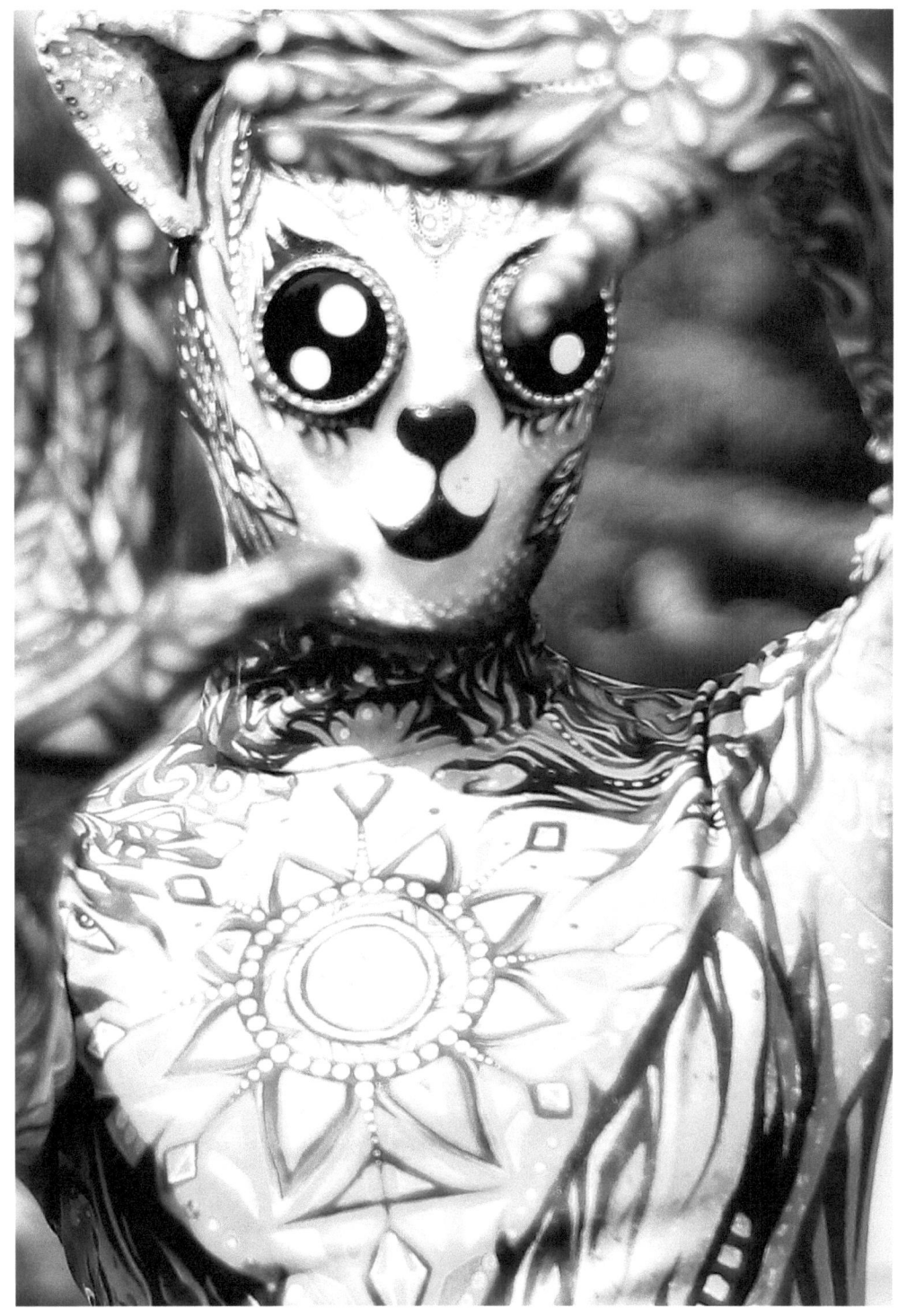

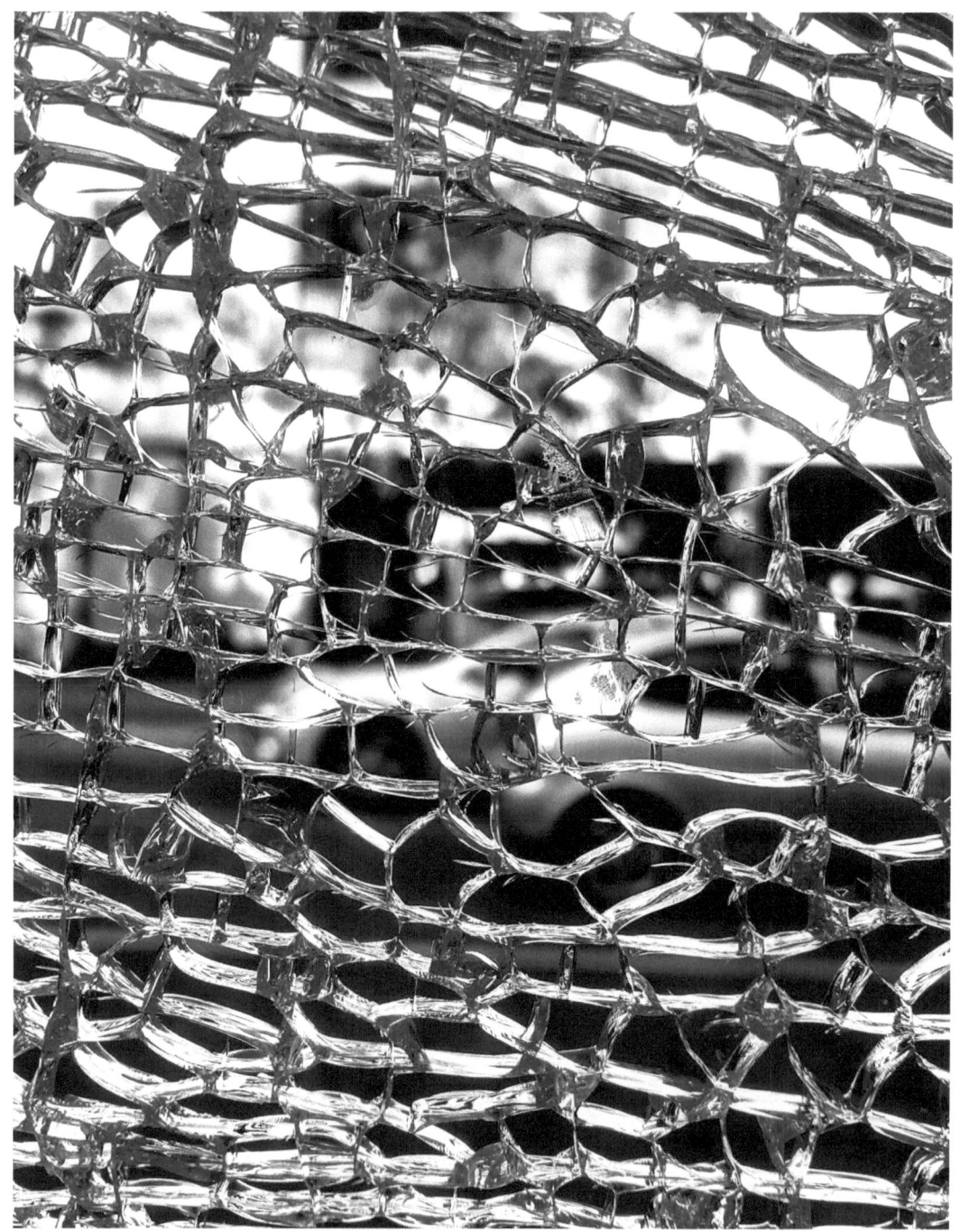

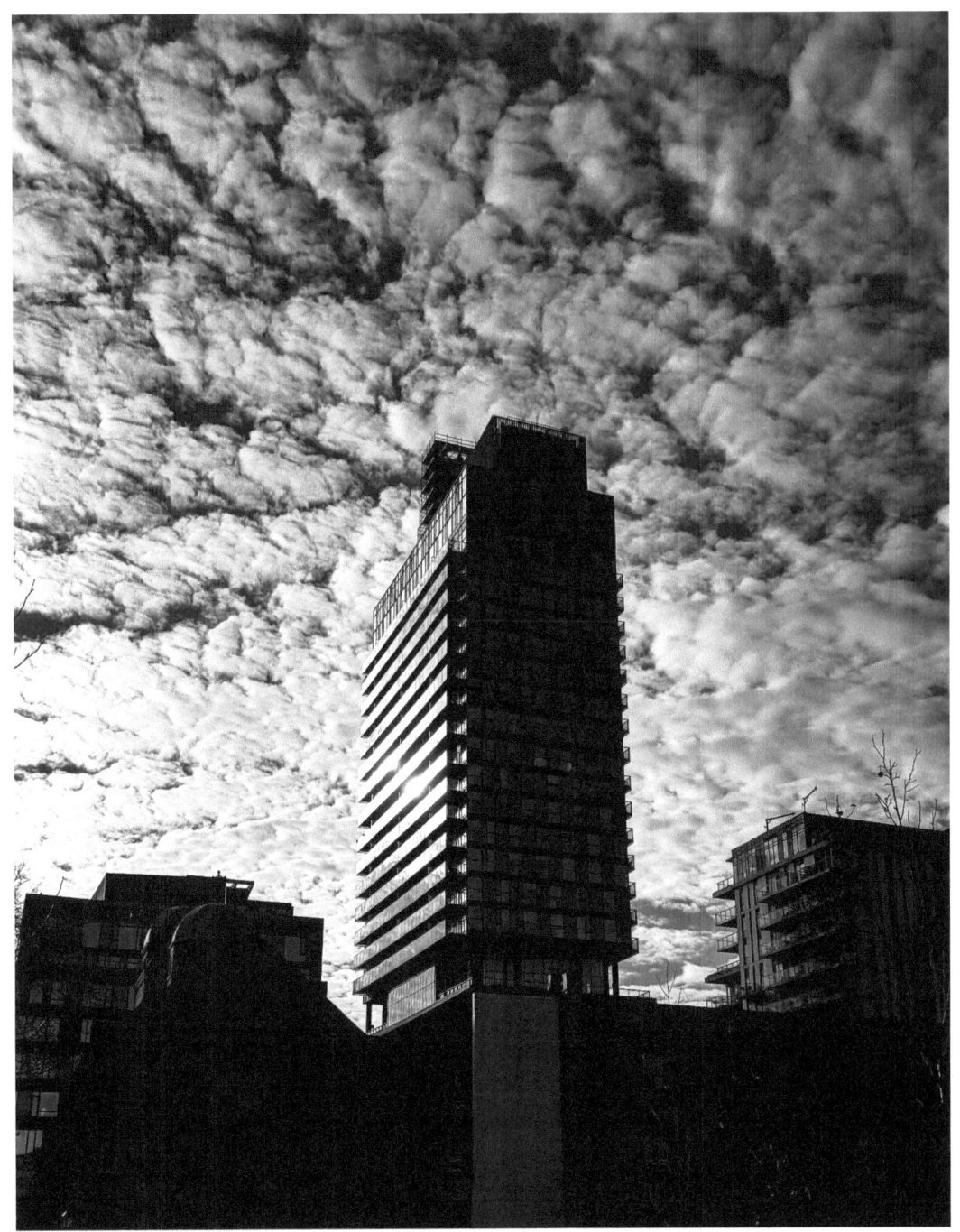

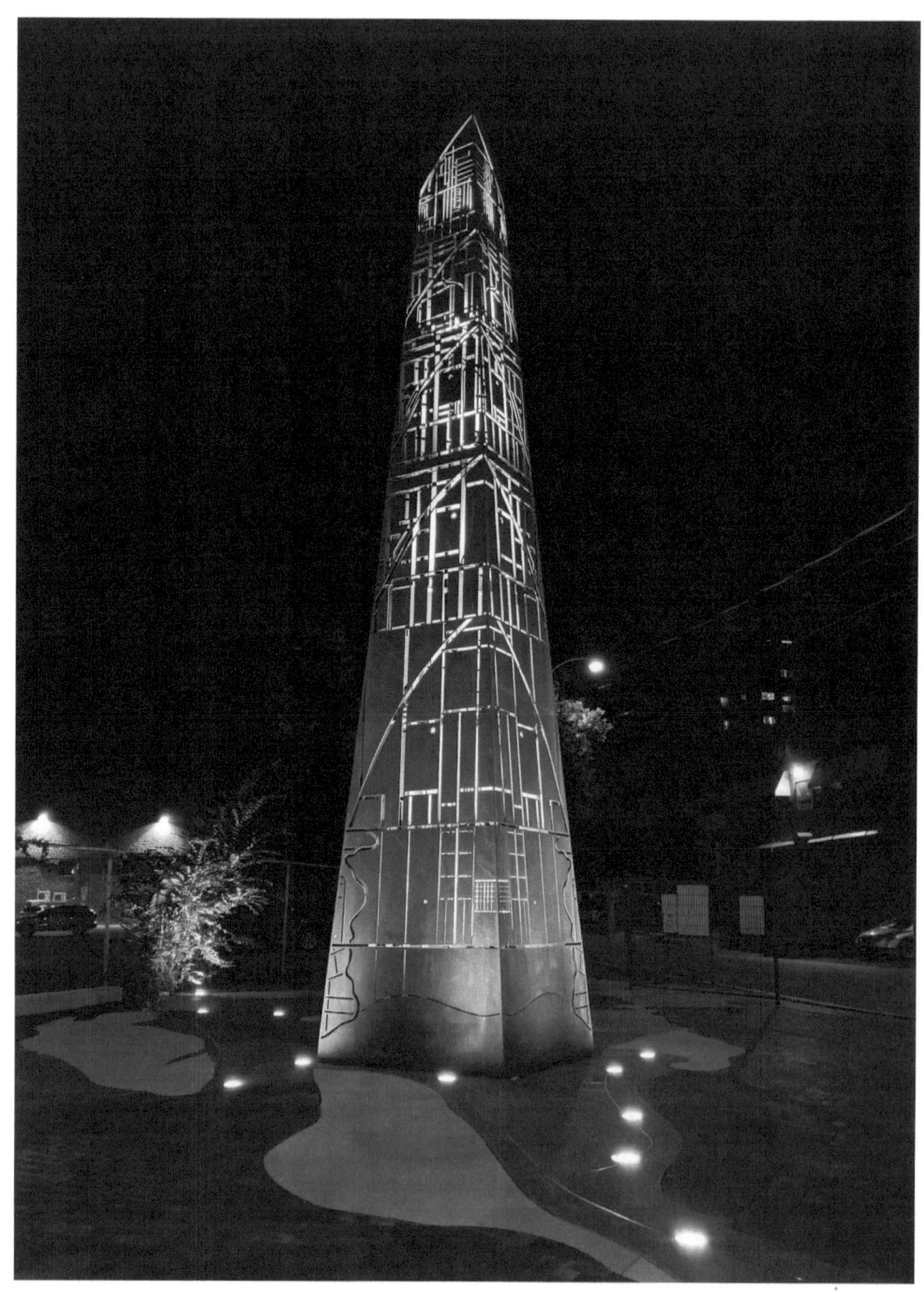

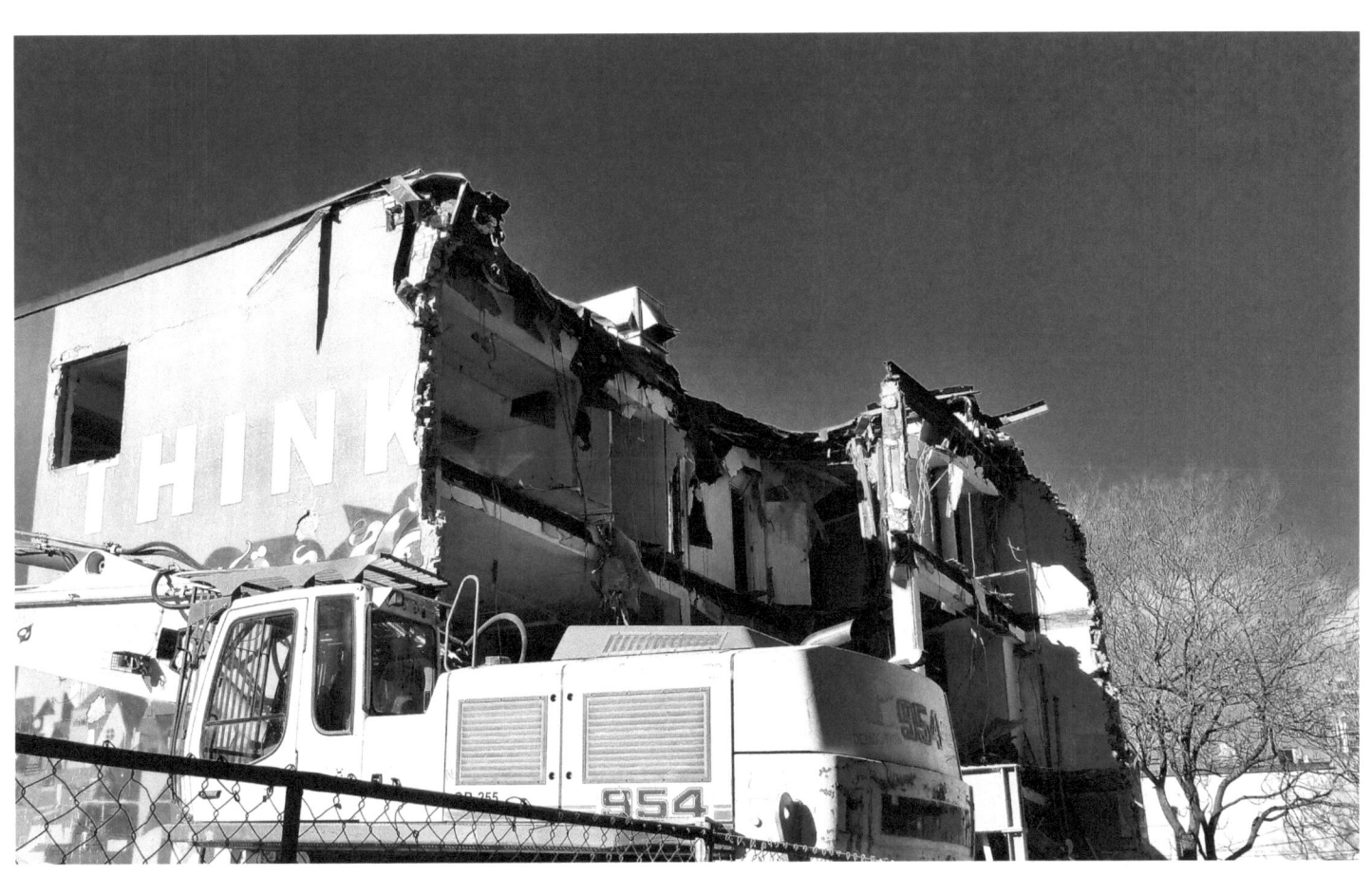

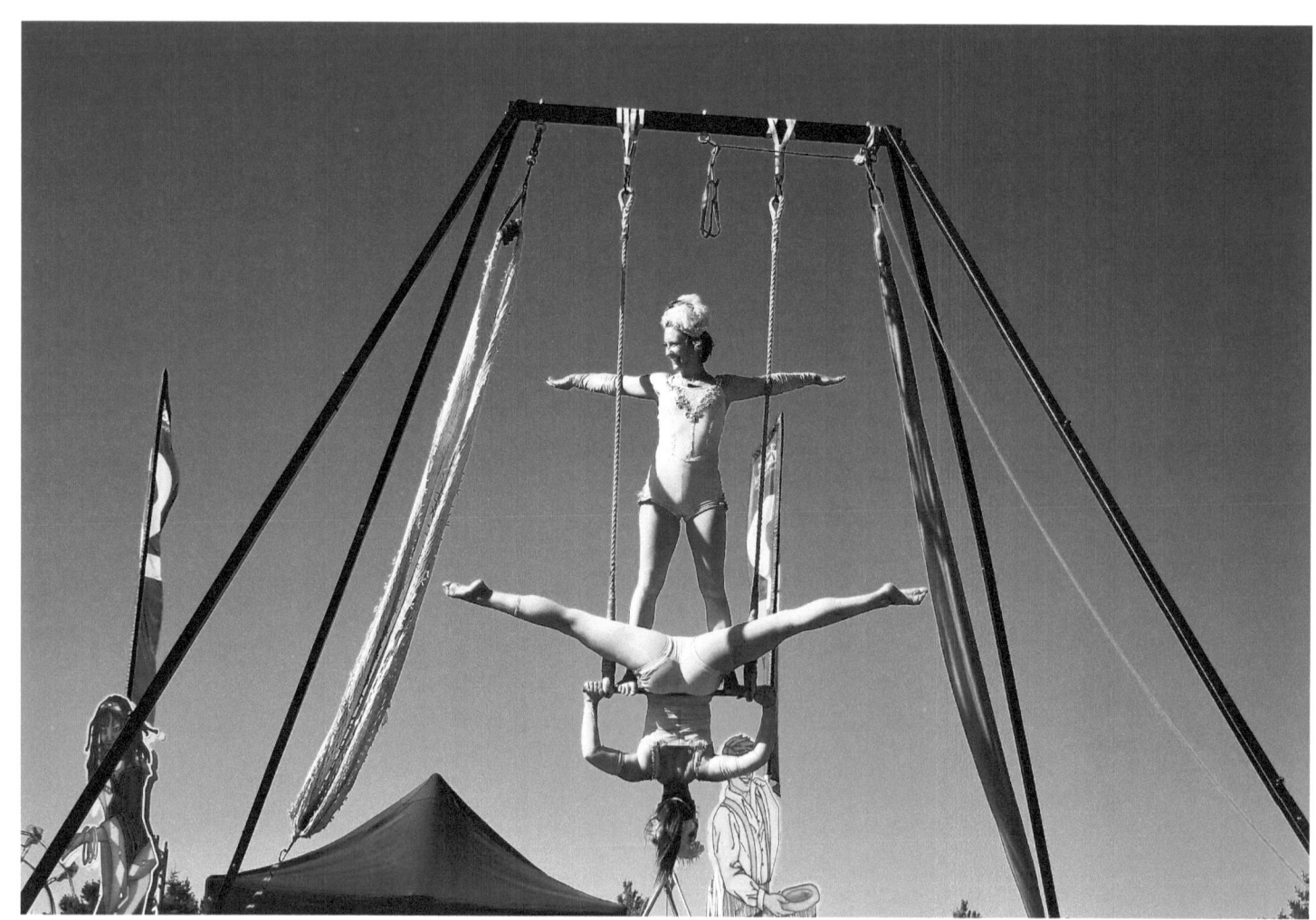

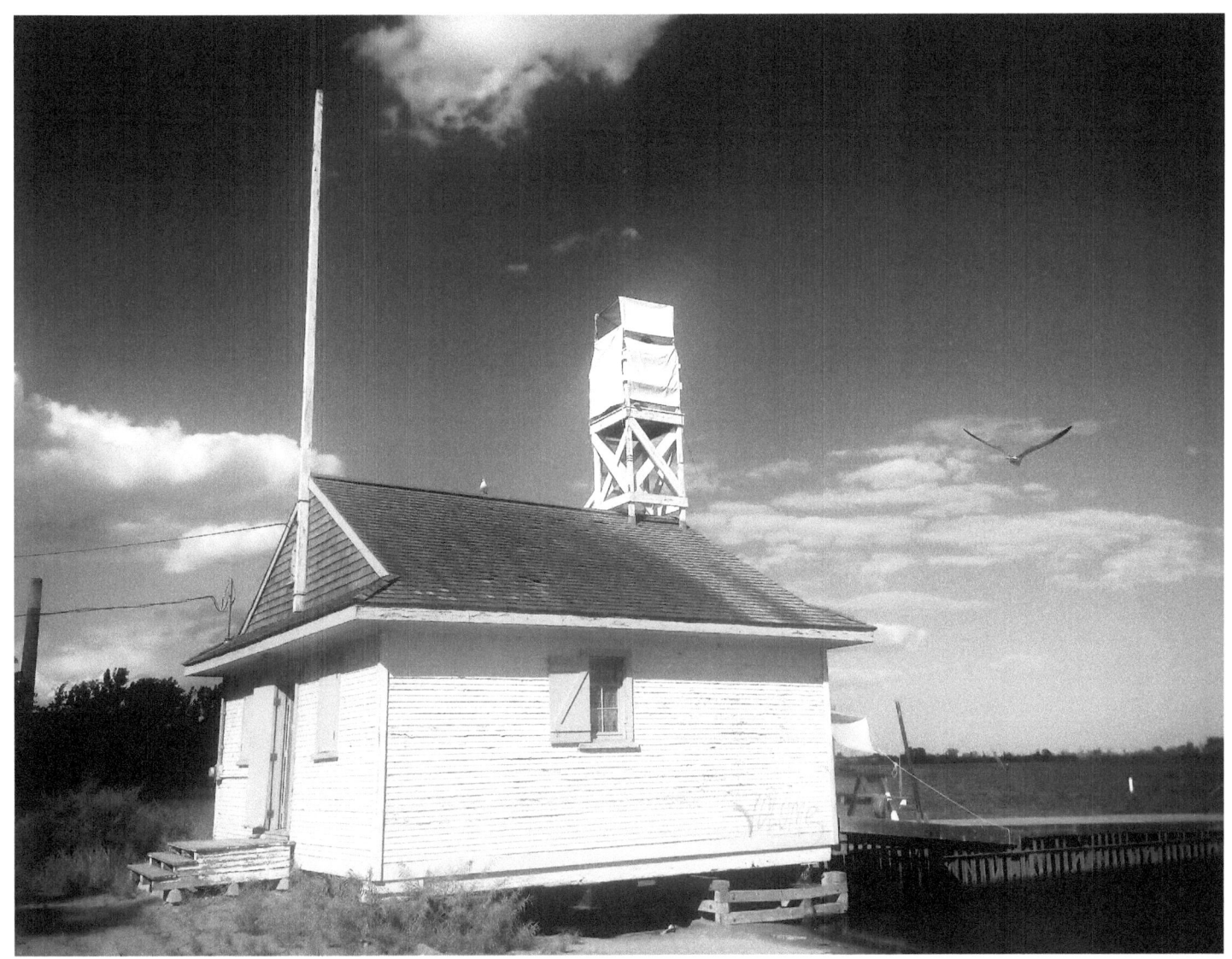

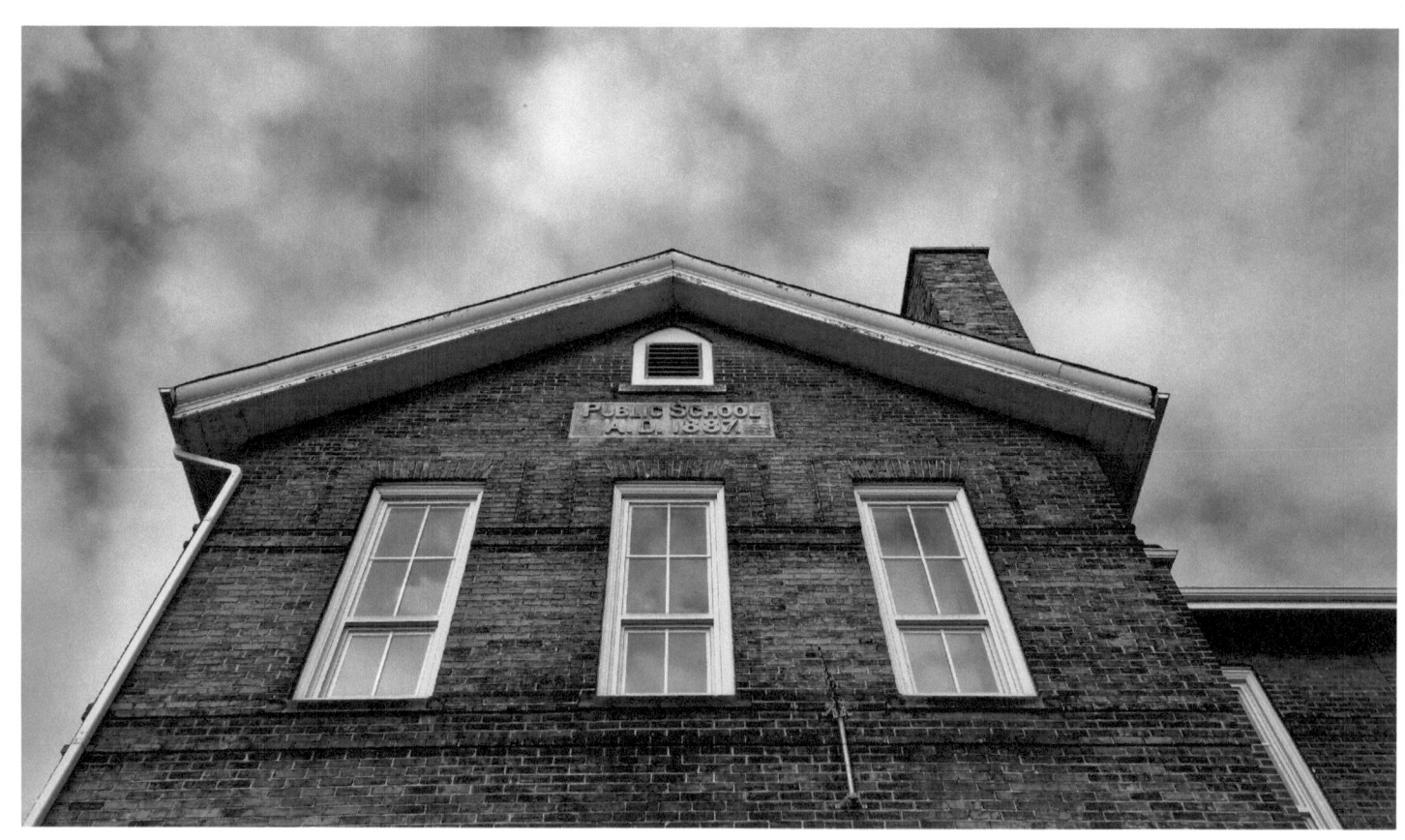

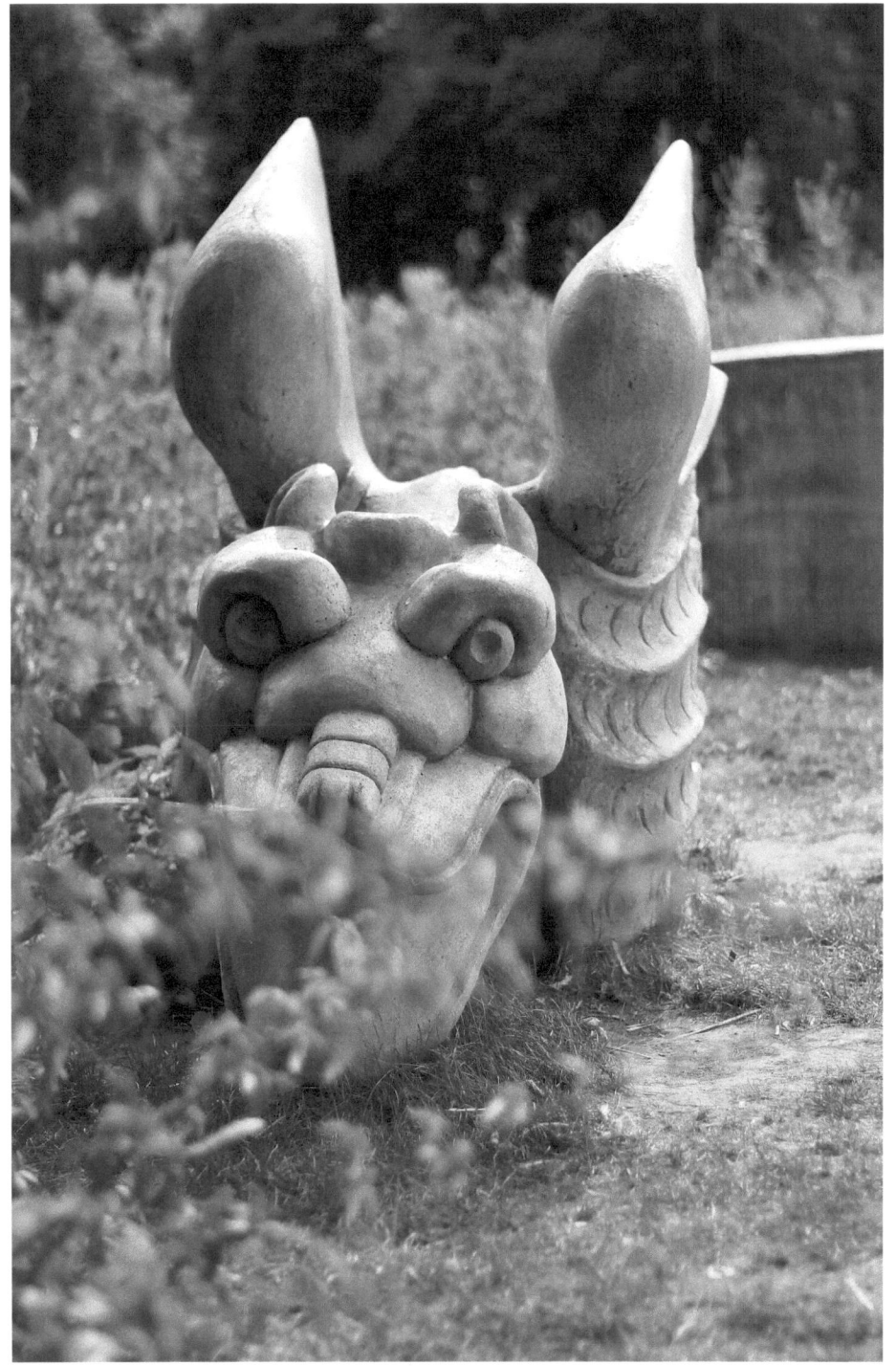

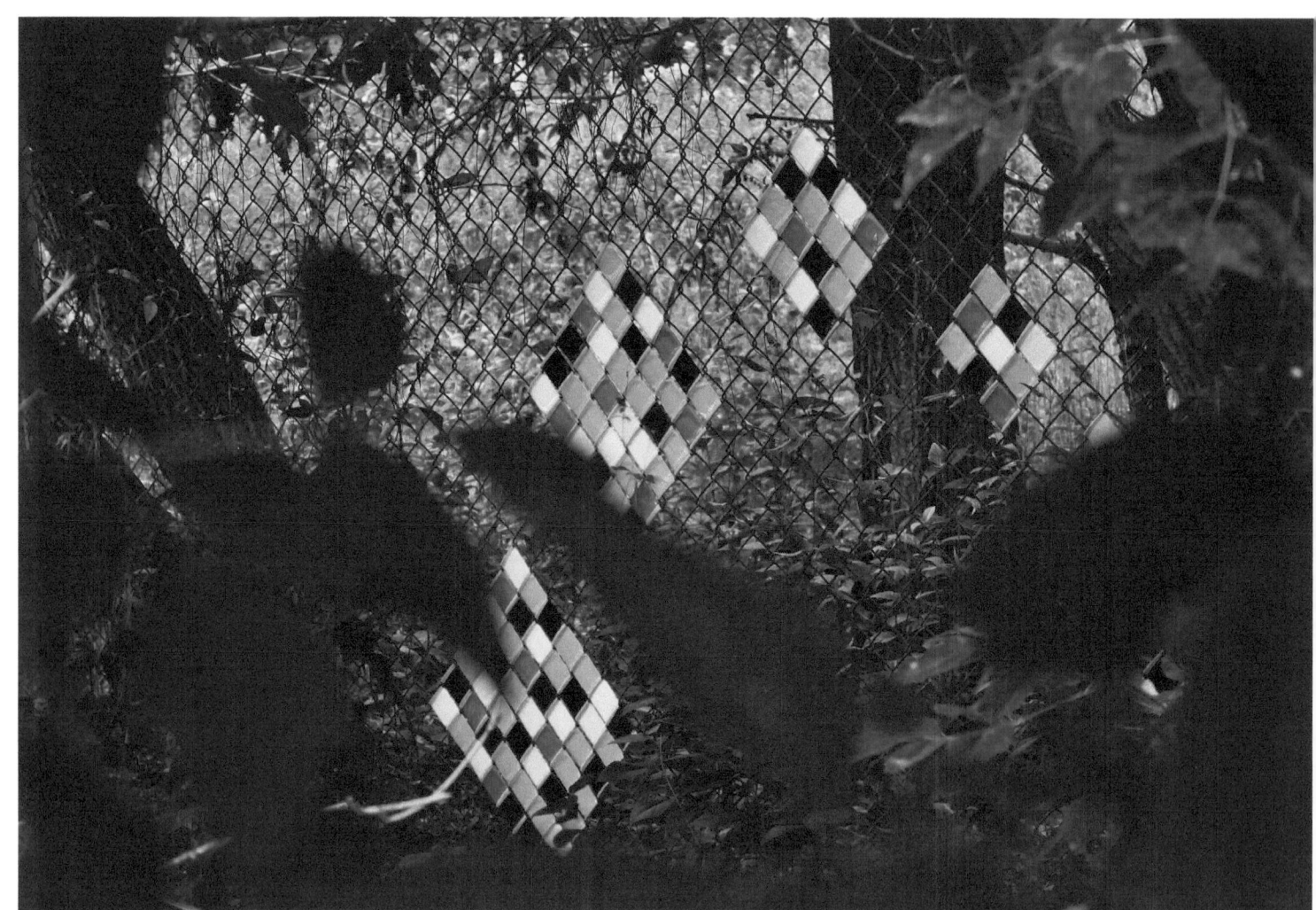

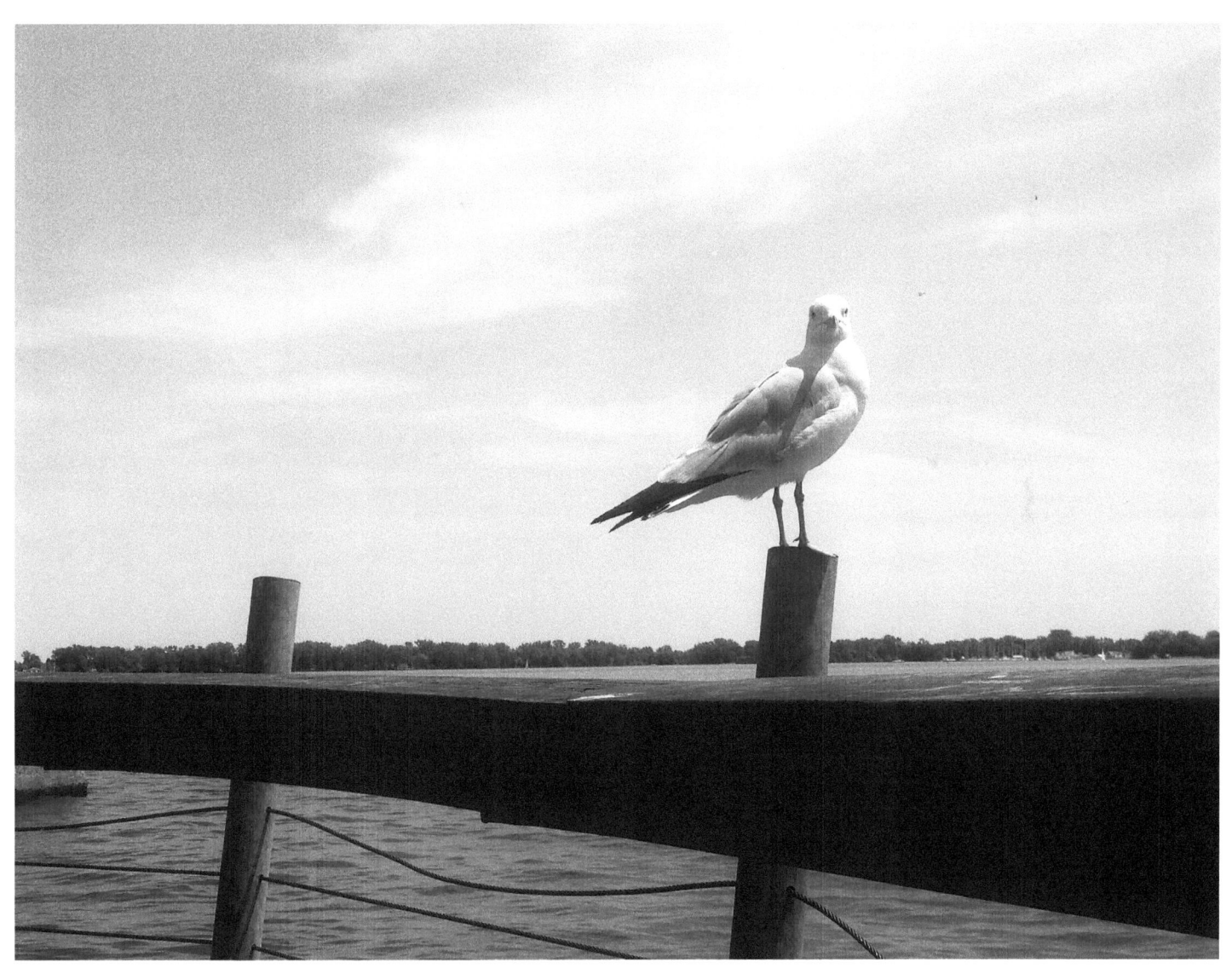

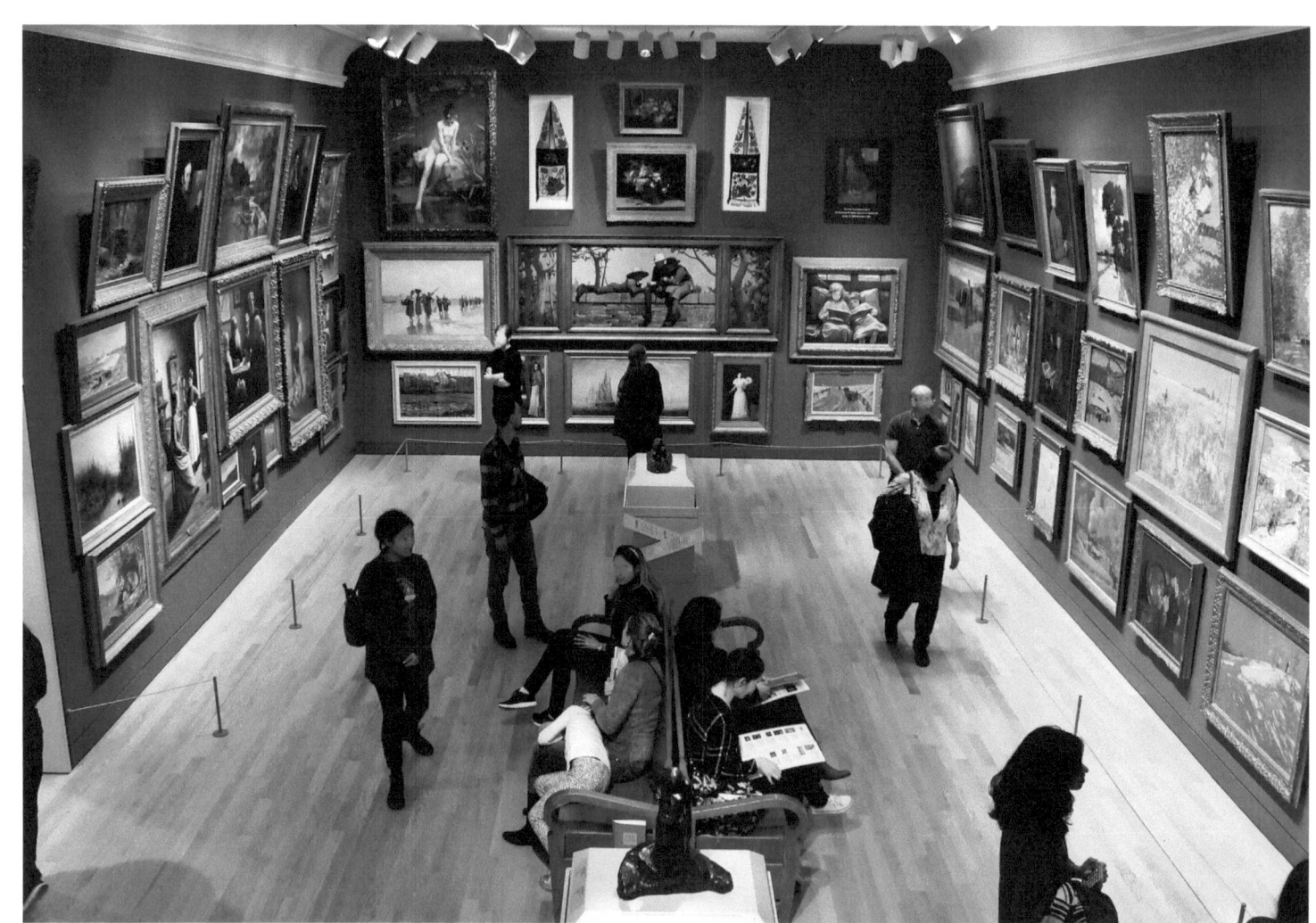

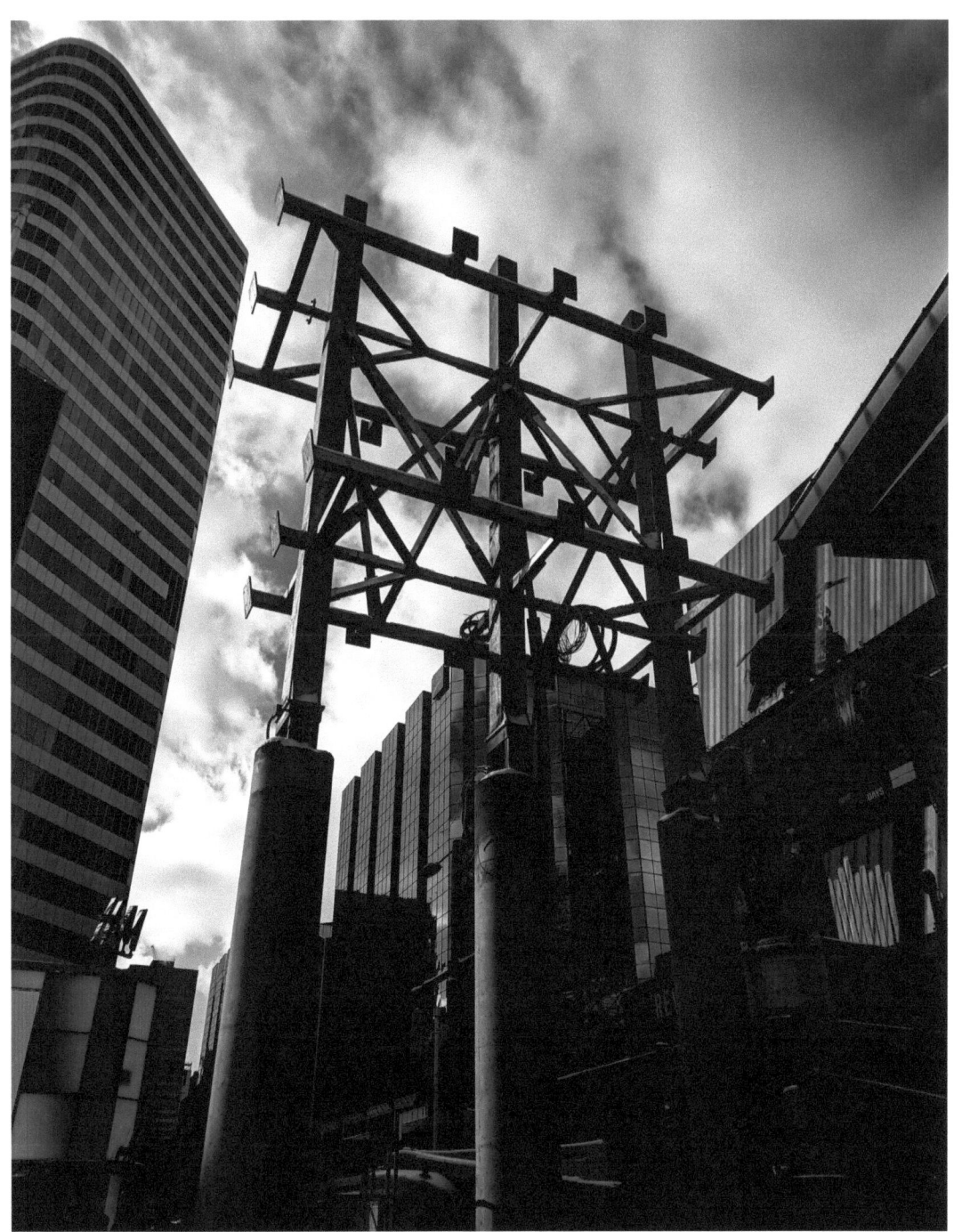

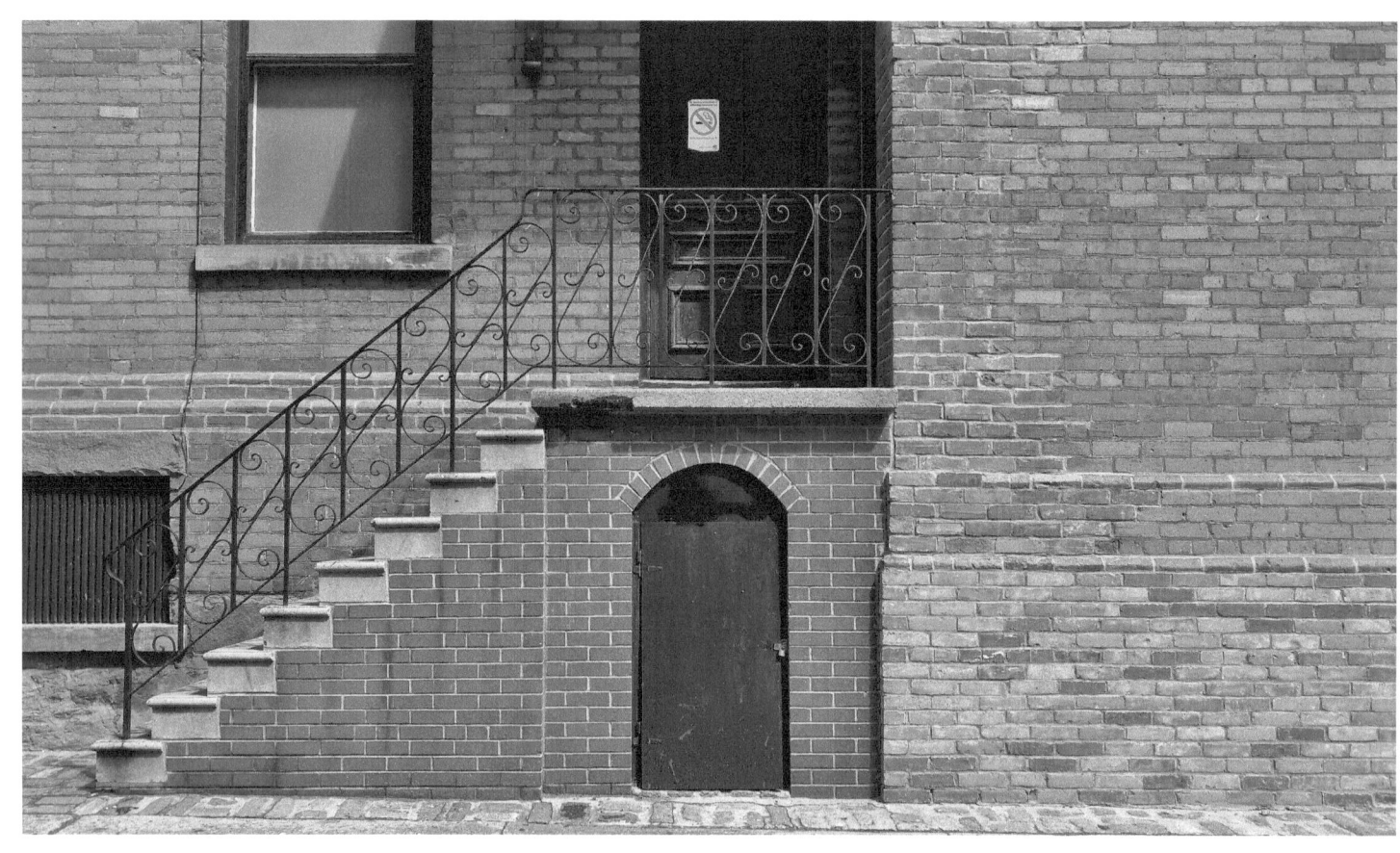

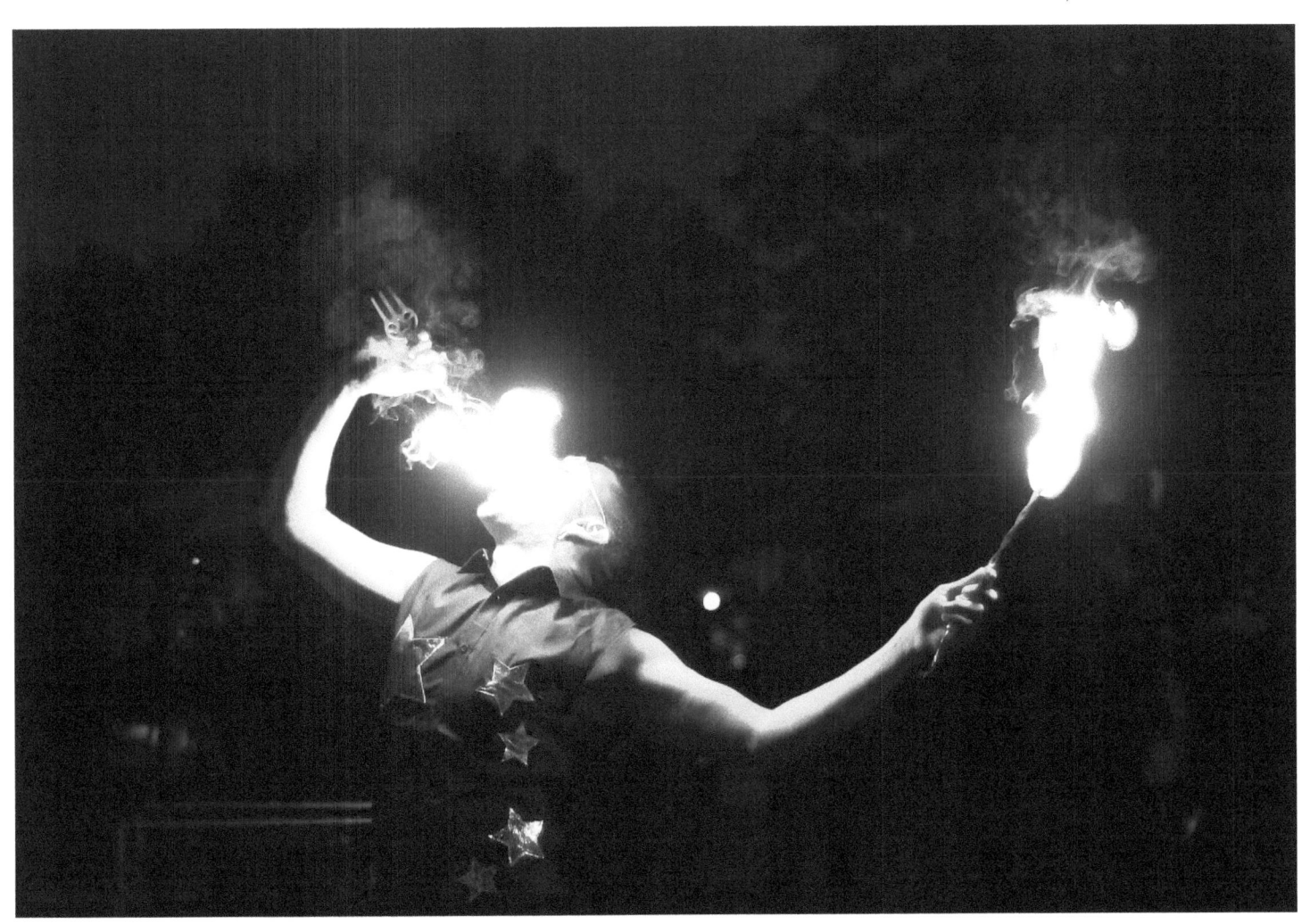

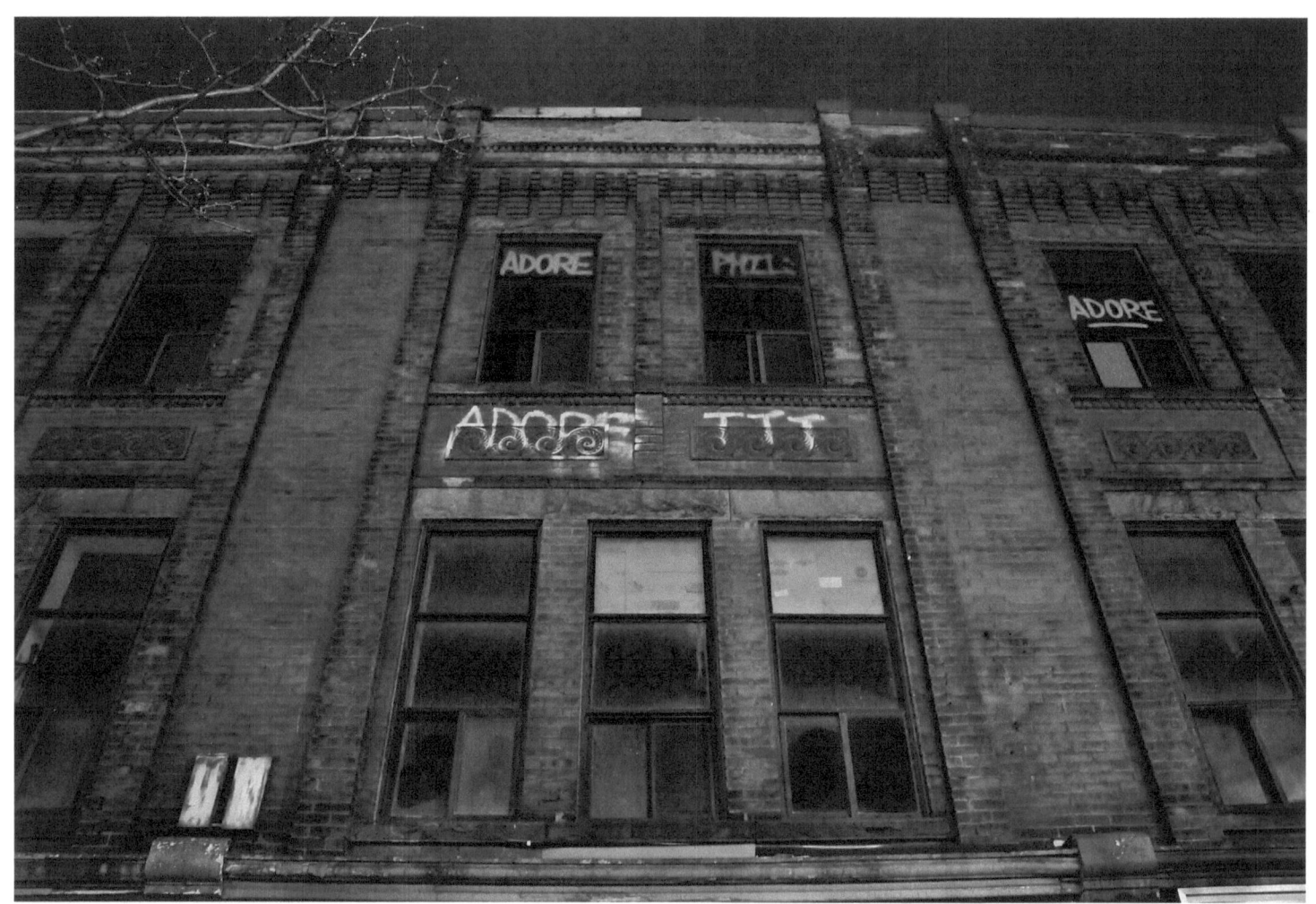

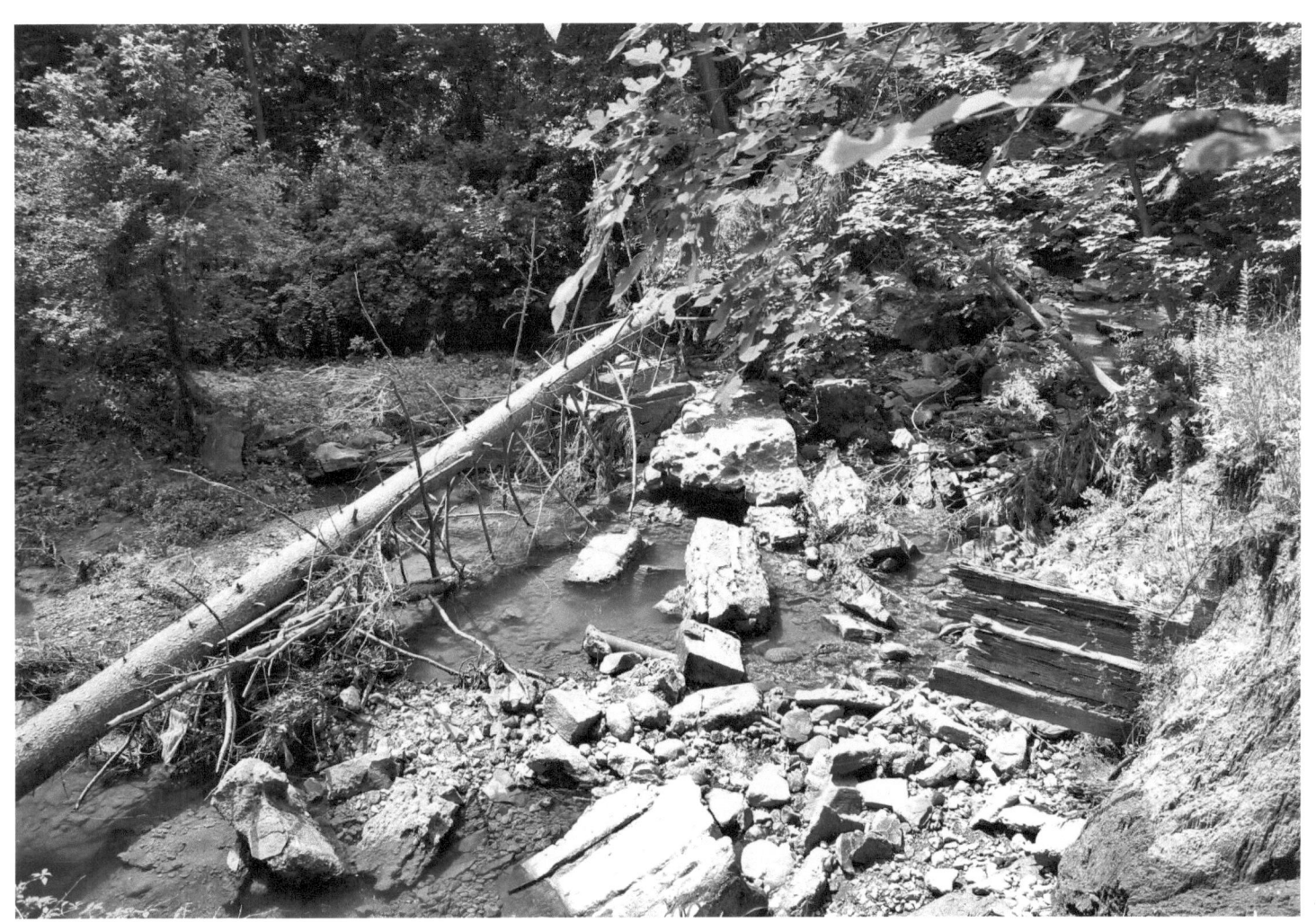

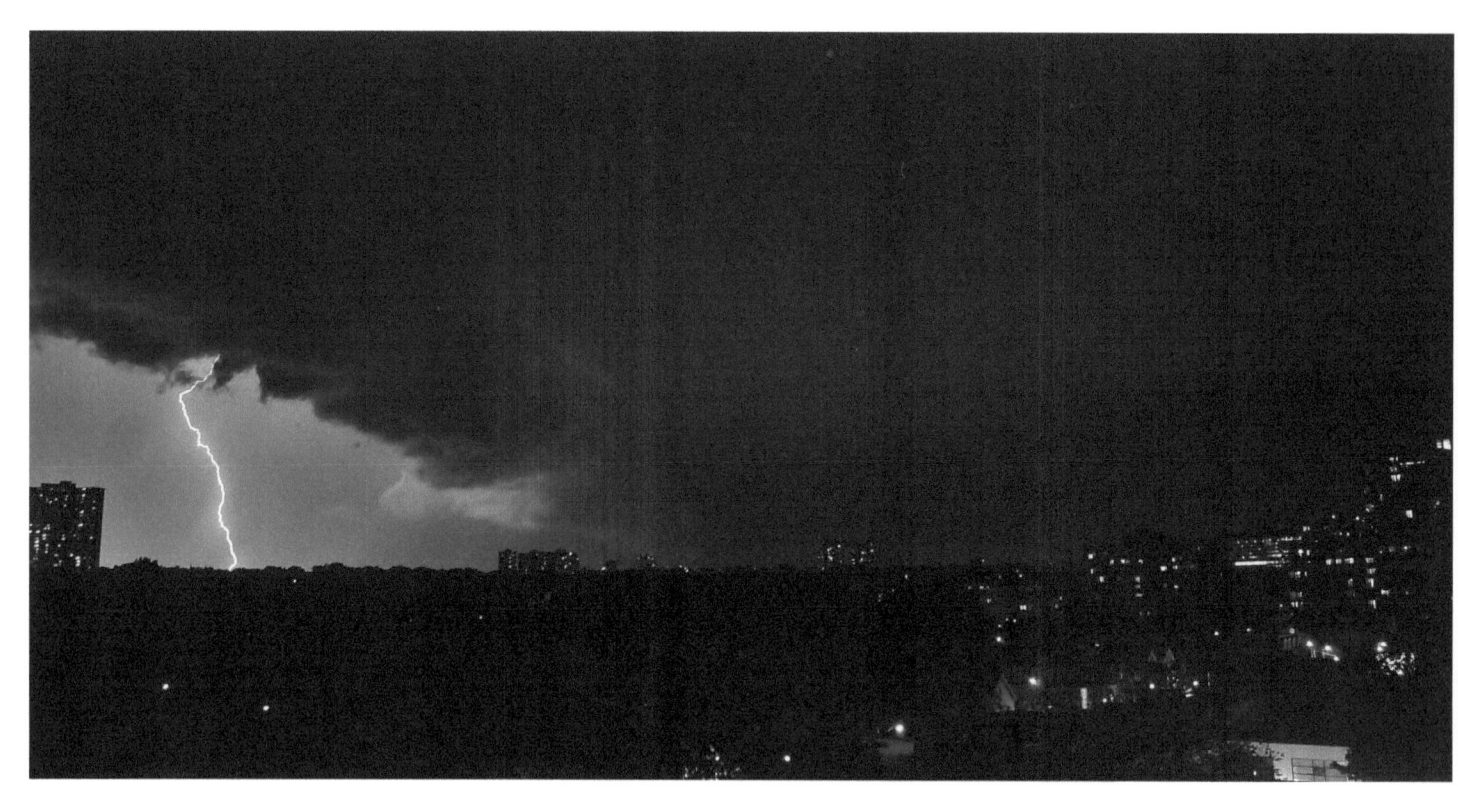

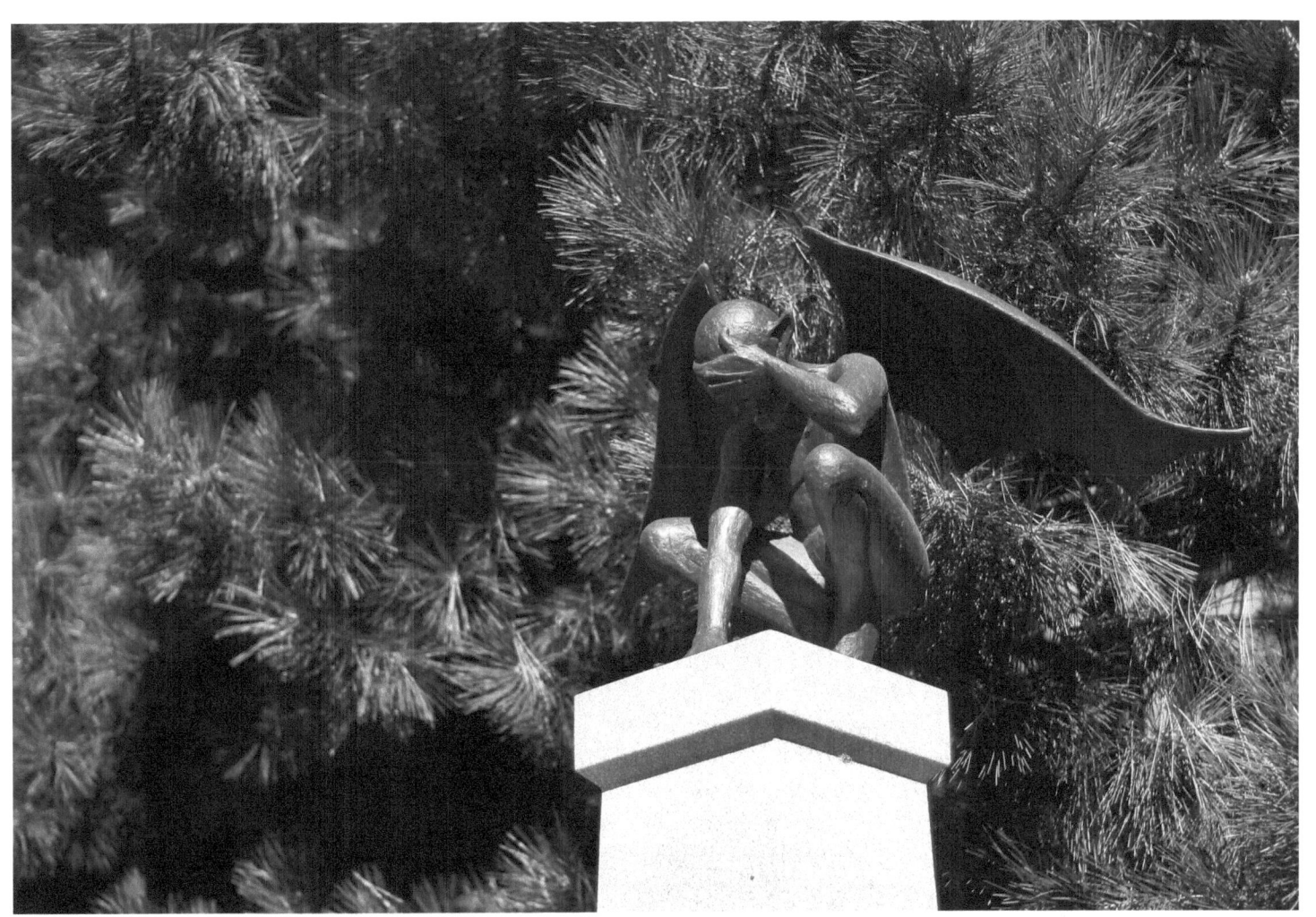

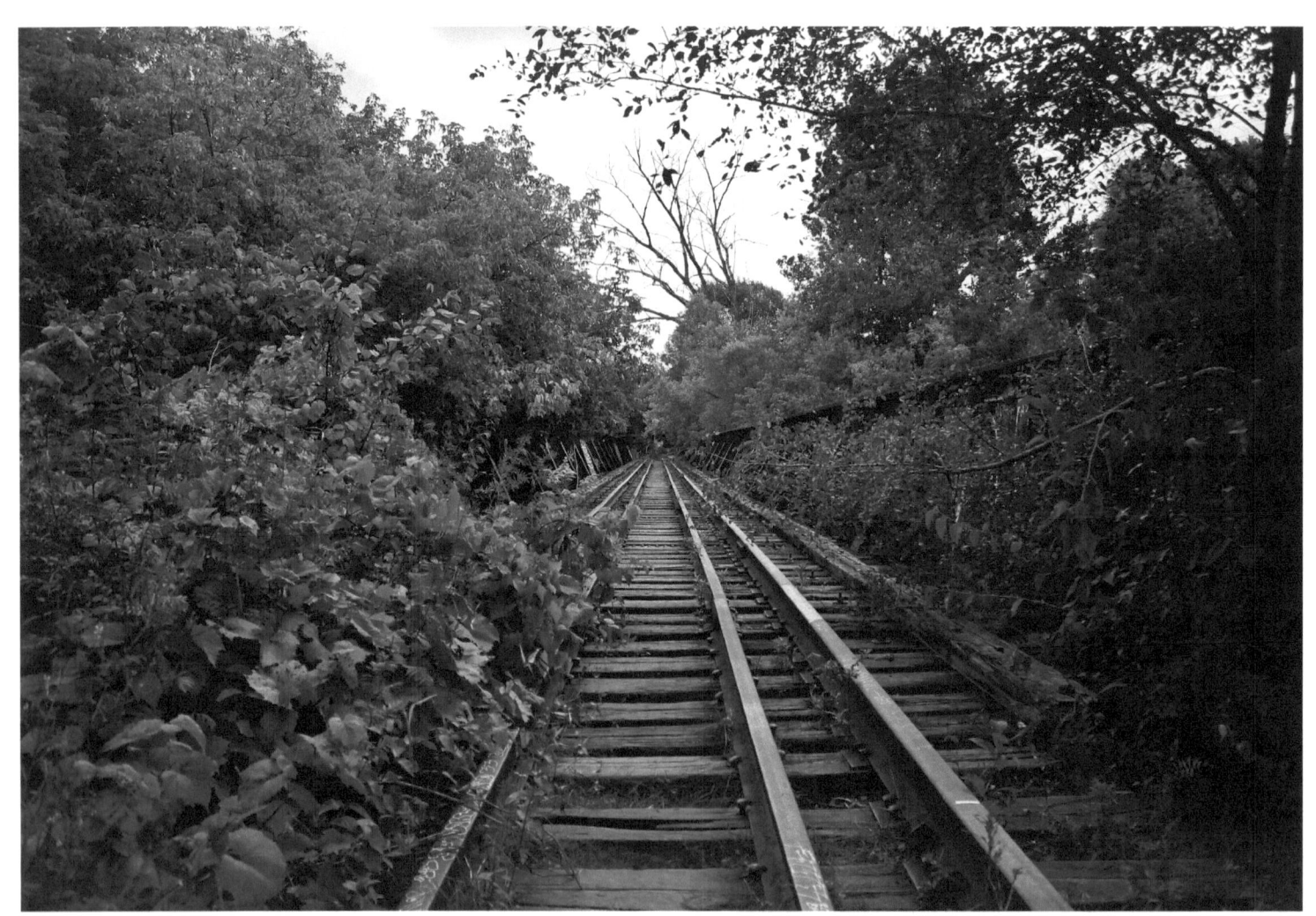

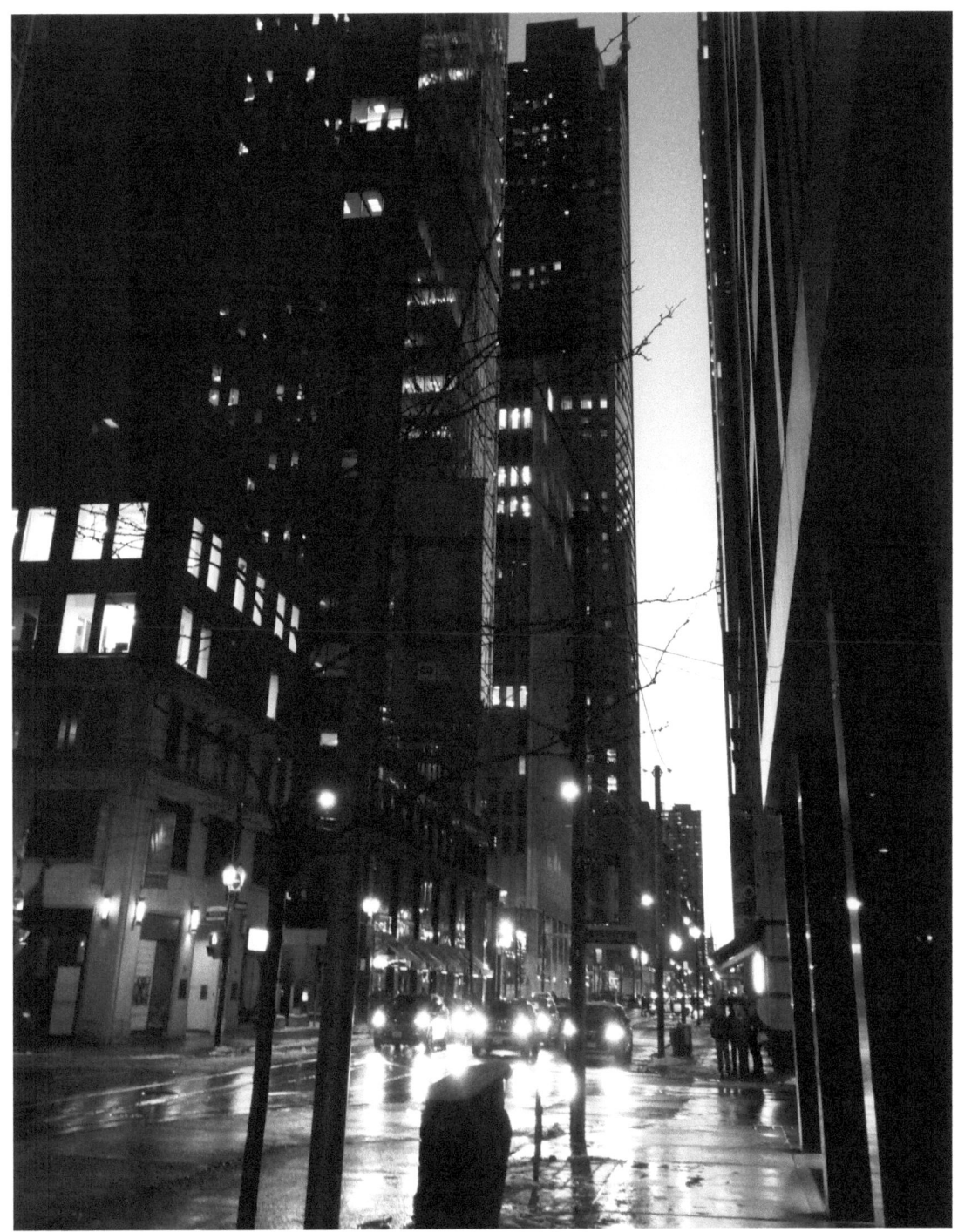

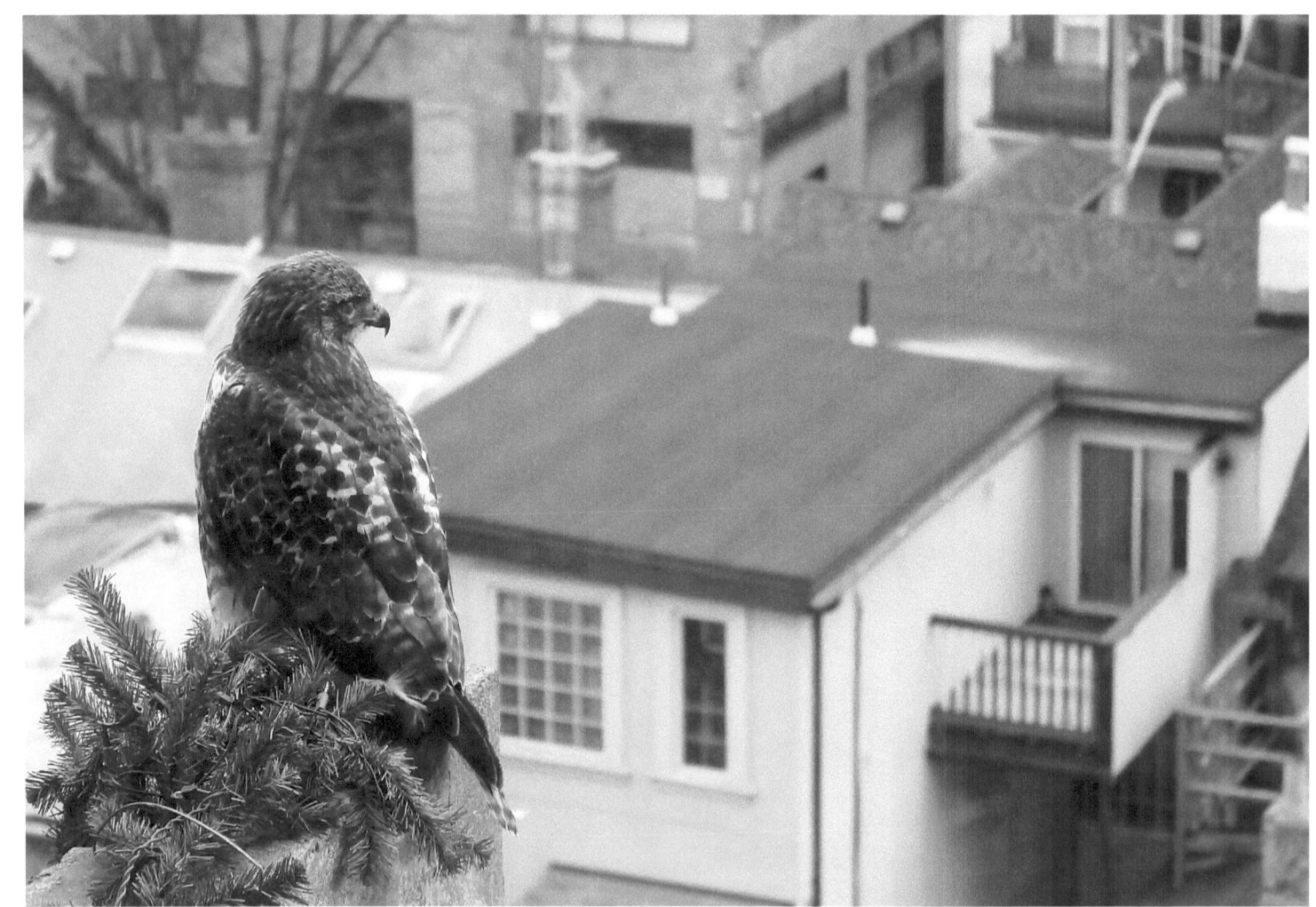

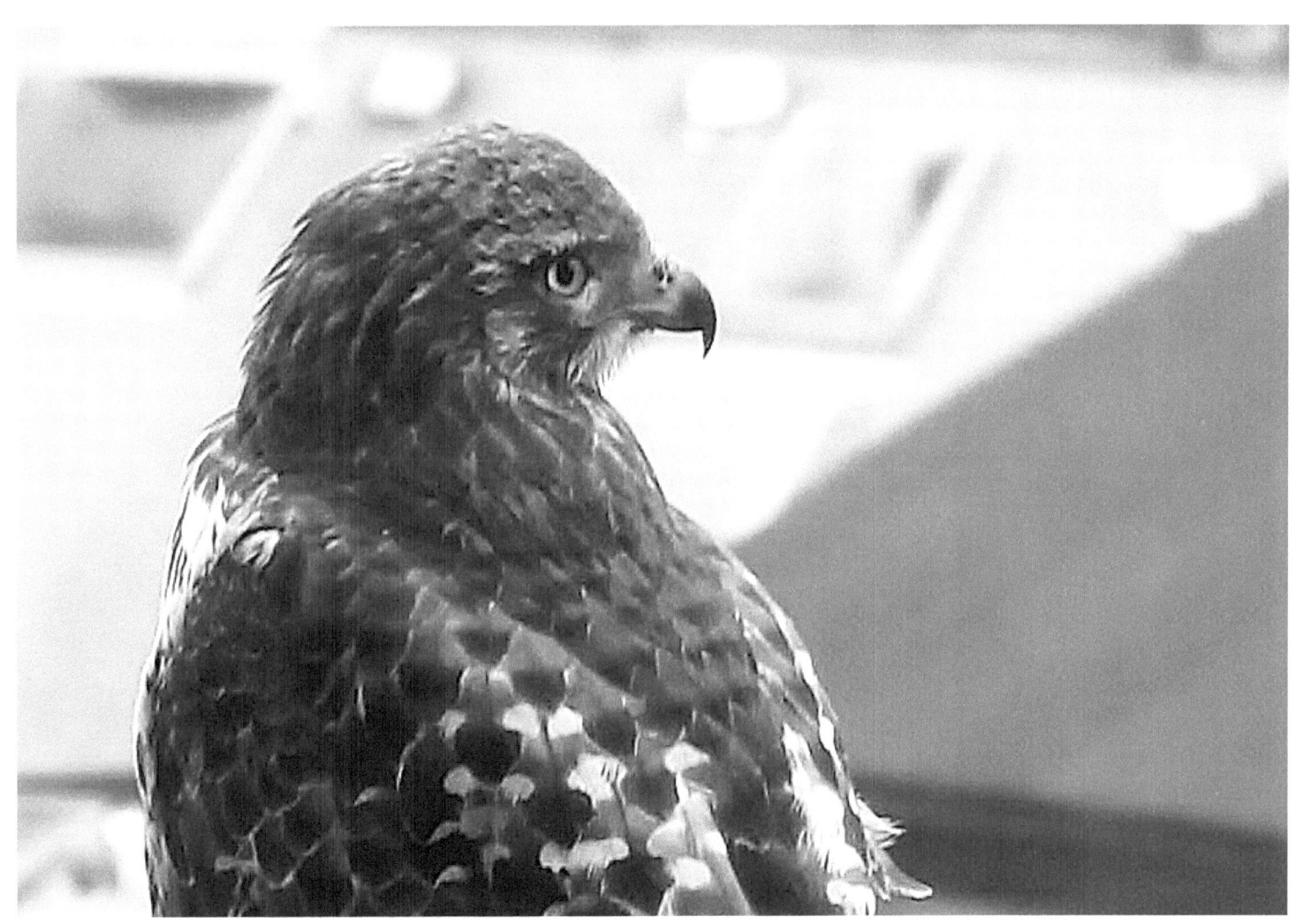

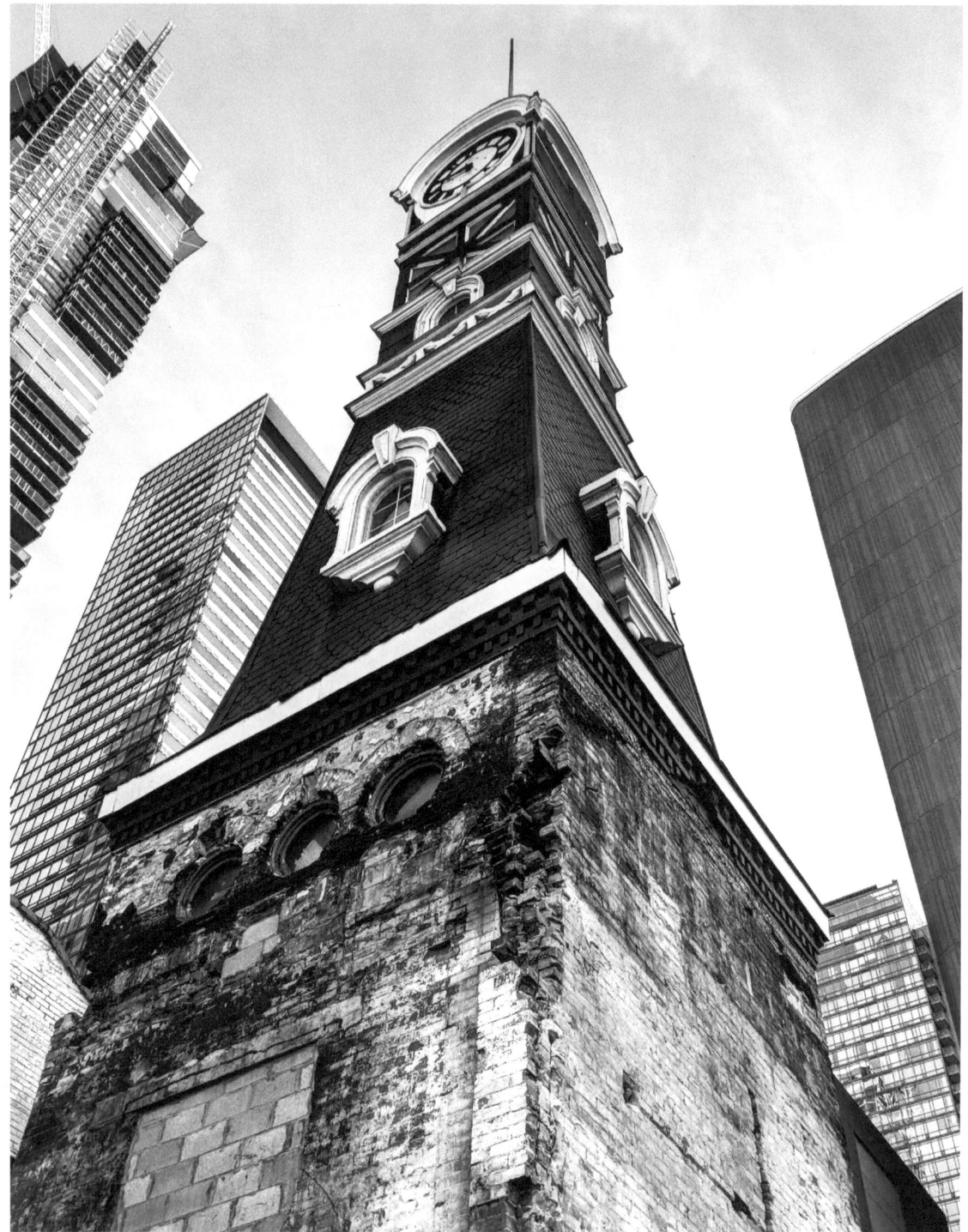

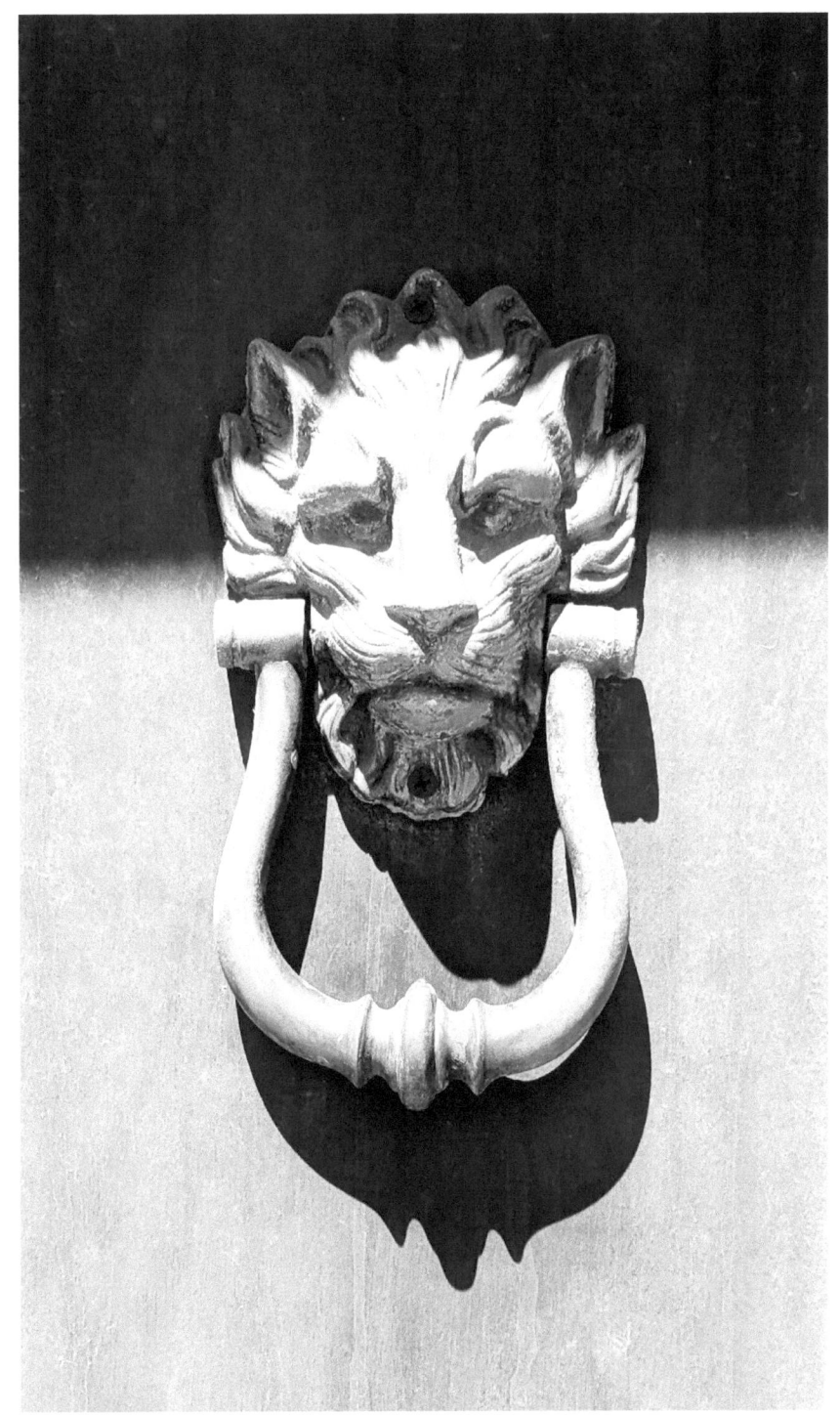

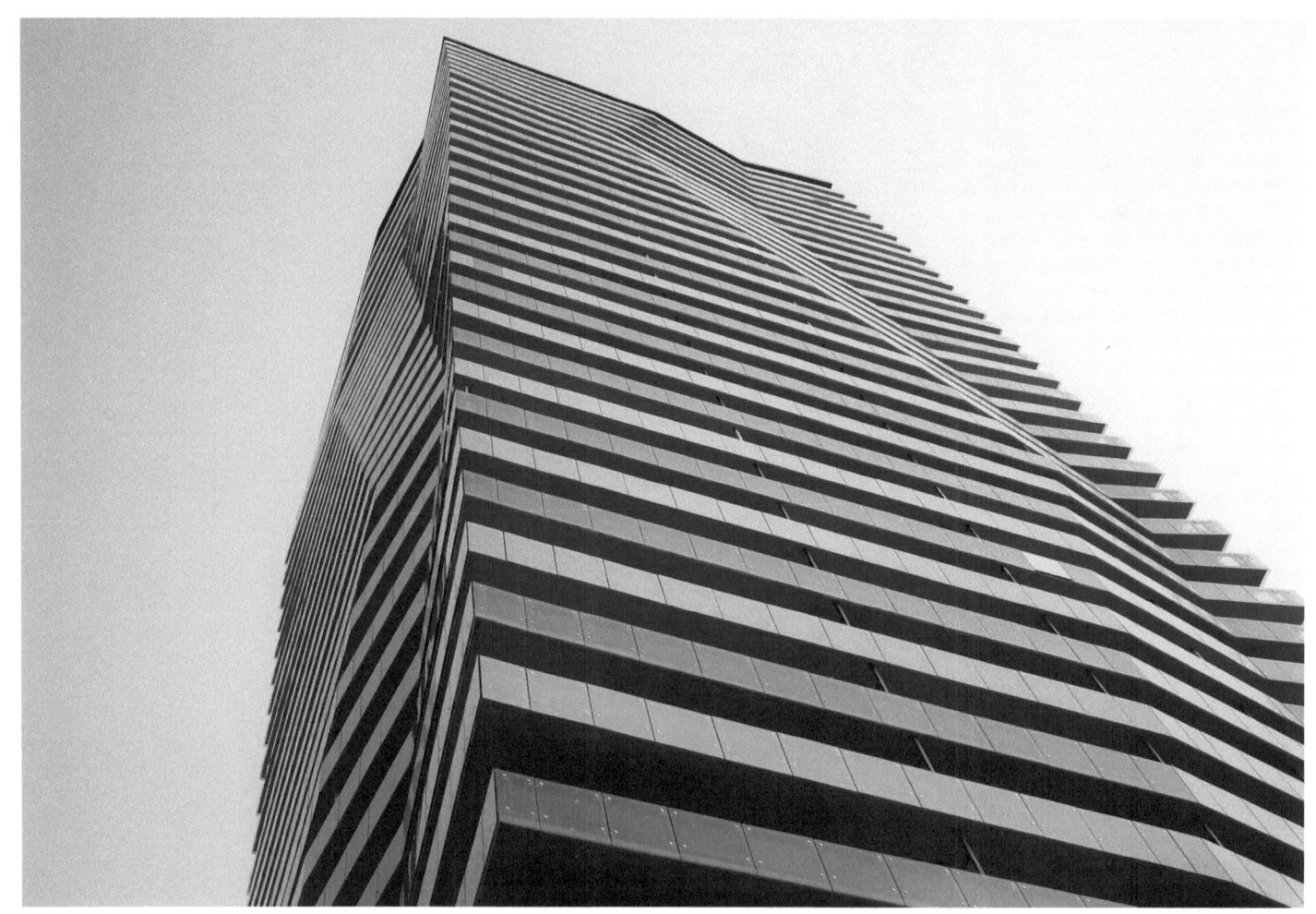

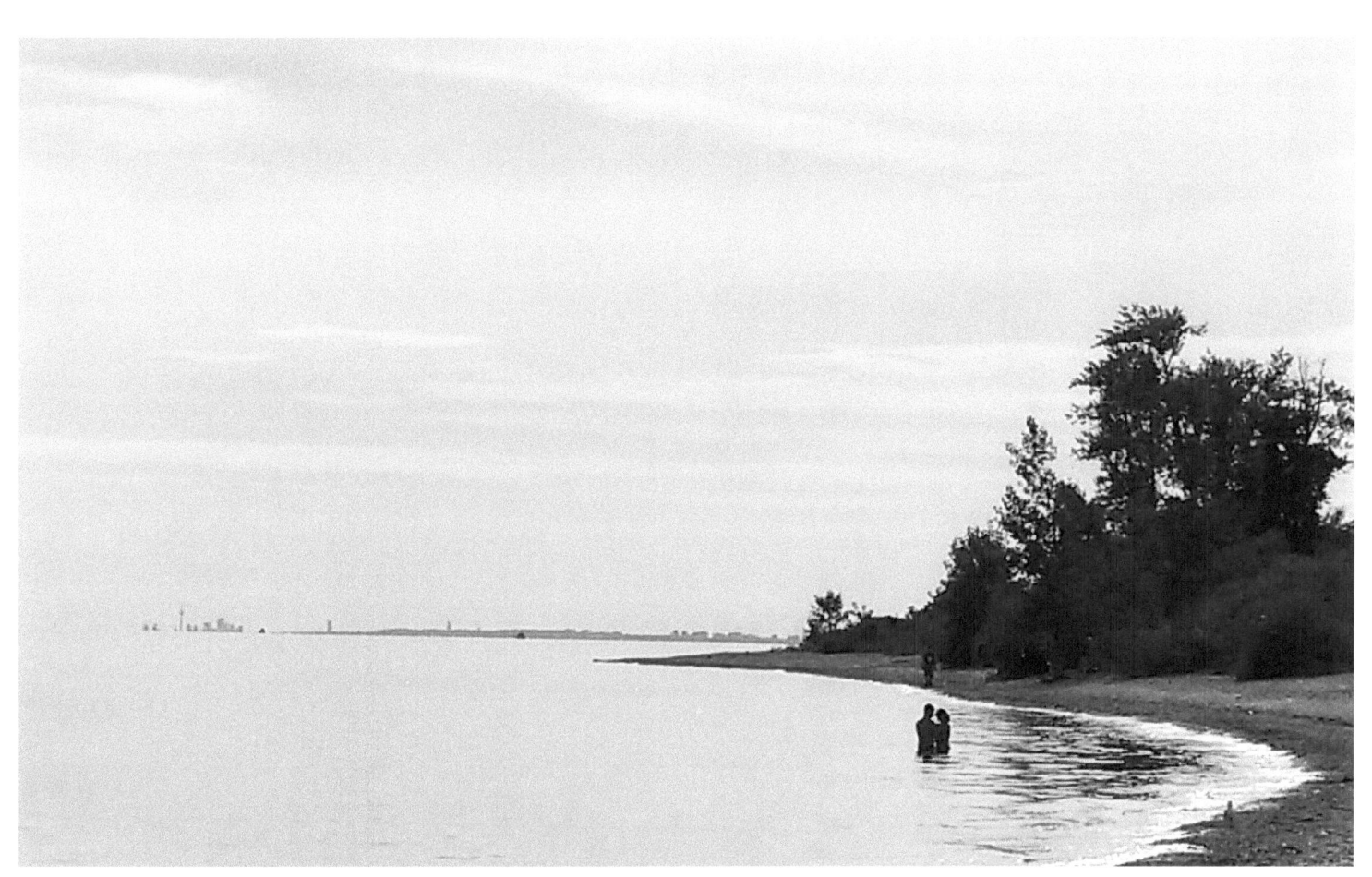

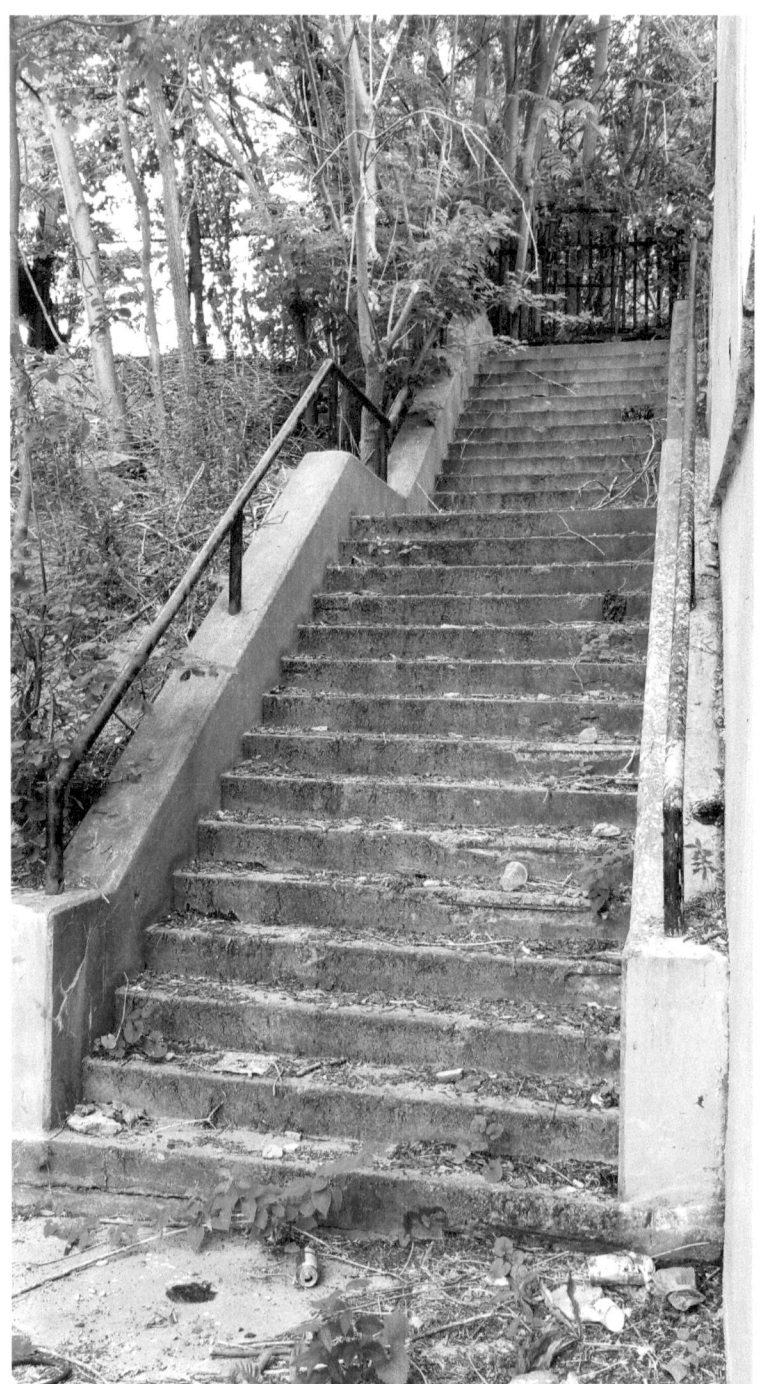

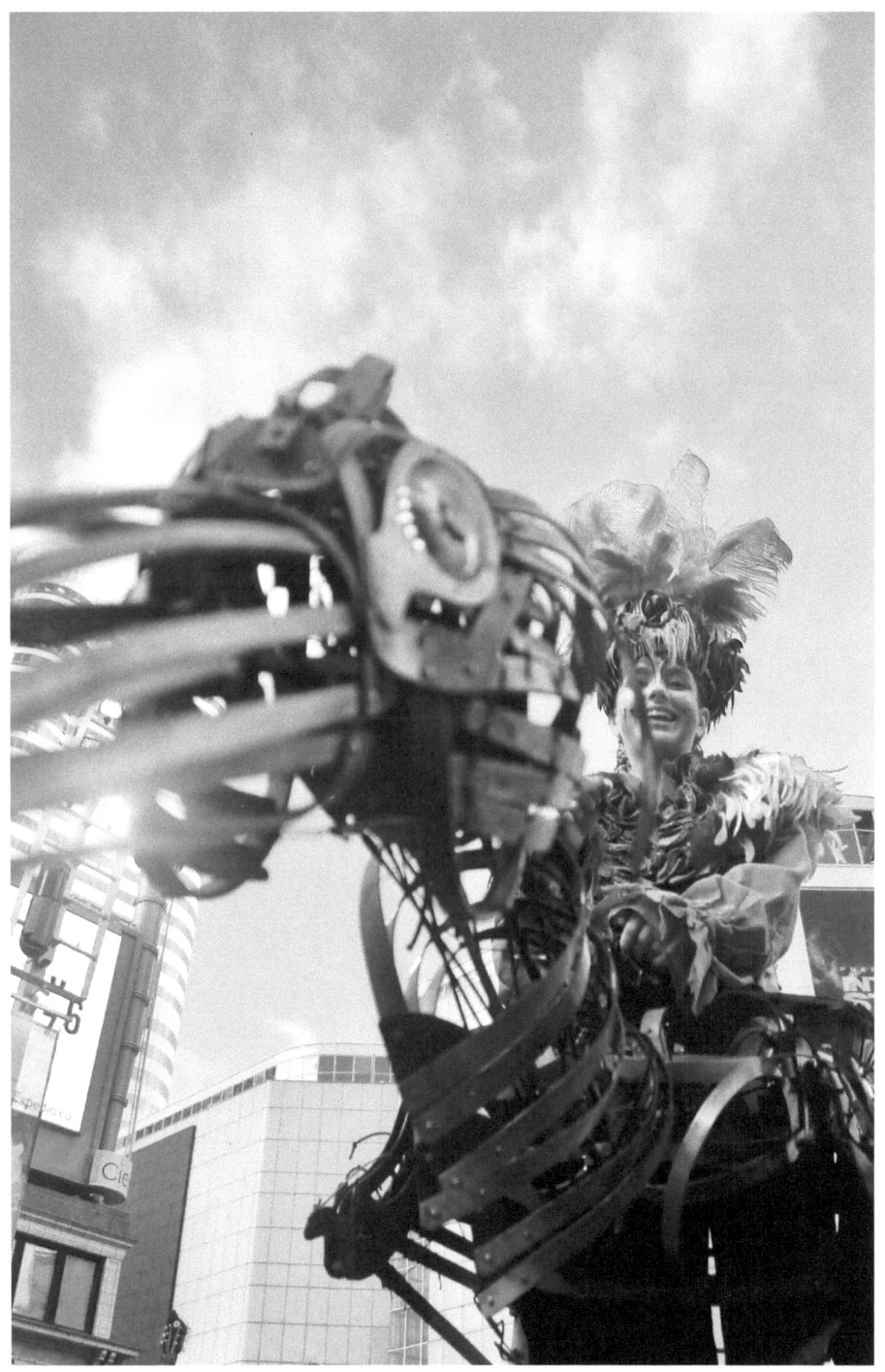

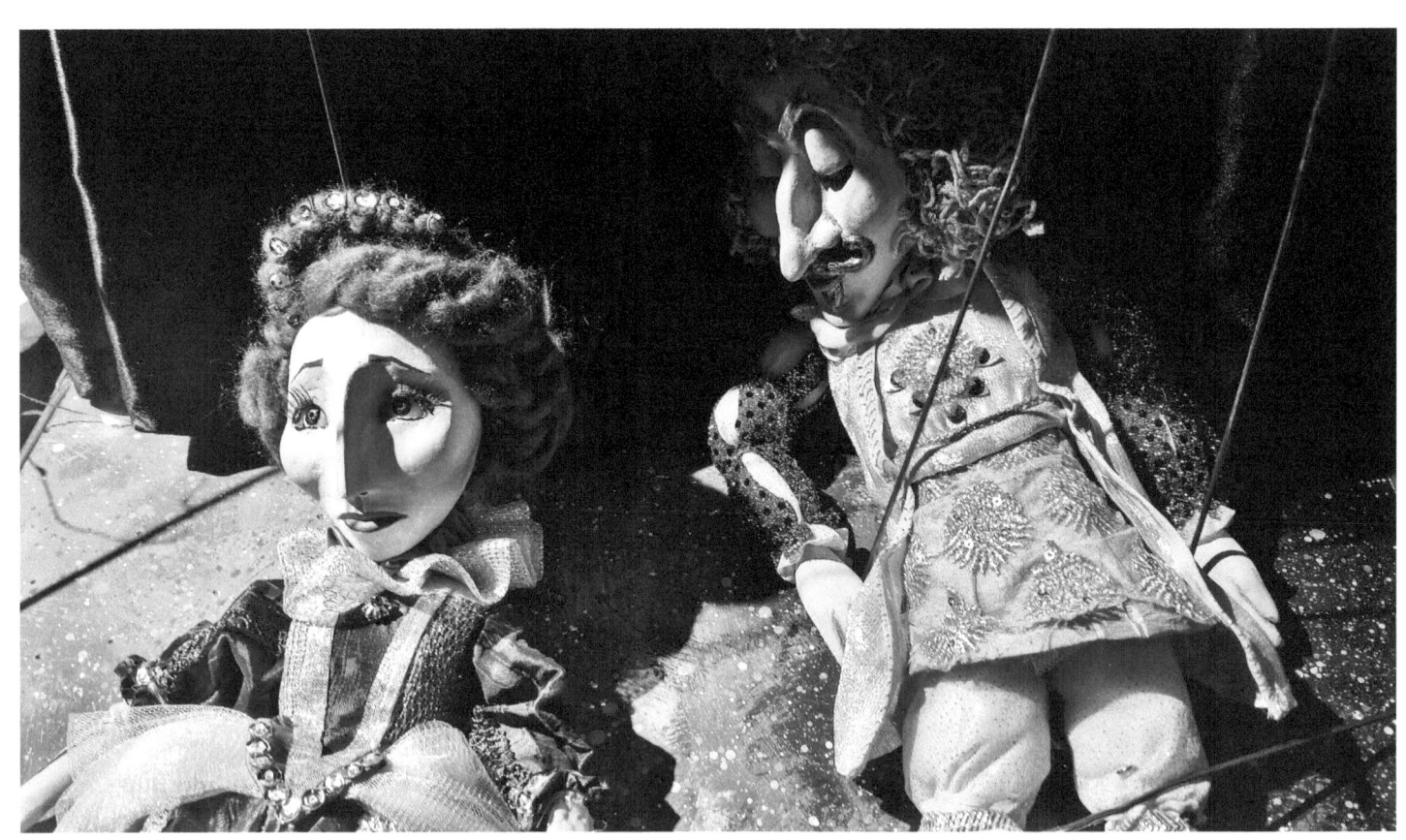

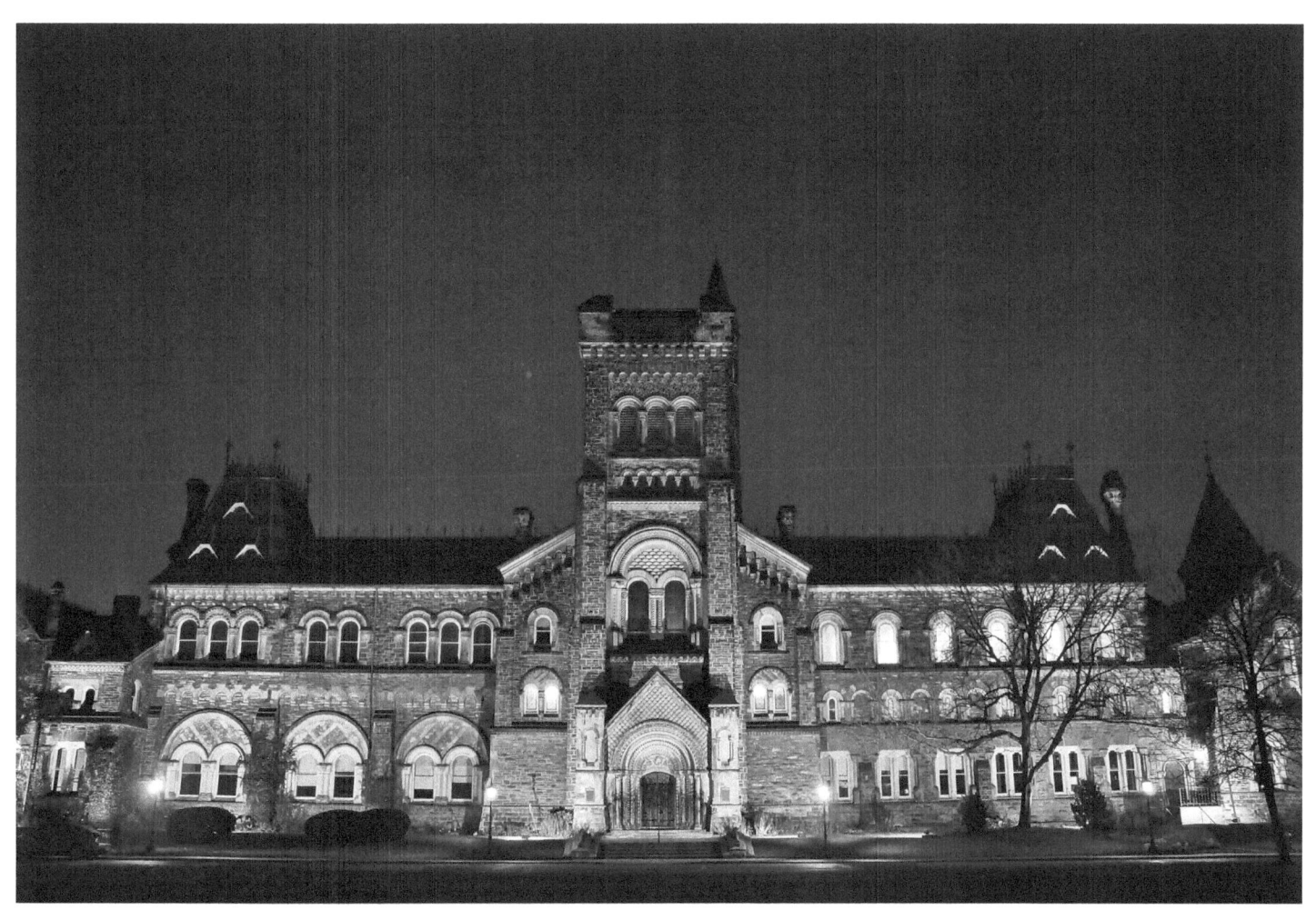

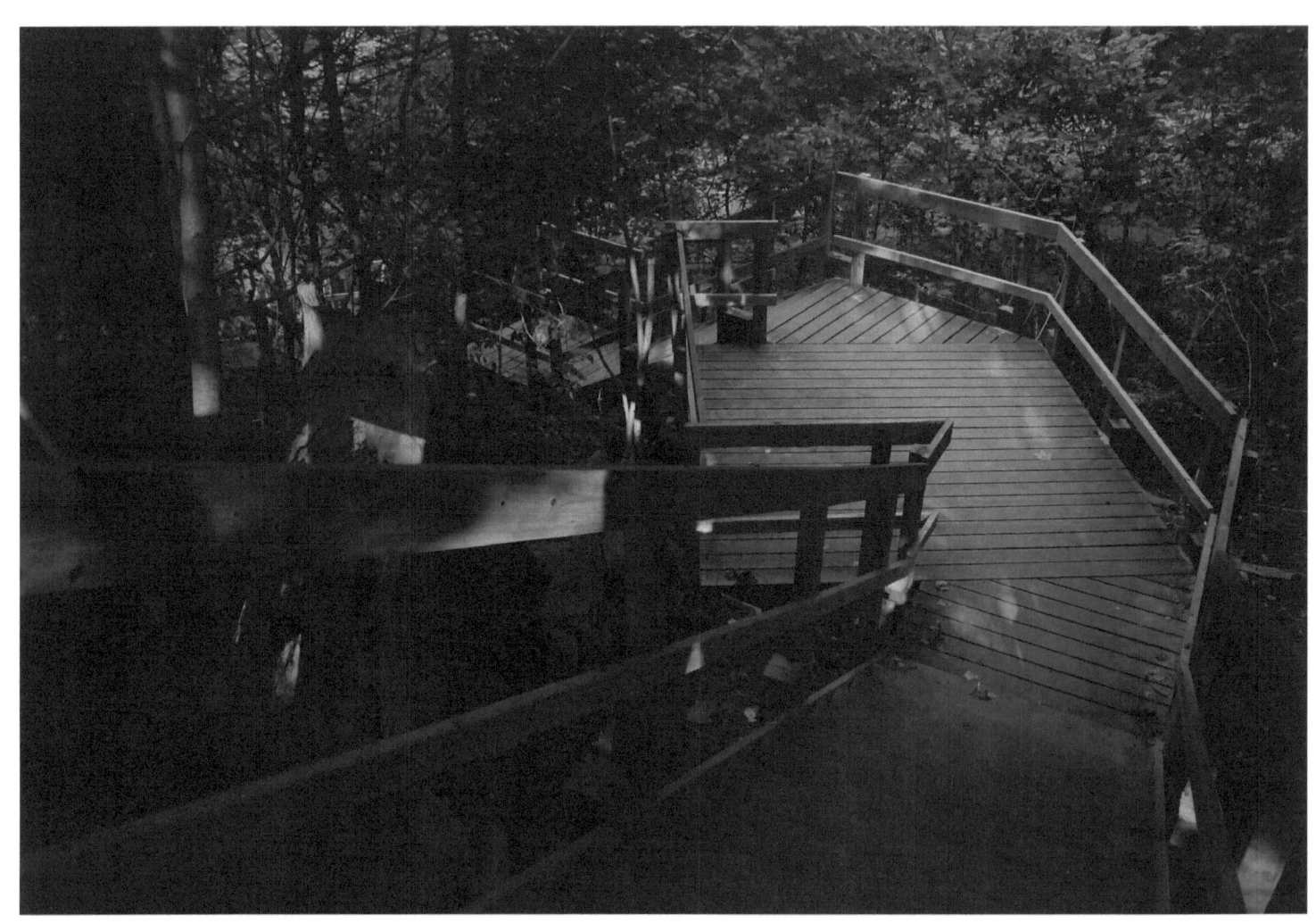

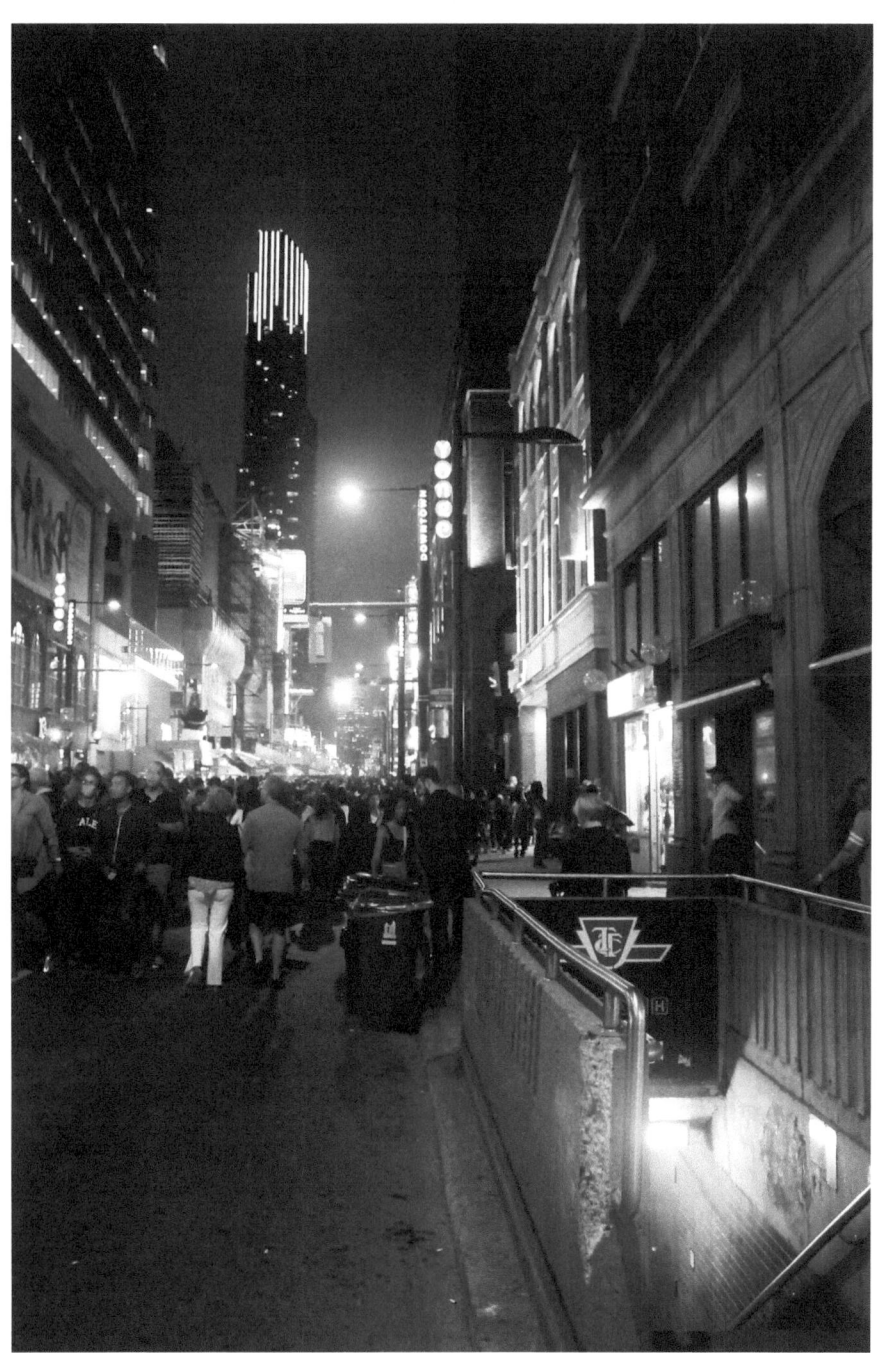

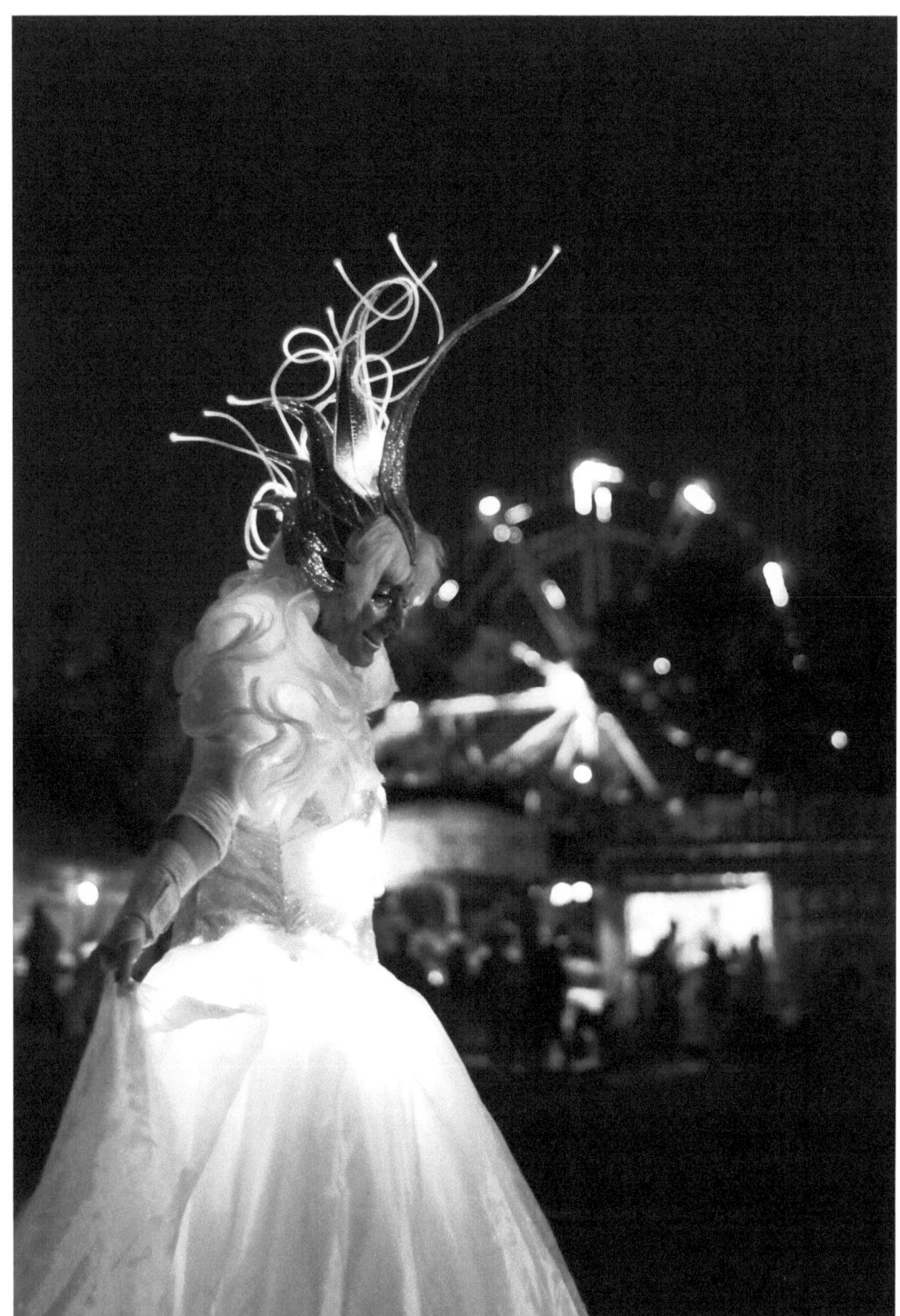

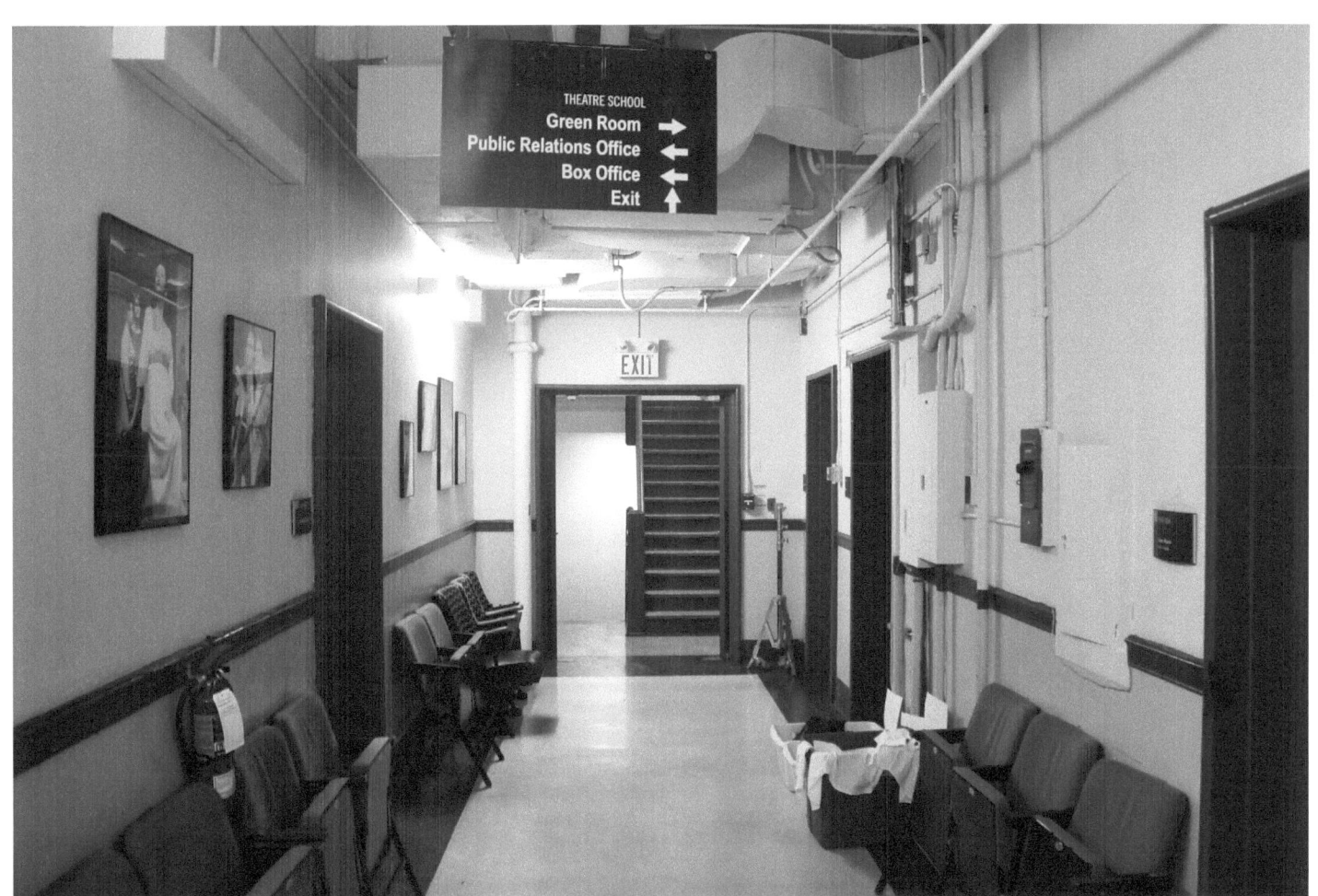

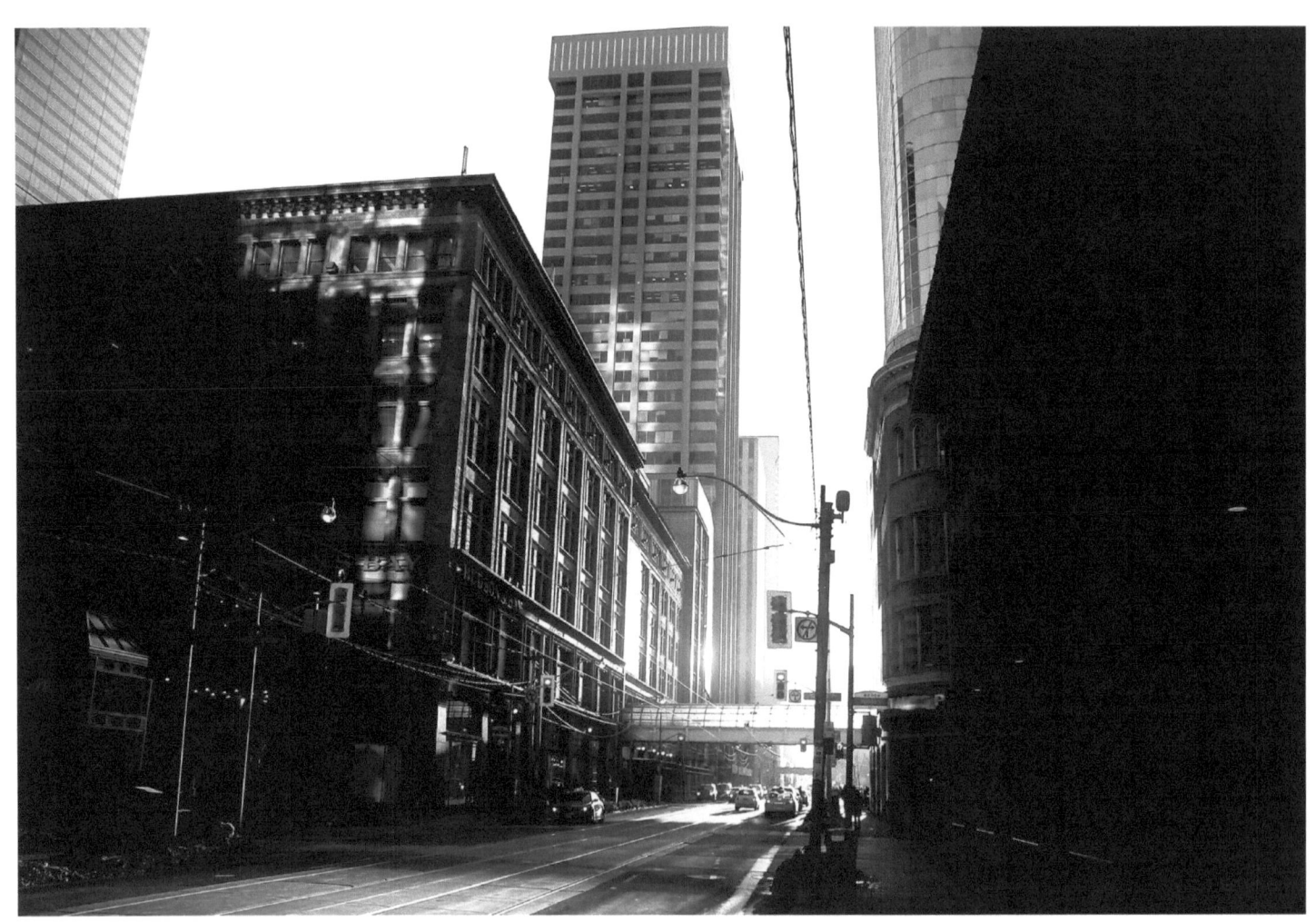

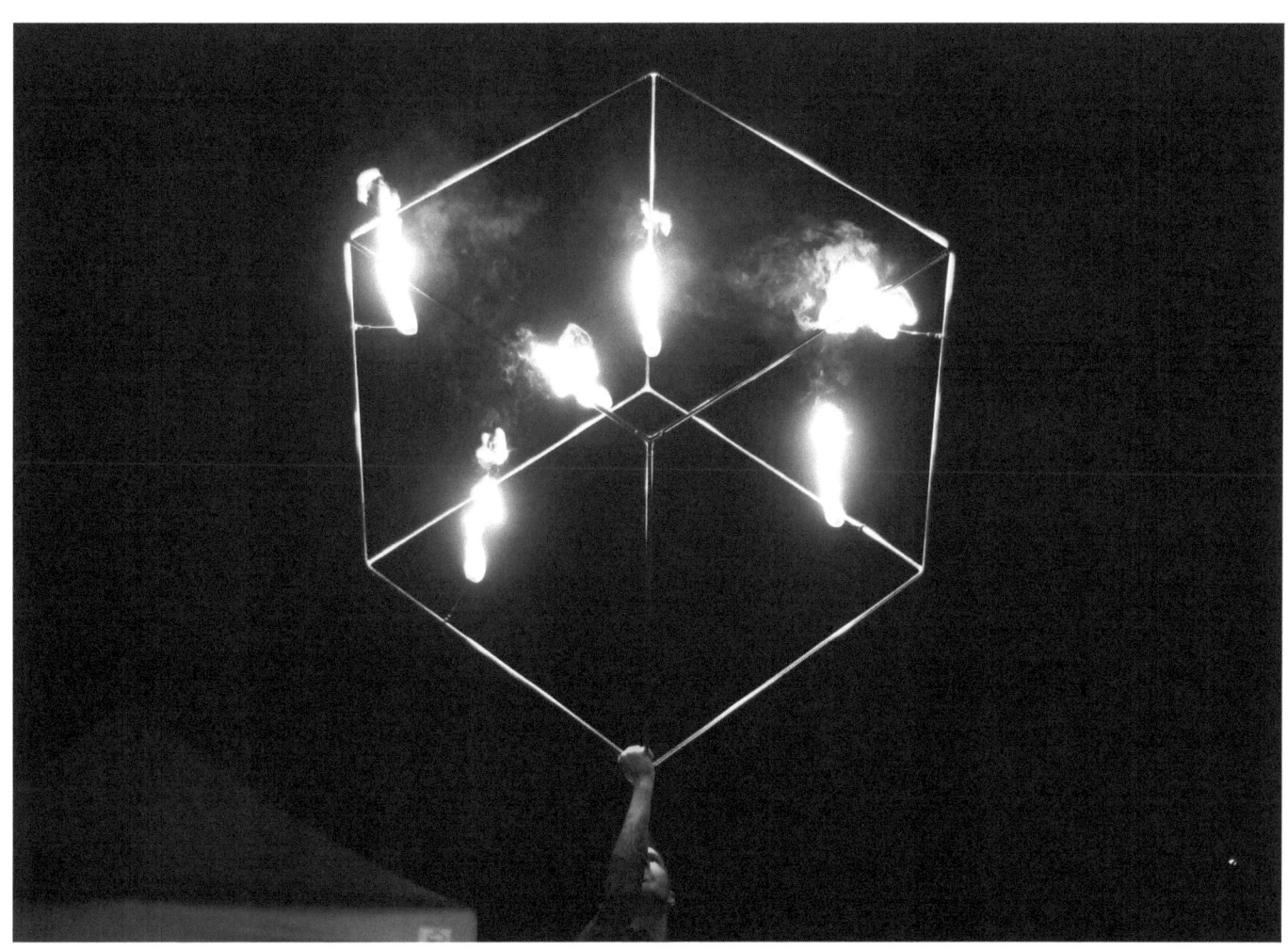

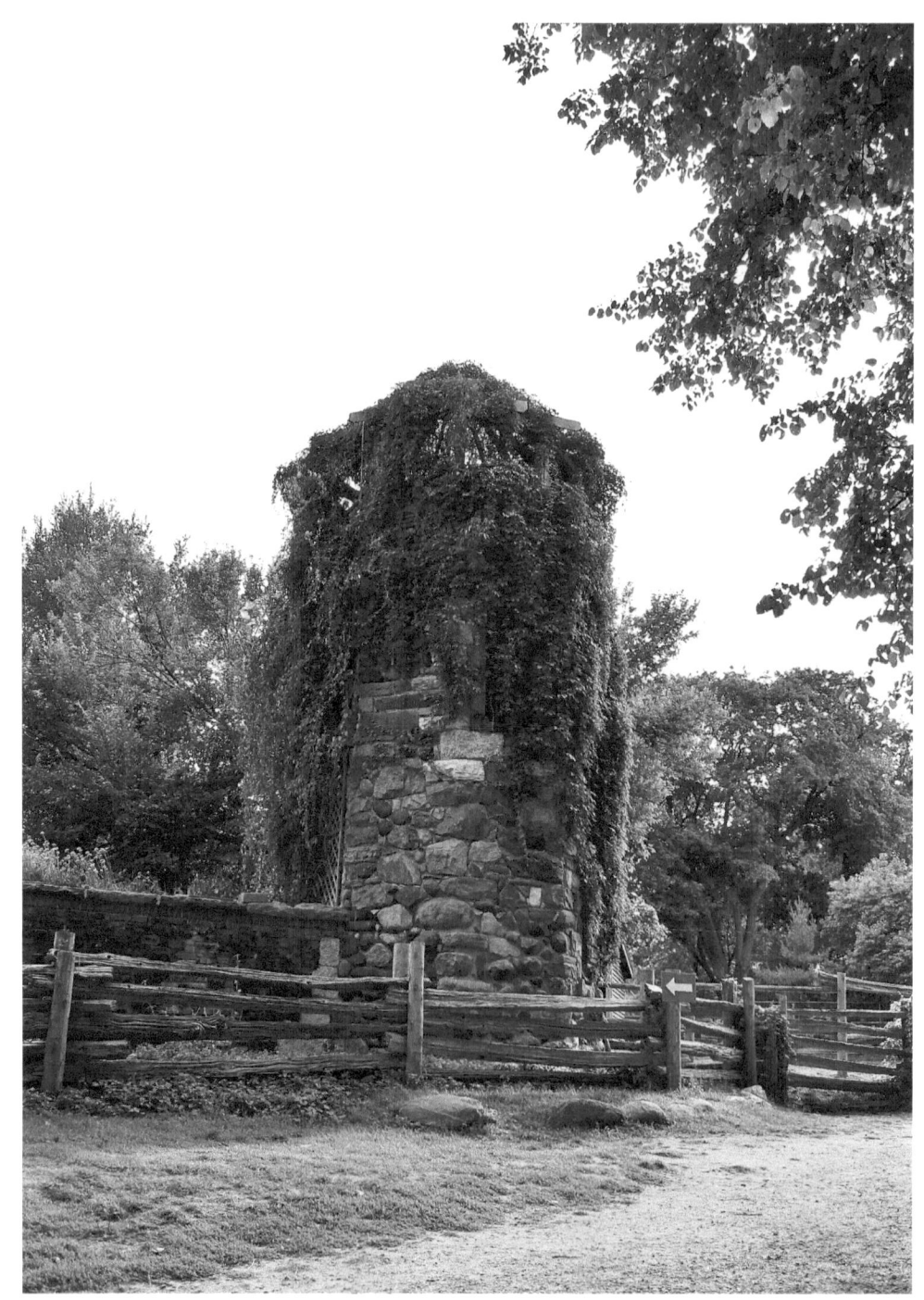

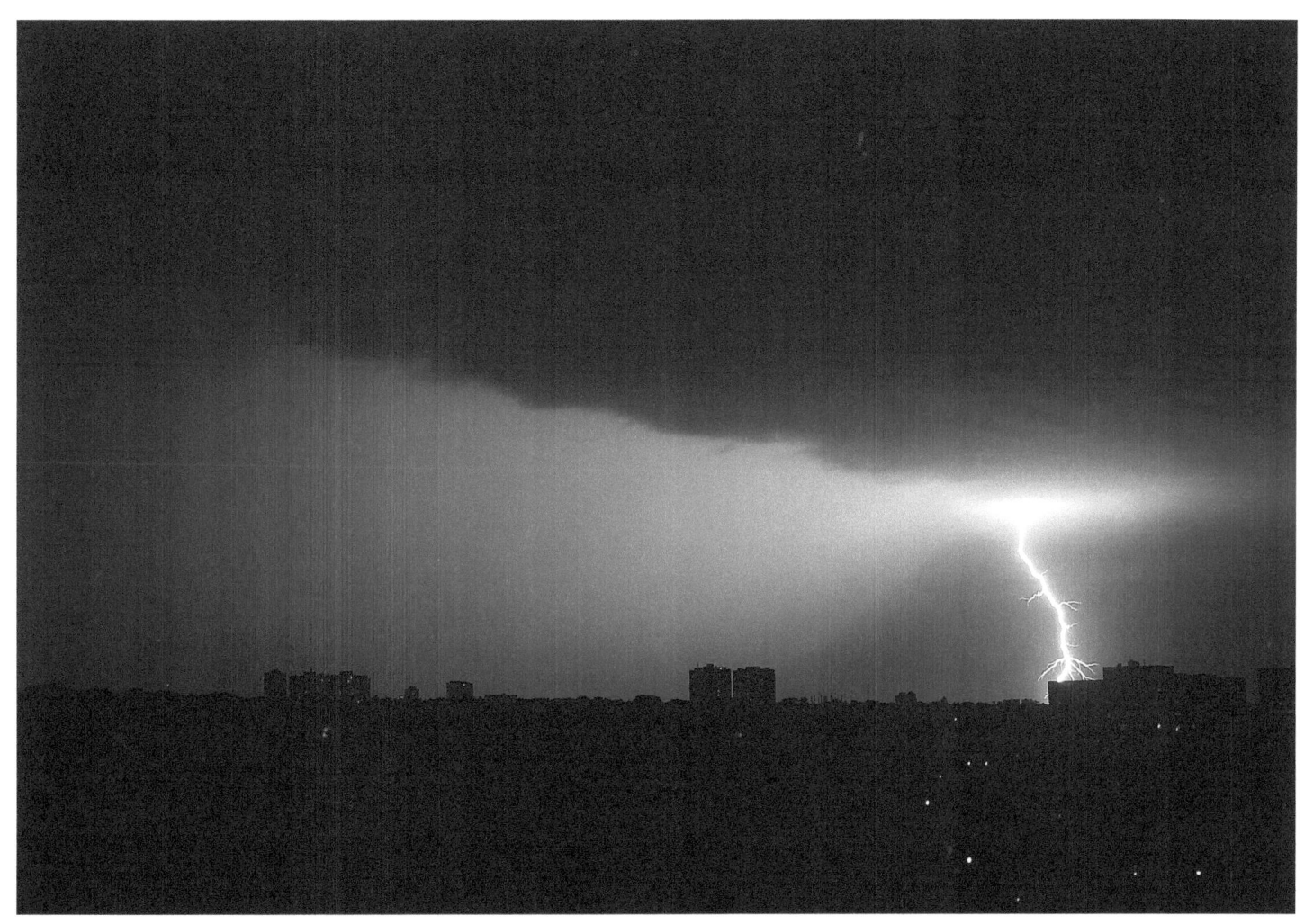

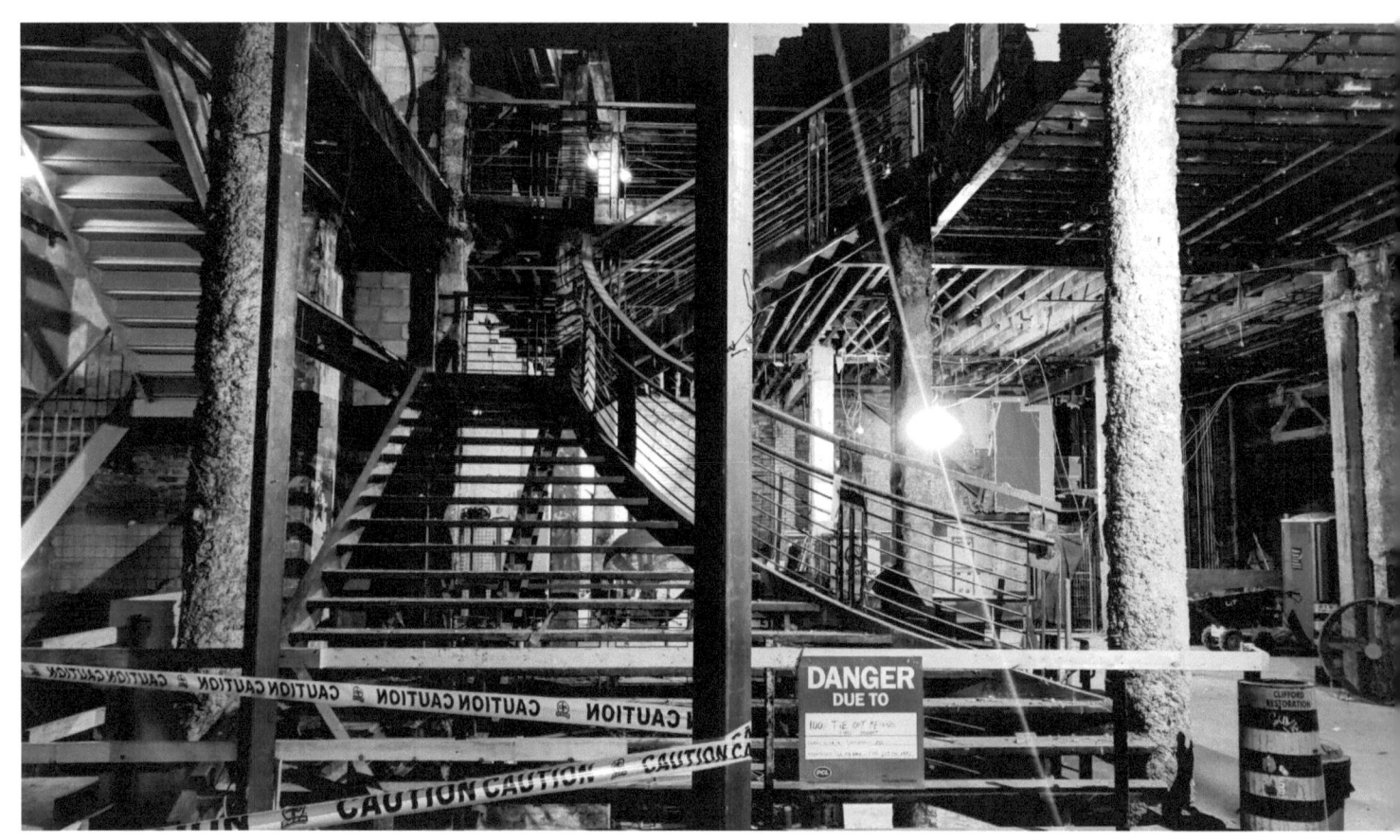

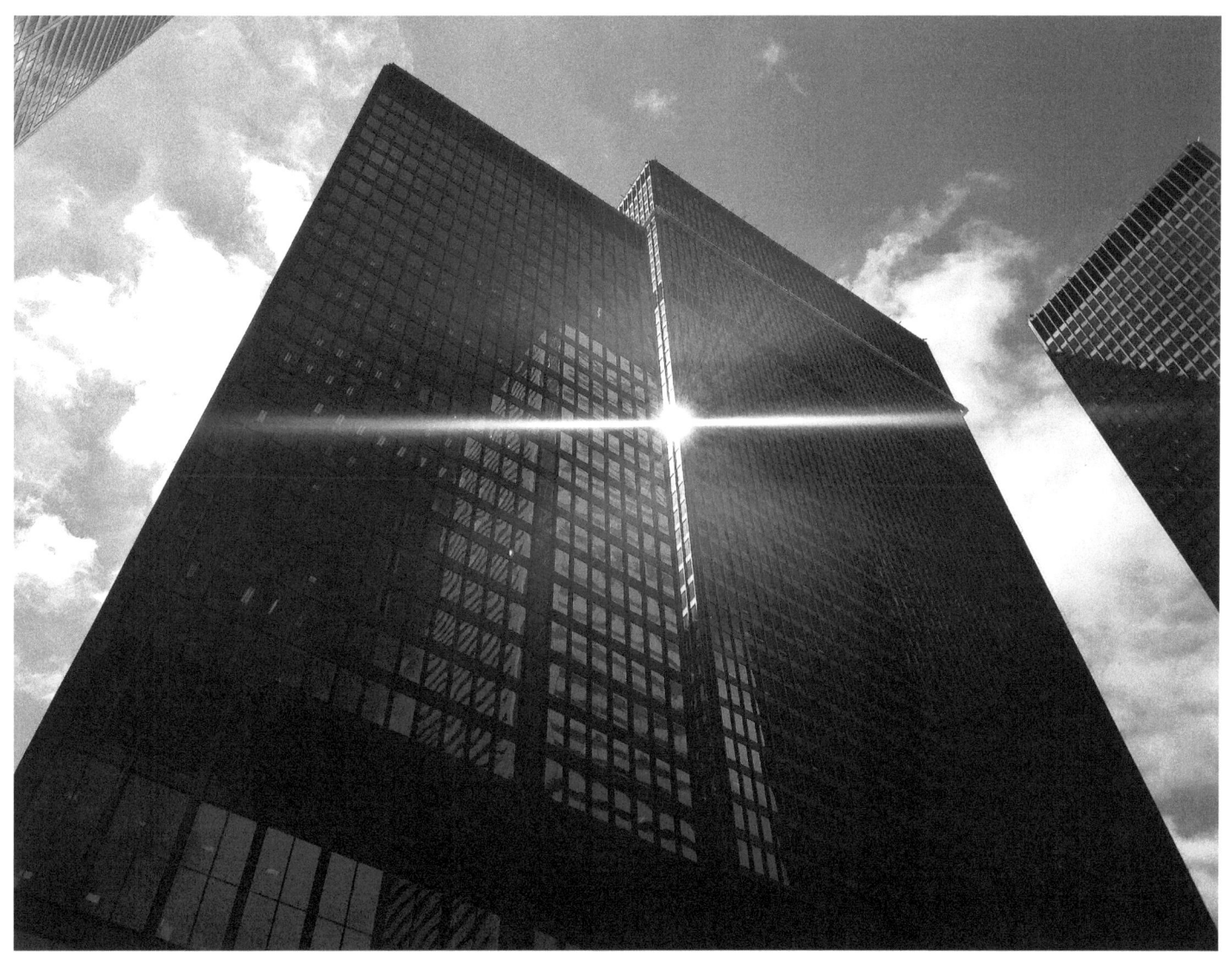

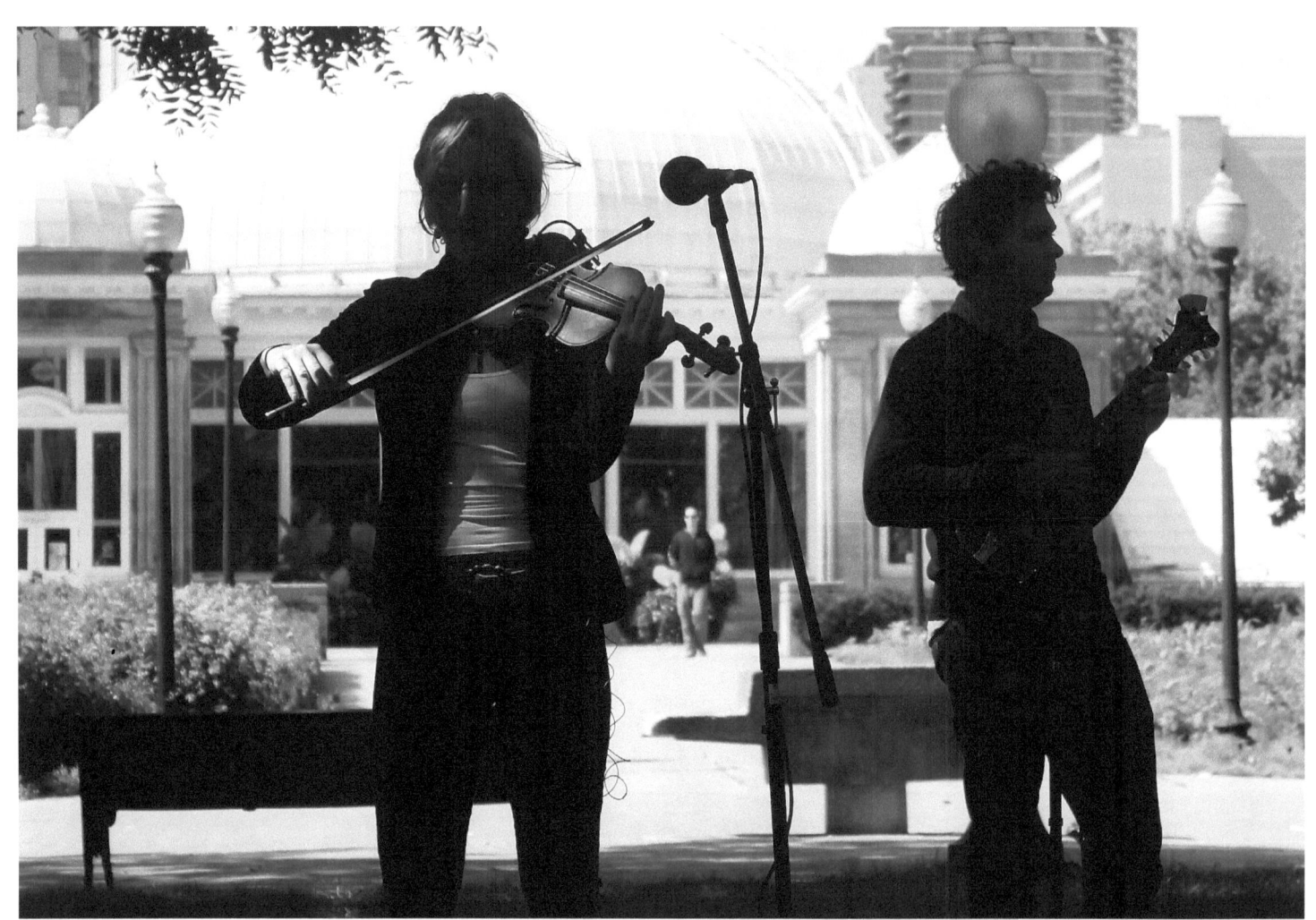

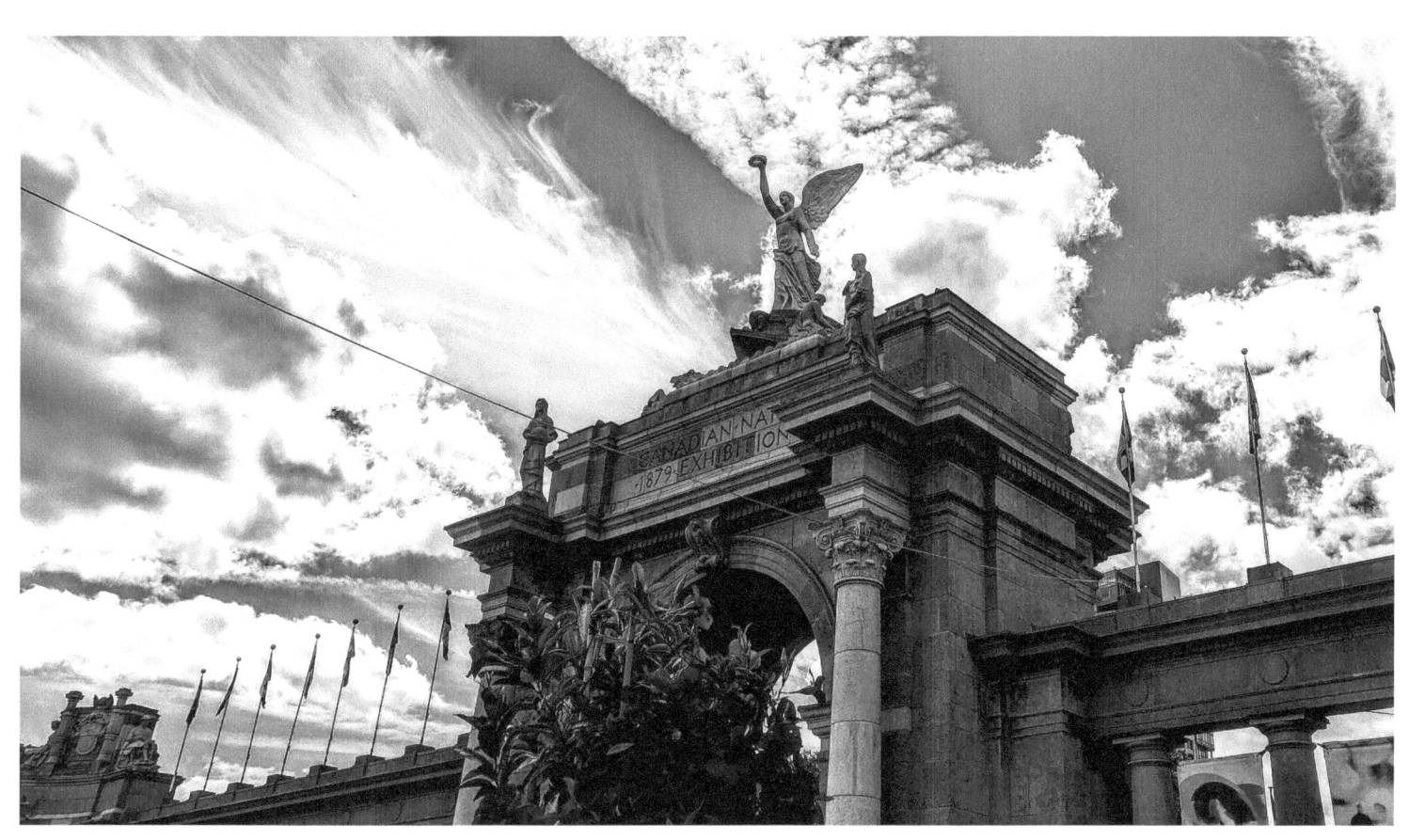

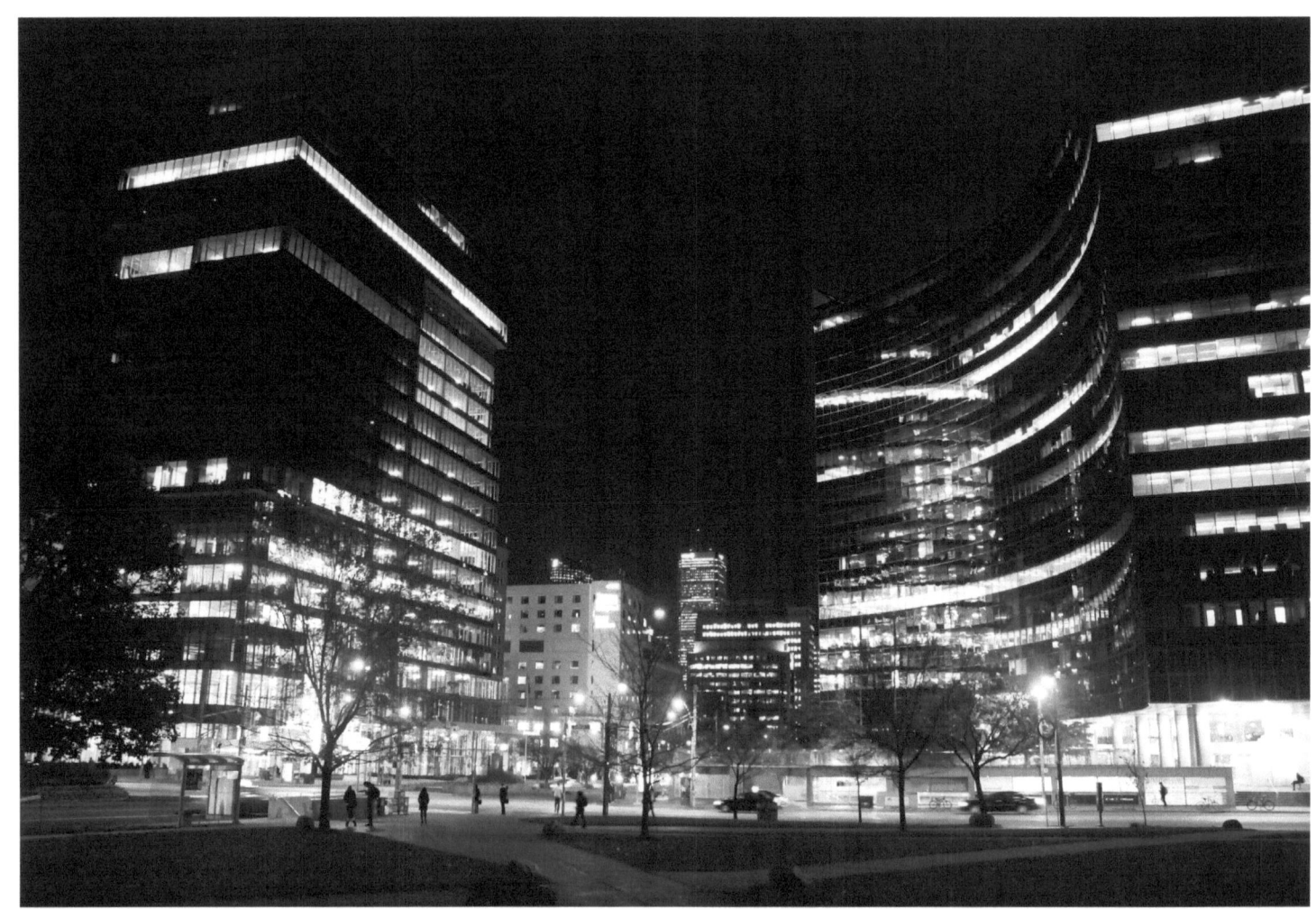

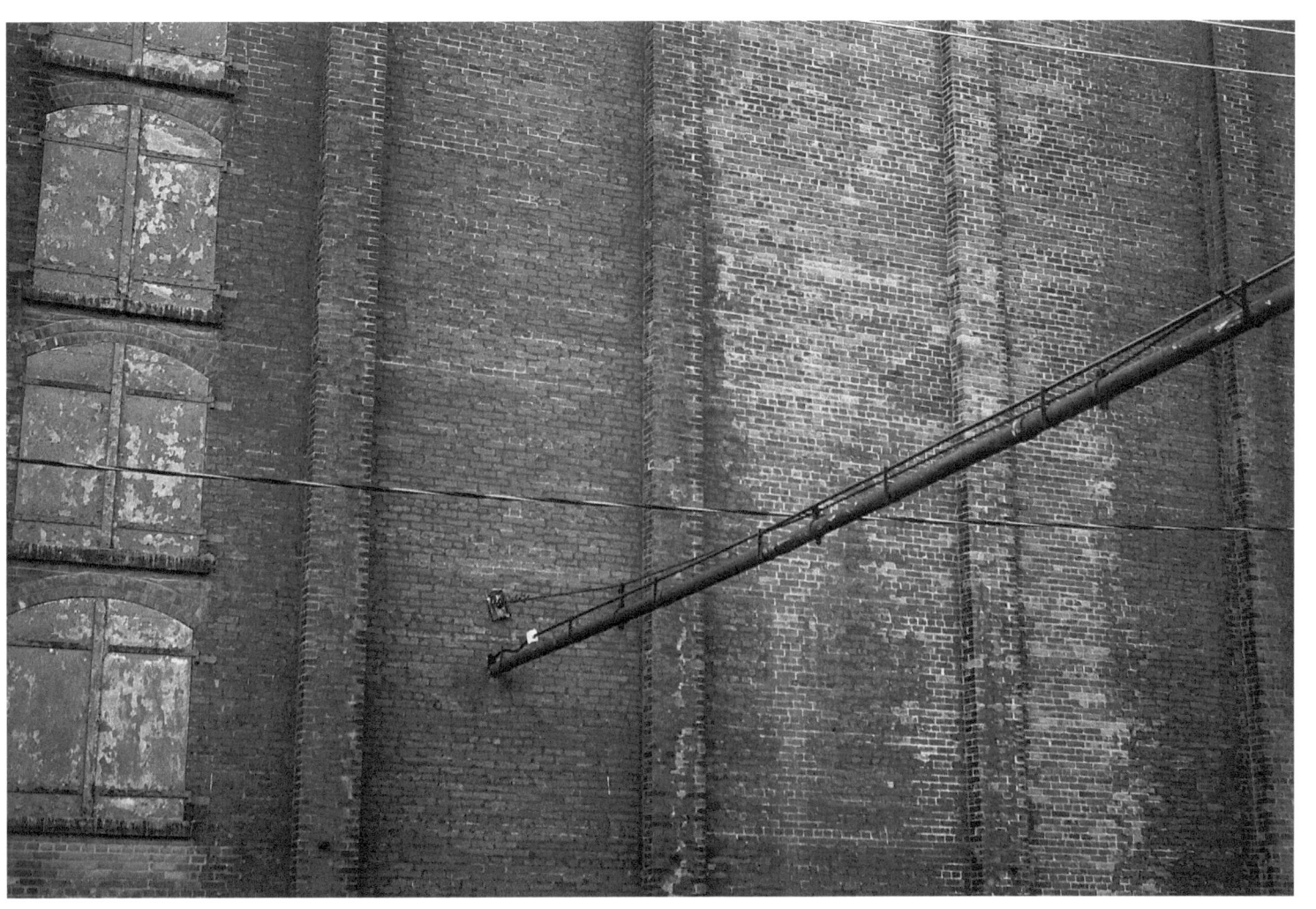

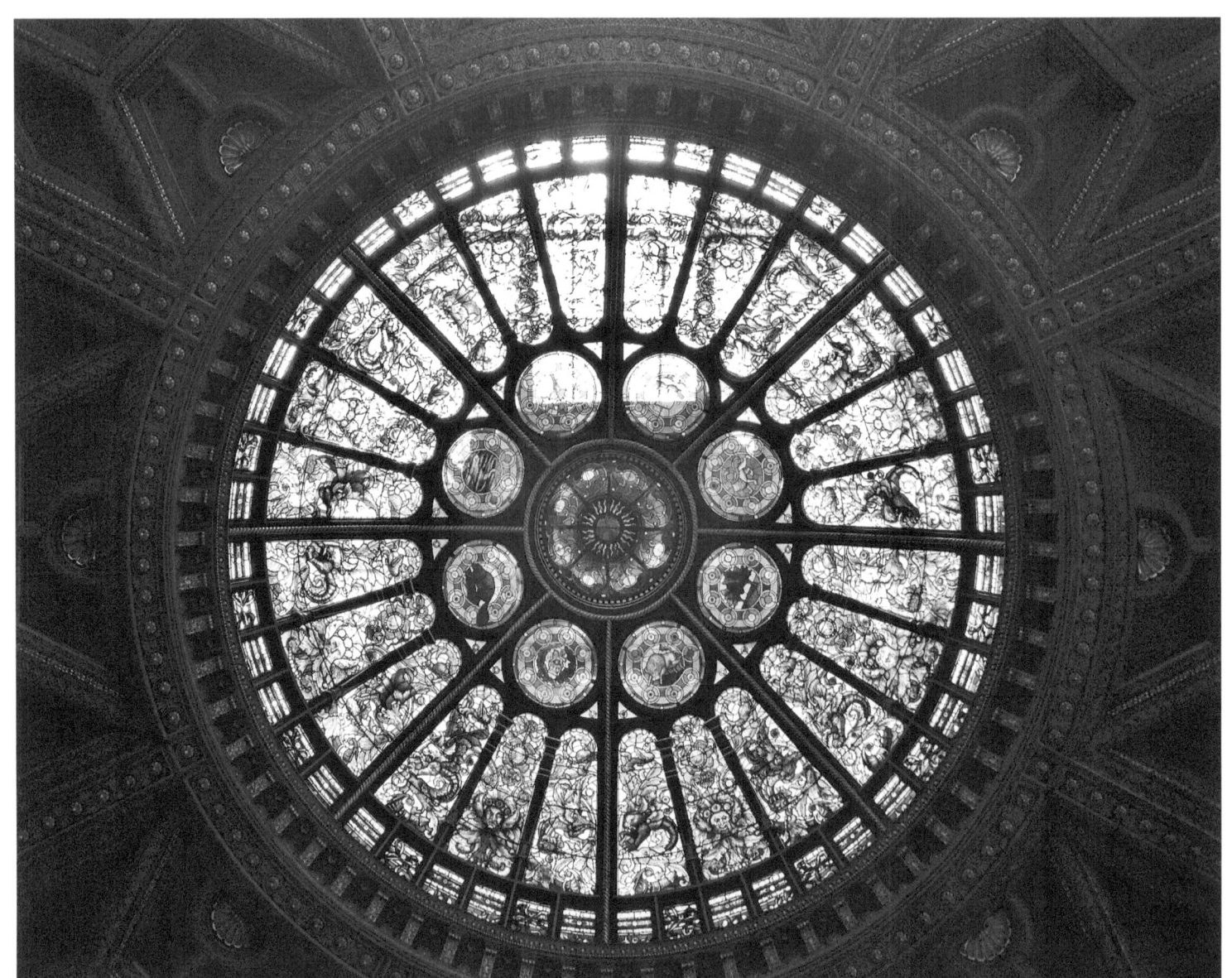

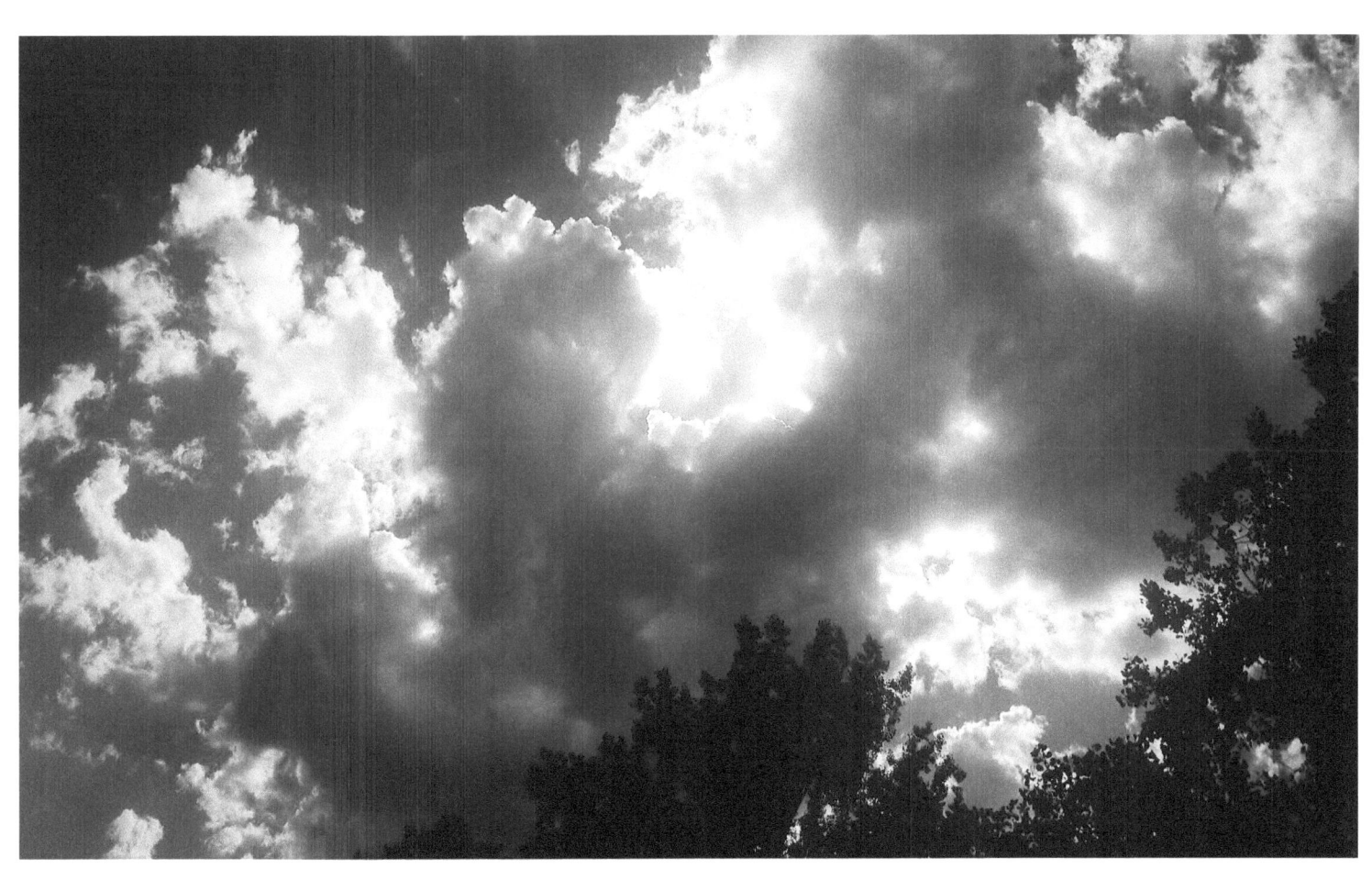

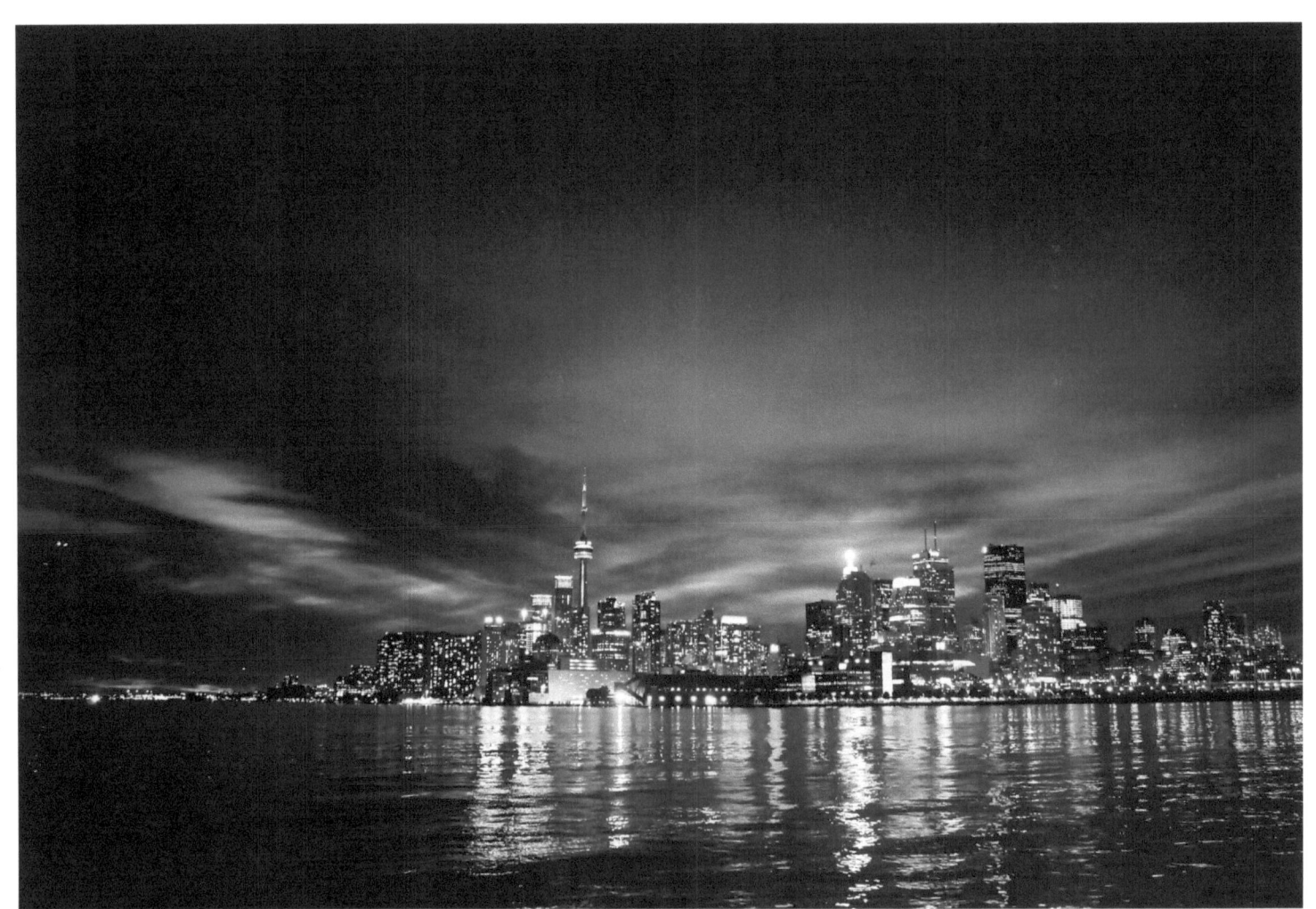

The following artists were kind enough to grant me permission to reproduce their likeness, property and creations in this collection:

Page 3: Andrew Lopatin (AndrewLopatin.com)
Pages 38, 45, 109, 131: NorthFIRE Circus (NorthFIRECircus.com)
Pages 42, 46: Mental Floss Sideshow (Mental-Floss-Sideshow.com)
Page 49: Zoossemobile (BikeArt.ca)
Pages 59, 64: Perch Creek (PerchCreek.com)
Page 69: Hercinia Arts Collective (HerciniArts.com)
Page 90: The Grand Salto Theatre (TheGrandSaltoTheatre.com)
Page 94: The Chalk Chick (The ChalkChick.com)
Page 95: Meow Mur - The Psychedelic Cat (Instagram: MeowMur_psychedeliccat)
Page 100: The Silver Starlets (TheSilverStarlets.com)
Page 123: Les Chasseurs de Reves (leschasseursderves.com)
Page 124: Marionettes by Kira Duff and Sophie Moynan
Page 128: Hala On Stilts (HalaCircusArts.com)
Page 136: Jessica Deutsch and Ozere (JessicaDeutsch.com)

Thank you to everyone for your support and encouragement:

Mom & Dad, always my light.
Tim, Mel, Emmet, Jill, Dave, Jack, Josephine, Mark & Liv: family.
Ms Crangle, for teaching me to look.
Michael, for chilling on the porch.
Heidi, for drinks and discussions.
Karl & Lesley, Kiki, Matt, Natalie, Jo, Molly & Danielle, Hala, Jocelyne, Natasha, Andrew, Kira & Sophie, Eileen & James, Jessica, Zita & Myque, and Paul, for saying yes.
Melanie & Tiffany, for giving the world the Freedom Factory.
David & Brianna, you are missed on the 9th floor.
Natalie, Diana and Emily, for (Un)usual Spaces.
Kiran, for an afternoon at the park.

About The Author

Patrick Lemieux is a Canadian artist, writer and taker of photographs who makes his home in Toronto, Ontario. He has exhibited his artwork in galleries and venues around North America. He is currently working on the fourth novel in the *Orchard Bend* series. For his photography in this book, he used a Canon Rebel T3 with both Canon EF-S 18-55mm f/3.5-5.6 IS II and Yongnuo YN50mm f/1.8 lenses, with a Velbon Victory 450 tripod, as well as the following smart phones: Motorola Moto Xplay, Google Pixel XL and Google Pixel 3a.

You can follow Patrick on Twitter @MadTheDJ and on Instagram at PatrickLemieuxArtist.

Visit AcrossTheBoardBooks.ca

Copyright © 2020, Patrick Lemieux

www.ingramcontent.com/pod-product-compliance
Lightning Source LLC
Chambersburg PA
CBHW051910210526
45473CB00006B/1967